AF279483

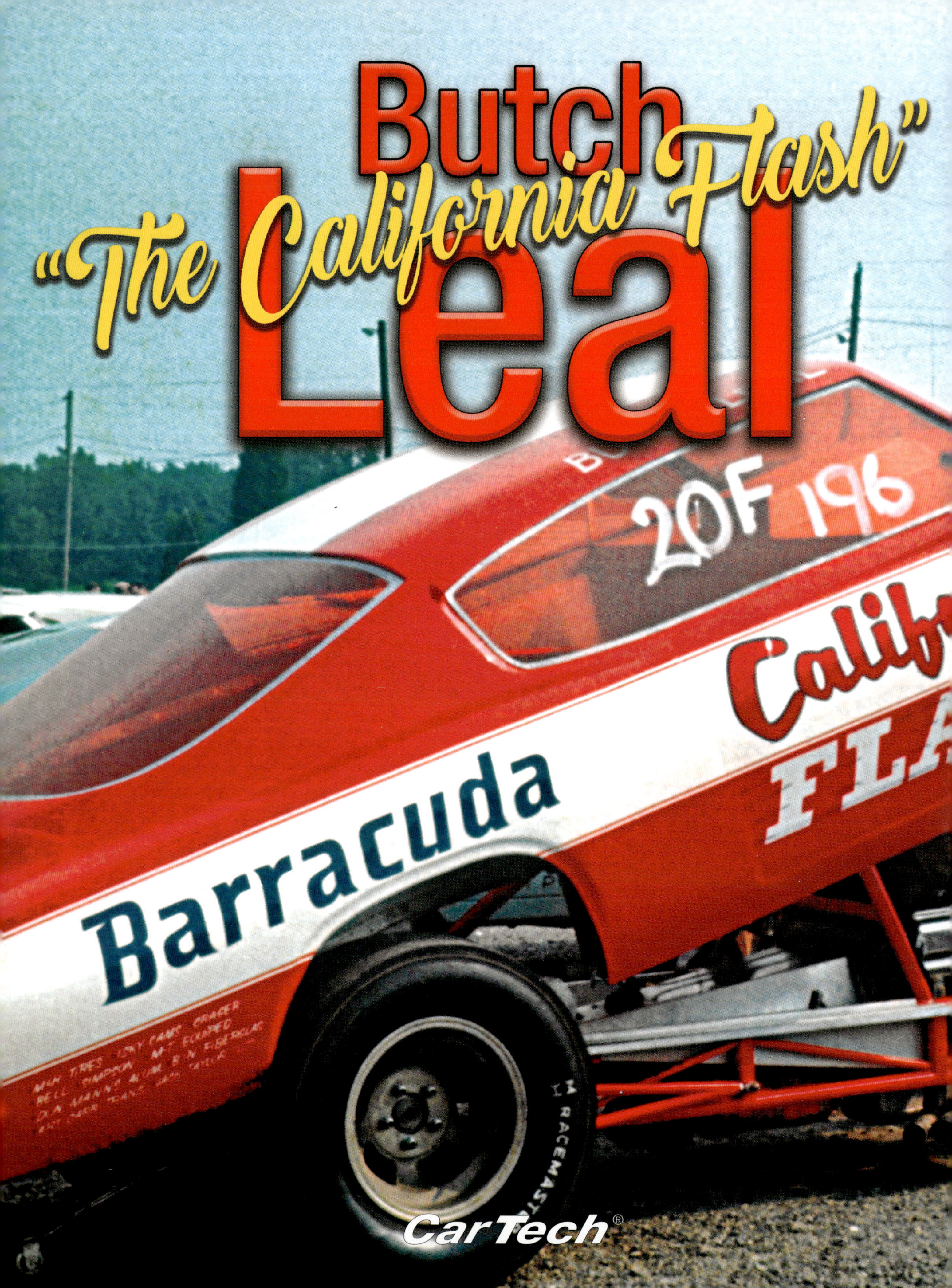

Butch
"The California Flash"
Leal
20F 196
Califo
FLA
Barracuda
CarTech

Bob McClurg

CarTech®, Inc.
6118 Main Street
North Branch, MN 55056
Phone: 651-277-1200 or 800-551-4754
Fax: 651-277-1203
www.cartechbooks.com

Edit by Bob Wilson
Layout by Connie DeFlorin

ISBN 978-1-61325-710-4
Item No. CT685

Library of Congress Cataloging-in-Publication Data Available

Written, edited, and designed in the U.S.A.
Printed in China
10 9 8 7 6 5 4 3 2 1

PUBLISHER'S NOTE: In reporting history, the images required to tell the tale will vary greatly in quality, especially by modern photographic standards. While some images in this volume are not up to those digital standards, we have included them, as we feel they are an important element in telling the story.

DISTRIBUTION BY:

Europe
PGUK
63 Hatton Garden
London EC1N 8LE, England
Phone: 020 7061 1980 • Fax: 020 7242 3725
www.pguk.co.uk

Australia
Renniks Publications Ltd.
3/37-39 Green Street
Banksmeadow, NSW 2109, Australia
Phone: 2 9695 7055 • Fax: 2 9695 7355
www.renniks.com

Canada
Login Canada
300 Saulteaux Crescent
Winnipeg, MB, R3J 3T2 Canada
Phone: 800 665 1148 • Fax: 800 665 0103
www.lb.ca

TABLE OF CONTENTS

DEDICATION

This book is dedicated to the memory of H.L. Shahan (1936–2020) who, through his mechanical wizardry, furthered the driving career of Butch Leal and was also extremely instrumental in guiding the driving careers of Shirley Shahan-Bridges, Ronnie Broadhead, Hank Taylor, Doug Thorley, and Carroll Greer. May he long be remembered.

ACKNOWLEDGMENTS

Thanks to Mike Bagnod, Bill Bagshaw, Jim Baker, Jack Beckman, Norman Blake, Boss Performance, Brandon Bregel, Shirley Shahan-Bridges, J.V. Brotherton, Ron Butler, Rich Carlson, John Callies, Jesus Christ our Lord and Savior, John Clinard (Ford Motor Company), Tim Costello, Steve Chrisman, Gary Victor Dubin (Attorney at Law, Honolulu, Hawaii), Bob Frey, Don Krenzer, Gina's Photos, Roy Hill, Tom and Linda Jacobson, Tom Jacobson Jr., Debbie Jacobson-Wilson, Jim Kelly, Gil Kirk, Dave Koffel, Bob Lambeck, Denny and John Laube, Donna, Bret, Burt Leah, Lisa, Laurie, Harrison, and Maddison Leal, Ray Mann, J.B. and Brayden Myer, Gary Nastase, U.S. Senator Devin Nunes, Ron and Donna Ogilvie, Bob Perkins, Hayden Proffitt, Paul Rossi, Donald N. Sarian Photo & Graphics, Steve Reyes, Bob Riffle, Richard Shute (Auto Imagery), Geoff Stunkard, Danny Thompson, Doug Thorley, Dick Towers (Matchracemadness), Linda Vaughn, Clayton "C.W." Waites, Les Welch, Mark "Willy Boy" Wilson, and Lynn Wineland.

ABOUT THE AUTHOR

Bob McClurg has been writing about cars and car people for the last 55 years. He is a widely acclaimed automotive photojournalist whose specialty was photographing erratic Fuel Altereds, wheel-standing Gassers, vintage Funny Cars, fire-breathing front-engine dragsters, and early-era Pro Stock cars back in drag racing's halcyon days. In doing so, he has stood on the starting lines of some of the most famous drag strips in the history of the sport and has pretty much seen and done it all.

As a youngster, McClurg grew up in Southern California's post–urban sprawl era when many smaller communities were still separated by orange groves and rows of Eucalyptus trees. The city of Orange was where the McClurg family ultimately settled (upon migrating from upstate New York in July 1954) along with countless others seeking milder climates and seemingly unlimited opportunities that the Golden State had to offer.

Bob's father, Robert H.S. McClurg, had grown up as part of a sizeable Irish immigrant family in New York's post-depression recovery era that haplessly evolved into the World War II era. As with countless other young Americans, Bob's father went off to war and was among the fortunate ones to return. However, with a growing family and five mouths to feed, there was never enough money or leisure time in the McClurg household to indulge in something as expensive and irrelevant as hot rods. As far as Bob's father was concerned, cars were strictly a mode of transportation to get from Point A, to Point B.

"Unfortunately, my father used to call hot rods 'jalopies,' or even worse, 'junkers,'" Bob said. "I was absolutely befuddled by that; he just had no use for cars other than as basic transportation. He just didn't see the beauty in them or marvel at the incredible amount of engineering put into them. I remember the time he tried to change the main bearings on the flathead V-8 engine in his 1941 Ford work car. I learned a whole new (and quite colorful) vocabulary that weekend. But then again, he *was* a former sailor in the U.S. Navy!"

Fortunately for Bob, there were outside (automotive) influences from which to draw. The late Jack Hart, who went on to become the first competition director for the fledgling National Hot Rod Association (NHRA) and owned Hart's Texaco Automotive Service at the corner of Chapman Avenue and Parker Street, took him under his wing. One block down was Towne Barber Shop where Bob worked as a shoe-shine boy. It was during that time that he discovered *Hot Rod* magazine and numerous other car magazines stuffed in the barber shop reading rack. Directly across the street from Towne Barber Shop was Selman Chevrolet's A-1 Used Car lot, which usually had a handful of Tri-Five Chevrolets and a Corvette or two parked there.

Walking across town to St. John's Lutheran School every day was another adventure with plenty of places for a car-crazy kid to get sidetracked. Along the route, directly across the railroad tracks was Selman's new-car showroom, and right across the street was Bill Corwin Ford. If that wasn't sufficient enough temptation, there was also a Goodyear tire retreading shop, the Blake & Nation Body Shop, Hoffman's Radiator Shop, and the local Mobil gas station. You get the picture.

In the early 1960s, the McClurg family moved across town to Villa Park, which seemed light years away from Bob's old hangouts. Fortunately for him, there were three hobby shops located on nearby Tustin Avenue. Two of them had slot car tracks, and all were easily within walking distance.

"I was a sophomore on half-day session at Orange High School and would walk down to either Gish's Toys or Frank's Hobbies every morning, race slot cars until about 11:30 a.m., and then go to school," Bob said. "On the way home again, it was even more slot car racing."

To help pay for his slot car "addiction," Bob took a weekend job at Gish's Toys. One afternoon, owner Roger Clausen asked Bob if he would like to accompany him to Lions Associated Drag Strip. "Big Daddy" Don Garlits was match racing Chris "Greek" Karamesines, Don "the Snake" Prudhomme, and Kenny Safford. Talk about sensory overload! The sights, sounds, and smells of nitro and burnt rubber—wow! You just don't get that from simply reading a car magazine. From that point on, he was hooked!

Although he was hooked, there wasn't much he was able to do about it.

"I didn't get my first car until I was 18 years old, so I had to 'mooch' rides to the drags from whomever I could," Bob said. "I usually was the one who paid, and sometimes, I got left there. Even worse, I had almost zero mechanical skills, so for me, becoming a big-time drag racer was pretty much out of the question. There had to be another way."

Fortunately, McClurg excelled in journalism. He wrote his first real newspaper article on traffic safety for the *Orange Daily News*, and had it published when he was in the fifth grade. That led to a brief stint as editor of the ninth-grade junior high school newspaper. Then, it was on to high school yearbook class, but all the writing jobs had already been taken. His journalism teacher, John Osborn, handed him the school camera, a couple of rolls of film, and gave him a little piece of advice, "You can either take pictures or transfer to another elective."

"I knew very little about photography," Bob said. "My uncle had given me his old 35-mm Argus C3 a few years before, but it involved quite a bit of math, and I was lousy at math."

Then, one night McClurg snuck out onto the starting line at Lions Associated Drag Strip with his high school camera in hand. It was a short visit, just enough time to click off about a half dozen pictures before being escorted back to the stands by track security, but it proved to be a real game changer.

"From then on, all I wanted to do was photograph drag racing," Bob said. "Fortunately, I was able to obtain a starting-line photo credential through the sports editor at the *Orange Daily News*. By then, I was attending Fullerton Junior College and met a classmate there who photographed football for the *Anaheim Bulletin* newspaper. I wasn't particularly interested in photographing football, but Sports Editor Doug Miles made me a deal that if I would do that on Thursday and Friday nights, he would arrange for a permanent starting-line photo credential for me at Lions, Irwindale, and Orange County International Raceway (OCIR). He also made good on the deal by publishing a weekly feature story I did on one of many local Orange County racers."

In April 1969, Bob got his first big break with *Super Stock & Drag Illustrated* magazine and headed east. His first assignment was none other than photographing Tasca Ford's last in a series of Mustang Funny Cars, the Tasca *Super Boss*. The prolific McClurg has gone on to become published in practically every car magazine in America as well as a number in Europe and Asia. Along the way, he worked for the *Los Angeles Times*'s Orange County Bureau, as photo editor for Petersen Specialty Publications, as photo editor for *Hot Rod* magazine, and as editor for *Hot Rod Corvette* and *Petersen's Kit Car* magazines. He taught school at Chatsworth, California's Learning Tree University, was editor at McMullen & Yee's *Mustang Illustrated* magazine, and was editor for the McMullen/Argus *Ford High Performance* magazines. Today, Bob and his dog, Jake, reside just outside Hilo, Hawaii, and he still writes and takes in select car events on the mainland.

"After all those years, I finally have my own toy shop on the property," Bob said. "I also have an IHRA-sanctioned drag strip (Hilo Raceway Park) 3 miles in one direction of town and a dyno shop less than 3 miles in the other direction of town. This truly *is* paradise."

FOREWORD
BY "FAST JACK" BECKMAN

I've done a lot of fun things in my life, and I've done lots of rewarding things in my life. Those two terms aren't necessarily mutually inclusive. Many fun things simply aren't very rewarding, and often what's considered rewarding isn't really very fun.

Being asked to write my first foreword for a book initially seemed to check off both the fun and rewarding boxes until I sat staring at my computer screen, cursing my apparent attention deficit disorder and the writer's block it had produced.

I know drag racing, I know Bob McClurg, and I know Butch Leal, and whoever actually reads this foreword certainly won't experience a life-changing moment. So, why all the fuss?

Well, like most of you, I like to put in an honest effort with the hopes that it yields a quality result. Bob deserves it, Butch deserves it, and the sport deserves it.

Now that I am on version 3.0 of this text, I have come to appreciate that "fun" isn't what I'm going after by writing this, nor is it necessary; I'll be completely content with "rewarding."

I'm beginning with a heartfelt thank you to Bob for entrusting me with this. Among my heroes of the sport are many announcers, writers, and photographers. They are the ones who preserve the sport for history, as well as serve up current information to keep the fans entertained

I count Bob as one of the major icons.

I think nearly every fan of drag racing would put Butch into that category.

It's not surprising that Butch and I share many similar experiences, but there are some interesting commonalities: we both made our first runs down the strip as teenagers driving El Caminos. His was a 1960 version; mine was a 1968 (which I own to this day). Both of us hail from California, and both of us go by nicknames. I'm not talking about the "California Flash," or "Fast Jack." Butch was born Larry; I was born John.

Butch sold his 1968 Barracuda Funny Car (his first Funny Car that featured a supercharger, and one that he never ran) to my future boss, Don Schumacher.

The question I am asked more often than any other is what I consider the greatest accomplishment of my career. Although my answer likely isn't what the interviewer was thinking of, I think this sums it up: I am most proud of the fact that I have become close with so many of the sports pioneers, legends, and icons.

(Photo Courtesy Mark Gerwertz)

To digress for a moment, I often don't think of myself as a 50-something man who is married with two children and has dozens of trophies and a couple of World Championships. I often don't think of myself as someone who has earned a good living driving 10,000-hp, 335-mph beasts for the better part of 15 years. I often don't think of myself as someone who has been interviewed for television hundreds of times, set multiple records, and has signed tens of thousands of autographs.

No, I often (and clearly) remember that 7-year-old version of myself sitting in the stands at OCIR. No amount of wishful thinking, daydreaming, or wishes granted could have teleported me 47 years into the future, sitting here typing this, surrounded by an enviable trophy collection. I simply wasn't prepared to dream that big.

From the instant my Uncle John got my brother Ted and me into the facility, I was completely drawn in and totally hooked. I was in awe of *every* machine that went down that quarter-mile strip of asphalt. Sure, the nitro cars were something out of a dream—with push starts, huge burnouts, dry hops, and backup girls. The nitro stung my eyes in the most satisfying way imaginable, and the exhaust blast pounded my chest. Overwhelming is an understatement.

But, unlike Uncle John, who even to this day thinks the Pro Stock class is his official reminder to go down and watch the work in the nitro pits, I could not be pried out of the stands when the factory hot rods came up. In fact, *because* they made less noise, in many ways they were more enjoyable. If the announcers were earning their pay, getting the fans riled up to cheer for their favorite brand just added to the pageantry that was Pro Stock in the early and mid-1970s.

The first time I saw Butch was at OCIR, in either 1973 or 1974. He truly had it all: mechanical ingenuity, driving prowess, movie-star looks, and a killer car with a great name: *The California Flash.*

Again, allow me to digress:

This was also a very, very special time for drag racing. Back then, the sport was as much (or more) entertainment than sport. Today's fans truly missed a marvelous era where ultimate performance wasn't the only way to win the crowd over. In fact, in that era, even the dominant cars still were doing the rituals that added so much to overall enjoyment, beyond how the car accelerated for a quarter mile.

Gradually, the burnouts became shorter, the dry hops in VHT (resin) were less prevalent, and the practice hit at the line fell out of favor. Race cars were becoming more sophisticated and expensive, and better track preparation plus the desire to expedite the show simply made superfluous many of the pre-race antics that were just plain bitchin'.

That is not to say that the sport has suffered, although I will forever cherish and miss all of that asphalt hyperbole. In fact, most of that milieu I'm describing had not been a part of drag racing for very long. When the sport began taking off in the 1950s, none of that would have been necessary. However, advancements in tires, tracks, clutches, and driveline components (and perhaps that cultural phenomenon that was the 1960s and 1970s) helped shape the sport into what it was at that point, and that was something very special.

Although its seeds were planted in the 1970s, the 1980s became the age of corporate involvement in drag racing. To be certain, independent racers could still compete (and some even thrived) but not like a decade before. The drivers who contended for championships were now strapped into machines that bore sponsors' names, and they raced for wins, for points, and for championships.

Knowing this makes Butch's accomplishments all the more impressive. He was able to win from the time he was a teenager until well into his 40s; he won in stick shifts and automatics; he won in Chevys, Fords, Dodges, Plymouths, and Pontiacs; he won in Super Stock, Modified, and Pro Stock. He was competitive for nearly 30 years, and he did it as a hired driver and as a team owner. He was ultra-tough as a privateer and formidable as a factory team member.

Butch also somehow possessed that elusive blend: he was passionately competitive and genuinely nice.

Years ago, I was signing autographs at the back of my pit area in Pomona and struck up a conversation with an obviously knowledgeable woman. I don't know how the conversation turned toward her racing experiences, but she mentioned that her father, a former racer, was attending this race with her.

When I found out that Butch was her dad, I did my best to keep my composure and asked (as coolly as I possibly could) if there was any way she could introduce me.

I don't think I can adequately describe the satisfaction of not only meeting Butch for the first time (notwithstanding the times that I stood at his pit to get an autograph as a kid) but also having him actually know who I was! You can get a sense of Butch's charisma by watching him be interviewed on TV. However, much like the sport of drag racing itself, it's just not the same as in person. He's easy to converse with, emits positive energy, and is just plain likeable.

I one-upped myself when I was asked to emcee a panel one evening at the NHRA Motorsports Museum. The panel, which was packed with legends, included Butch. I did my homework, came prepared, and knew how to set up each person to enable them to deliver an entertaining answer to the audience. I was getting good at "lobbing softballs" at many of these functions, and it is necessary for many of our past stars who struggle with public speaking.

With Butch, it was completely unnecessary. He literally could command the stage as a solo act and entertain the room for an hour straight.

I'd be honored if that opportunity ever avails itself to me.

For now, I am content to know that this endeavor of mine, for my friend Bob, has been rewarding. Heck, I suppose it even has been a little fun!

Butch, the International Drag Racing Hall of Fame has recognized your contributions to the sport by inducting you.

However, your life is really defined by much more than that. You've been a hall of famer in my eyes since the day I first saw you shifting gears and helped guide my life into the fast lane.

Thank you, Bob, and thank you, Butch! I'm humbled.

"Fast Jack" Beckman
2012 NHRA Funny Car
World Champion

INTRODUCTION

It has been said that regardless of the brand of car, with Butch Leal behind the wheel, it was worth an extra two hundredths of a second on the tree. Considered one of the best 4-speed men in the business, Larry "Butch" Leal was born on May 10, 1944, to parents Pansy and Frank Leal Jr. in the agricultural town of Tulare, which is located in Central California's San Joaquin Valley just 80 miles south of Modesto.

"My grandmother Donna, also known as "Doney," named me Butch the very minute my parents brought me home from the East Tulare hospital—her reasoning being that I looked more like a Butch than a Larry, and the nickname just sort of stuck," Butch said.

As a youngster, Butch resided in the agricultural town of Pixley but spent his summers on his grandparent's dairy farm, Frank Leal Dairy, in Hanford, California. Those were idyllic times: chasing cows, tossing cow chips, riding on his grandfather's tractor, and playing with Shemp, the family dog.

"The two of us would go out and herd the cows every evening," Butch said. "I ate well there. My grandmother was such a good cook that every summer I would come home 20 pounds heavier."

Butch's love of hot rods went as far back as the fourth or fifth grade.

"My teachers at Pixley Grammar School [where Butch excelled in stick and ball sports, winning numerous awards] became so frustrated with me, as I was more interested in drawing pictures of cars on my school papers than I was about learning about math and history," Butch said.

With the obvious staring them squarely in the face, Butch's mother eventually caved in and gave her son his own subscription to *Hot Rod* magazine for Christmas at age 12!

One of life's lessons that young Butch learned (and it wasn't from school, either) was that hard work has its own reward and with it came the value of a dollar as he became engrossed more and more in the family business called Frank Leal Trucking.

"I used to load cotton seed and hay," Butch said. "We also used to haul tomatoes from the Sacramento River Delta area. After delivering a load, I would run the steam cleaner, which was pretty nasty work. If the trucks were stopped, we weren't making any money, so I did all kinds of odd jobs around the yard to help out.

"My dad and I used to kid around with each other,

At age 9, Butch is at his grandparents' dairy in Hanford, California.

and he even proposed that we re-letter the trucks to say 'Frank Leal and Son Trucking' on the doors. Of course, that gave me a somewhat inflated sense of entitlement. One day, I think I was about 14, I had grown tired of loading hay and steam cleaning tomato haulers and walked into my dad's office and said, 'I've got to do something else with my life. I'm tired of steam cleaning trucks. Why don't you just buy me out?' Looking back, that was some pretty funny stuff."

Friends For Life

Quite typically, young Butch learned the ins and outs of rudimentary auto mechanics from his father, Frank, and put them to good use. However, Butch also had a willing helper in lifelong friend Doug Walden.

"Doug and I were friends all the way through school and beyond," Butch said. "We did almost everything together. When I was 14 [1958], there was a kid in town who was selling a Mustang motorcycle, so Doug and I snuck off together away from home and chopped cotton out in the fields around Pixley until we had saved up the $80 the seller was asking for it.

"We rode it around for a while before I ended up trading it for a 1946 Ford coupe that didn't run. Doug and I ended up installing a 1953 Mercury flathead V-8 with Edelbrock heads and three-twos [three 2-barrel carburetors]. We also installed a LaSalle 3-speed transmission, rebuilt the rear end, and bolted up a set of 1948 Mercury wheels with whitewall tires.

"One night, I was cruising Pixley, California's Three Brothers hamburger joint, and a friend of mine named J.C. was there with his 1931 Model A Ford coupe. At the time, Model As were all the rage, so I said, 'Let's trade straight across, but I'll keep my tires and wheels,' and we did.

"One day, Doug and I were loading hay for my dad down in Bakersfield and were having lunch at the local burger joint when he met this young lady named Betty, and it was love at first sight. Doug and Betty have been married for 57 years now, which I think is pretty neat. Today, Doug is retired, lives in Bakersfield, builds hot rods as a hobby, and regularly comes to the Southern California Auto Club–hosted California Hot Rod Reunion events where it's just like old times!"

Running Afoul of the Law

"That first night, as I drove my 'new' 1931 Model A home, the local California Highway Patrol officer pulled me over for not having a brake light. When the officer asked me for my driver's license, I told him that I didn't have one, and he wrote me a ticket.

"About an hour later, he pulled me over again! He said, 'I thought I told you to go home?'

"I said, 'No, you just wanted to know if I had a driver's license. You already gave me a ticket for that, so I'm just out cruising for the rest of the evening.'"

When Butch's father appeared with him at the Porterville, California, juvenile court, Frank Leal explained to the judge that the family lived out in the country, owned a fleet of agricultural trucks, and in times of immediacy, young Butch was called upon to drive.

"The judge wrote me a special pass, and I got my driver's license at age 14.

"The farmers around there had given me a total of six Model A Ford engines, which Doug and I took apart and were able to make one good motor out of all those parts and pieces. I raced that old Model A everywhere I could. With a set of 8.20 x 15-inch Atlas Bucrons mounted, it made enough horsepower to chirp the tires in second gear at Bakersfield, California's Famoso Raceway and top out at almost 70 mph, which was pretty darned fast for a stock 'A Banger' in those days!"

And so began the legend of the yet-to-be-christened "California Flash." In hindsight, you can only wonder what that California Highway Patrolman would have thought that fateful evening had he known that he was ticketing one of professional drag racing's up-and-coming superstars.

CHAPTER 1

EL CAMINO LE-AL!

*"When I drove the car home that night, I had to drive at a 45-degree angle
across the railroad tracks because it was so low.
My dad came out of the house giving me all kinds of static."*

"When I was 14, I made a deal with my father that if I worked real hard at the yard (Frank Leal Trucking in Pixley, California), he would buy me any new car I wanted on my 16th birthday—that is, anything except a new Corvette," Butch Leal said. "He didn't pay me a salary or anything like that, but over the next few summers, I accumulated three or four thousand dollars in 'credit' doing every type of odd job at the yard that my father could think of.

"At the time, *the* hot car to have [was] a 1960 Chevrolet Bel Air equipped with the 335-hp 348-ci W-Series Turbo-Fire V-8 complete with Tri-Power and a 4-speed. At first, I was going to get one of those, but then I read in *Hot Rod* magazine that the 348 El Caminos were rated at 350 hp. Basically, it had something to do with the fact that the El Caminos had bigger intake valves because they were slightly heavier and were classified as light-duty trucks. Since our family owned a trucking business, it all worked out perfectly!"

Butch ordered a Royal Blue (Frank Leal Trucking Company's official color) 1960 Chevrolet El Camino 348 4-speed that arrived at Pixley, California's Dale Munson Chevrolet on his 16th birthday, and he became the scourge of the San Joaquin Valley.

A Slight Hiccup

"Once the dealer washed the protective coating off the car and backed it out into the sun, I noticed a huge white cloud in the driver-side rear quarter panel. When I pointed it out to the dealer, he said that they would spot paint it. I said no and insisted that (with this being a metallic paint job) the dealership should repaint the entire car!"

Fortunately for young Butch, the GM district sales representative happened to be paying Munson Chevrolet a call that day.

"I'm looking at it, and I'm just totally blown away," Butch said. "Just as the conversation was starting to become a little heated, he [the GM representative] walked

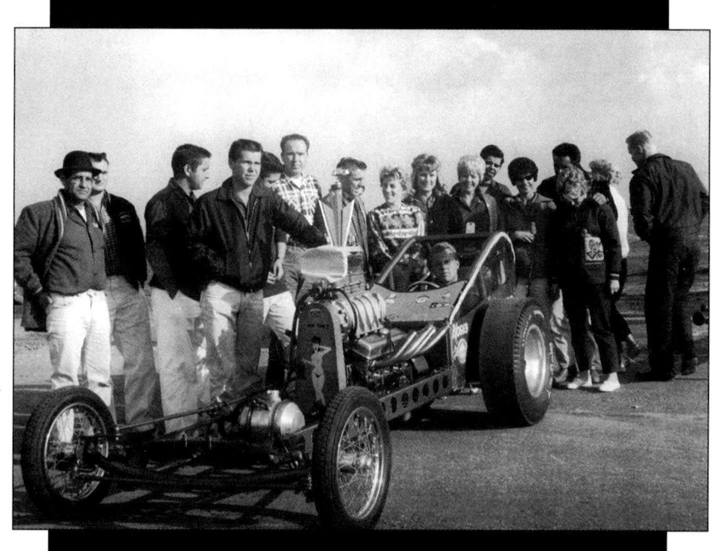

In this group photo taken in 1961 of the Vapor Trailer's Car Club of Tulare, a flat-top-wearing, 16-year-old Larry "Butch" Leal (fourth from left) can be seen admiring the club dragster. Also captured are H.L. and Shirley Shahan (seventh and eighth from left). Ed "Ace" McCulloch is also pictured, but his exact location is difficult to pinpoint due to photo quality.

out the front door of the dealership, took one look at it, and turned to the sales manager and said, 'We'll [re]paint the whole thing.'

"Well, they shouldn't have told me that!"

Rather than spend several weeks in the dealership body shop where projects such as this often get shoved on the back burner, Butch and his father drove the El Camino to Doyce's Paint & Body Shop in Tulare where the El Camino was repainted the original GM Code 912 Royal Blue Metallic with 20 coats of clear lacquer thrown in for good measure.

"Doyce's would spray on a couple of coats of clear and sand them down only to spray on a couple more," Butch said. "Once they buffed out the final coat, it just sparkled in the sun and turned purple under the lights at night. I mean, it was drop-dead gorgeous.

"I also had the first set of chrome-reverse wheels for it here in the valley. Everybody had their cars lowered back in those days, so during my lunch break at Tulare Union High School, I took the car over to a fellow in town who took a coil out in the front and half a coil out in the back. I mean, the car sat perfect.

"When I drove the car home that night, I had to drive at a 45-degree angle across the railroad tracks because it was so low. My dad came out of the house giving me all kinds of static. I stood my ground and said to him, 'Is this your car, or is it mine? I paid for it!'

"That ended the conversation."

This extremely rare photo shows the 16-year-old Tulare Union High School student posing with his pride and joy, a mild custom, H.L. Shahan–engine 1960 Chevrolet El Camino W-Series 348 and 4-speed. Butch ran his El Camino in the SS/S class for a year and a half and won well more than 100 trophies while clocking a best ET of 13.80 at 104 mph. The unfortunate irony of this photo is that after trading the car back in to Dale Munson Chevrolet for his 1962 409 Biscayne, the second owner stalled the car at a Union Pacific Railway crossing in Tulare and the El Camino was unceremoniously cut in half!

The Lure of the Drag Strip

"At the time, my dad didn't want me to even think about drag racing, although deep inside, he knew that's where things were headed," Butch said. "The first time I took the El Camino out to Famoso Raceway (which was *the* place to hang out on the weekend) I let a friend of mine named Bobby Dykman drive because I was a little nervous. He ended up getting beat. The next month, my girlfriend Susann and I went. This time, I decided that I would drive, and I won.

"Well, that got me completely hooked on drag racing. Then, I went back the next month and won again. When I came home, I was holding this trophy behind my back, and they [Mom and Dad] asked me where I had been? I figured that my dad wouldn't like hearing that I had been out drag racing against his wishes, but once I showed him my trophy, he got pretty excited about it. In fact, he and my mother went to the track with me the very next month, and I won again."

"In September 1961 the 409 Impalas came out, and they were wicked fast—so fast that my friend Bobby was constantly outrunning me with his. The next day, I walked outside of the house. Dad had the hood up on the El Camino and said, 'If you're going to do this, then let's do it right!'

"We pulled the motor and took it over to H.L. Shahan's Precision Automotive shop in Tulare. We changed out the pistons (a couple of them were cracked because I had been street racing the thing for a while), and H.L. replaced them with a set of Forgetrue Pistons. Then, we balanced the motor. Otherwise, the rest of the engine remained stock."

Butch ran the El Camino in the SS/S class for a year and a half and clocked a best elapsed time (ET) of 13.80 seconds at 104 mph. In the process, he won more than 100 trophies.

"My mother cleared off a shelf in our den to show off my trophies, but after my winning so many, she gave up trying to dust them all," Butch said. "Man, I raced that thing everywhere I could—even circle track. They had a quarter-mile circle track in Hanford called March Bank Stadium where they raced NASCAR. We would race down the straightaway, and then when you would go to shut it off, you would coast around the corners.

"I would race twice a week at the small tracks around here when I could. I even raced San Fernando once. I'll be darned if 'Dandy Dick' Landy wasn't there driving Andy Andrews's 406 Ford. I out-ran Dick with the El Camino, and he said, 'Where did you come from, young boy?' Yeah [laughing], he called me a 'young boy.'

"In those days, good tires were always a problem. We didn't have cheater slicks back then. I would run Atlas Bucron tires, which were really soft. I can't remember how many sets of those I went through. Actually, I ran two classes with the El Camino. I would run the three-two class, and then I would switch back to the factory 348 intake and run the car in the single 4-barrel class!"

In late 1961, Butch pulled the H.L. Shahan–prepared 348 drivetrain out of the El Camino and replaced it with a stock one. Chevrolet Division's 1962 409s had just been released, so Leal drove over to Dale Munson Chevrolet and traded the El Camino in on one. Suffice it to say, vintage 1960s NHRA Division 7 Super Stock Eliminator class racing was never the same.

Family Ties

Ronnie Broadhead and his 1960 Tri Power 389 Pontiac Catalina are caught in action at the 1963 NHRA Nationals at Indianapolis Raceway Park in Indianapolis, Indiana. It was a banner year for Broadhead, as he won the NHRA Stock Eliminator World Points Championship. In 1966, cousin Butch Leal won class at the NHRA Winternationals driving the very same car. (Photo Courtesy Jeanette Broadhead)

In 1961, Porterville, California, custom car upholsterer Ronnie Broadhead (Buster's Custom Upholstery) decided to get in on the fun. He was encouraged by the reasonable degree of success that his cousin Butch Leal was experiencing drag racing his Chevrolet El Camino big-block at AHRA and NHRA racetracks up and down the Golden State.

A Pontiac man by preference, Broadhead fielded a number of "Tin Indians" throughout his driving career, including an H.L. Shahan–prepared and tuned 1960 Pontiac Catalina Tri-Power 4-speed car that Ronnie campaigned in the C/Stock class to take the 1963 NHRA Stock Eliminator World Points Championship.

"We were close—just like brothers," Butch Leal said.

After running Pontiacs, Ronnie Broadhead transitioned to Oldsmobiles. Toward the end of his racing career, Broadhead teamed with racing great Joe Alread on a Mopar small-block program, but after a heart attack in 1975, Broadhead was forced to hang up his driving gloves for good.

CHAPTER 2

GIDDY UP, GIDDY UP 409

". . . if Butch Leal ever beat you out of the hole, you needed all the horsepower and driving skills you had just to catch him." – Hayden Proffitt

In the fall of 1961, Butch Leal ordered a Royal Blue Metallic W-Series 1962 409 Chevrolet Biscayne that was factory rated at 409 hp and equipped with twin 4-barrel Carter AFB carburetors and a BorgWarner 4-speed transmission (QB-8-409) through Pixley, California's Dale Munson Chevrolet.

"Being that the 119-inch-wheelbase Chevrolet Biscayne was a lighter car, weighing approximately 3,405 pounds, I reasoned that it might be a bit more competitive than the heavier SS 409 bubbletops that my competitors were running, and I ordered the car through the same dealership that I ordered my El Camino from," Butch Leal said.

As it turned out, Munson Chevrolet became the soon-to-be-christened "California Flash's" first associate sponsor.

"My family knew Dale Munson personally and helped set up a meeting with him," Butch said. "I told Dale what I was going to do and that I wanted to order this factory hot rod through his dealership but needed a little help.

"Munson enthusiastically replied, 'No problem!'"

What Dale Munson actually did was discount the sticker price on the Biscayne to the degree that it enabled young Butch to put together a first-class racing program at the age of 18.

"I remember the car had 13 miles on the odometer when we took it to H.L. Shahan's shop," Butch said. "We tore it completely apart. I got under it and lightened it as much as I could. We moved the body back on the chassis about an inch and a half. In fact, I even went as far as to cut every other spring out of the rear seat frame to save weight—and God help anyone if they ever sat in the back seat!

"That car was real, real fast. The first time out it ran low 13s at 109 mph. I would routinely run at Lions [Drag Strip] on Saturday night outrunning the likes of 'Dyno Don' Nicholson and [at times] Hayden Proffitt with their 409s, as well as winning class at the Pomona Drags on Sunday."

At this juncture, 1962 NHRA Nationals Top Stock Eliminator Champion Hayden "Old Folks" Proffitt offered his take on the subject.

"I've always regarded Butch Leal, Ronnie Sox, 'Dyno Don' Nicholson, and myself as four of the best 'leavers' in the sport," Proffitt said. "But, if Butch Leal ever beat you out of the hole, you needed all the horsepower and driving skills you had just to catch him."

This National Dragster *newspaper clipping shows Butch competing against soon-to-be-appointed NHRA Division 7 Director Bernie Partridge. At the time, both Butch and Partridge campaigned 1962 409 Chevrolet Biscaynes in the Top Stock class. On this particular outing, Butch took Top Stock honors at Inyokern, recording an ET of 12.06 at 118 mph.*

Obtaining pit passes was a lot simpler back in the day. These are examples of Butch's 1962 NHRA Winternationals and 1962 NHRA Nationals pit passes.

Leal's 409 also made a good showing at the 1962 NHRA Nationals on Sunday (where eventual winner Hayden Proffitt beat him in the semifinals) and on Monday (where Butch again lost in the semifinals to the Ramchargers, the eventual Top Stock Eliminator runner-up). Ultimately, the car ran a best ET of 12.82 at 114 mph, and more importantly, it established Butch as an up-and-comer in the Super Stock Eliminator ranks.

Old Race Cars Never Die

Old race cars never die; they just keep on winning. Case in point: the ex–Butch Leal 1962 Chevrolet 409 Biscayne acquired by Southern Californian's Tom and Linda Jacobson in the fall of 1963.

"We bought the Biscayne after Butch ordered his '63 Z11 car," Tom Jacobson said. "I think we paid $2,500 for it. I remember we financed it through the local bank where my wife worked. We used to run the car at Lions on the weekends and did pretty well with *Old Blue*."

Old Blue?

Tom Jacobson continued, "Whenever Butch came to town, he would always stay at his Aunt Pauline Dellingham's house in nearby Carson, California. When he would come back home from the races in the evening, she would always ask, 'Well, how did *Old Blue* do?'

"That's how the car got its name."

Old Blue was a known killer in AHRA Stock Class racing and won the AHRA A/Stock National Championship in 1966. Tom Jacobson raced *Old Blue* from 1963–1966 (with running upgrades allowed by an ever-changing AHRA rule book regarding the cam, cylinder heads, etc.) and ran a career best ET of 11.60 at 123.60 mph with the car.

In 1965, *Old Blue* developed sort of an alter ego (in a manner of speaking) when Tom Jacobson transplanted its 409 engine into Tom Sturm's *Just 4 Chevy Lovers* 1964 Chevelle match racer. The car was in dire need of a shakedown engine and was also known as "Sturm & Jacobson."

Evolutionary

As for the car itself, Tom briefly partnered with Ray Sledge (of Sledge & Jacobson) in 1963, Jack Upton (of Upton & Jacobson) in 1964, and Dennis Edwards (of Edwards & Jacobson) in 1965, only to sell the Biscayne in 1967 after it became heavily damaged when it slid off the lube rack during routine maintenance.

In the ensuing years, *Old Blue* changed hands numerous times and was eventually lost to the ages. Then, in 1983, Tom resurrected *Old Blue* using a donor body and frame. He also added the assorted 409 parts taken off and saved from *Old Blue* throughout its evolutionary development cycle. Today, a reincarnated version of *Old Blue* sits in quiet repose inside the Lions Drag Strip Museum in Long Beach, California.

In late 1962, Tom Jacobson purchased Butch's 409 Biscayne Old Blue *and transformed the car (with a series of three different partners) into an AHRA multi-class winner. (Photo Courtesy Tom Jacobson)*

CHAPTER 3

BEGINNING THE YEAR WITH ONE BRAND AND FINISHING IT WITH ANOTHER

". . . I pulled up to the time-slip booth, and wow, the thing ran 121 mph! Man, oh man, I felt like I was Keith Black, Ed Pink, and Sid Waterman all rolled into one! "

In 1963, Chevrolet Motor Division one-upped its potent 1963 SS 409 Impala street car package with the creation of its race-only RPO 427 Z11 Chevy Impala SS lightweight package that used a stroked version of Chevrolet's Code QM 409 cylinder block with a 4.3125-inch bore and 3.65-inch stroke. The car featured 13.5:1-compression pistons, a solid-lifter cam (at 325 degrees duration and 0.556 max valve lift), a set of staggered 2.19-inch-diameter intake and 1.72-inch-diameter exhaust valve W-Series cylinder heads, a two-piece cowl-induction aluminum intake sporting twin Carter No. 3815403 AFB carburetors, GM cast-iron headers, a deep-sump 8-quart oil pan, an aluminum water pump, ACDelco ignition, and 10,000-rpm ACDelco tachometer.

Conservatively rated at 430 hp at 6,000 rpm and registering 530 ft-lbs of torque at 3,600 rpm, the 1963 427 Z11 Impala SS big-block was backed with a BorgWarner T10 4-speed transmission and a 4.11:1-geared live rear axle. However, that was only the half of it. The 1963 Z11 tipped the scales at 3,405 pounds. That's 300 pounds lighter than the production 1963 409 Impala SS in part due to the utilization of aluminum parts, including the front fenders, hood, doors, and front and rear bumpers and mounting brackets along with a bare-bones interior. The actual production number data on these cars varies, but it is generally agreed that between 50 and 57 of these low-11-second 427 Z11 Chevrolet lightweights were built with fewer than a dozen examples surviving.

The release of Chevrolet's "for drag racing only" 427 Z11 (the Bowtie Brigade also offered a similar package for NASCAR powered by its 427 Mystery Motor) attracted a virtual who's who in AHRA/NHRA drag racing, including Dave Strickler/Bill Jenkins, Hayden Proffitt, Ronnie Sox/Buddy Martin, Hubert Platt, Malcolm Durham, and many others. Being a relative newcomer to the world of GM factory politics, Leal needed to find someone with a foot squarely planted in GM's front door (politically speaking of course) to obtain one of these cars. That certain someone happened to be the prime mover and shaker behind Holman & Moody of Chevrolet Motor Division: Mr. Bill Thomas, CEO of Anaheim, California's Bill Thomas Race Cars, Incorporated.

"In 1962 I was outrunning Hayden [Proffitt] and 'Dyno' [Don Nicholson] at Pomona when Bill Thomas came up and invited H.L., my folks, and me to his shop in Anaheim, California," Butch said. "Bill came up with a set of some really trick rear springs for the '62 (which didn't please Hayden none too much) that really helped the Biscayne launch better. After that, Thomas helped get me hooked up with my 1963 Z11 deal through GM. We had the car shipped directly to Dale Munson Chevrolet in Pixley. Bill also got one for Hayden [Proffitt] and one for Shirley [Shahan], so obviously he was pretty well connected. To be a part of all that at just 19 years old, I thought was really, really cool."

In the book *Shirley Shahan: The Drag-on Lady* published by CarTech, H.L. said, "If I remember right, there

Bill Thomas helped Butch as well as H.L. and Shirley Shahan obtain 1963 Chevrolet Z11s.

In early 1963, Butch flexes his 1963 427 Z11's muscles at Lions Associated Drag Strip (LADS). Butch's Z11 ran a career-best ET of 12.06 at 118 mph and toppled No. 3-seeded Hayden Proffitt's Plymouth to take Top Stock honors.

were only 57 of those cars built. Of course, Bill Thomas was the one who got the cars for us. Butch Leal had one, and Shirley and I had one. Can you imagine that—having two of those Z11 Chevrolets in a little old town like Tulare?"

As could be expected, Butch's 1963 Z11 lightweight proved to be one of the fastest and quickest 427 Z11s in the country with ETs of 12.06 at 118 mph. Due to the car's rarity, the NHRA placed these cars in the Limited Production class at the 1963 NHRA Winternationals along with the Fords.

"I ended up beating [Richard] Brannan and [Bob] Tasca," Butch said. "Then, I ran Greg Sanders' Z11 in the final and got beat. But when we went to tear down, Sanders' Z11 got thrown out for valve spring pressure of all things, so I ended up winning the race!"

That year, Butch also challenged 1962 NHRA Nationals Top Stock Champion Hayden Proffitt and took the third spot away from Hayden (who was running a 426-ci 1963 Plymouth Max Wedge) in two runs with a best ET of 12.44 at 114.21 mph to Hayden's 12.62 at 109 mph

during the Lions One Hundred Dollar Challenge. At that time, Leal was ranked No. 10.

"Halfway through the year, Bill asked me if he could pull the aluminum front end off the Z11 and install an OE steel front end that GM had sent us," Butch said. "Then, he wanted to install a NASCAR-spec 427 Mystery Motor with three twos in the car. GM had shipped three of those engines to Bill's shop, and Bobby Unser would drive the car at the Pike's Peak Hill Climb. Well, I thought that was a pretty good idea, so we pulled off the aluminum front end, and just as we were getting ready to change out engines, Bill called me into his office.

"Bill said, 'Butch, Chevy just pulled the plug [by publishing its infamous *Moratorium on Racing*].'

There was no more NASCAR and no more NHRA/AHRA drag racing.

"Bill said, 'I don't know what you're going to do.'

"I was totally a Chevy guy at the time, and that wasn't by any means in my plans.

"Bill said, 'Well, I don't particularly care for the guy, but Pontiac called Mickey Thompson first and pulled the plug on his racing program, and he flew to Dearborn and got a Ford deal. You might call him.'

"So, I called Mickey and made an appointment to see him. At the time, John Garrison also worked at the Thomas shop as an engine builder.

Classified in the NHRA's Limited Production category, Butch defeats Bill Lawton driving Tasca Ford's 1963½ 427 R-Code Galaxie in the second round prior to facing Greg Sanders's Z11 in the final. Sanders won but was tossed out of teardown, which gave Butch the win.

Now, Mickey knew who John was but didn't know who I was. Anyhow, he hired the both of us. Long story short, I ended up selling the Z11 to a racer up in Washington, went to work for Mickey Thompson Enterprises, and that was the end of that."

Mickey Thompson and Ford to the Rescue

In 1963, Ford Motor Company made its answer to Chevrolet's 427 Z11 and Chrysler Corporation's 426 Max Wedge engines with its newly introduced cross-bolt-main, cast-iron-block 1963½ 427 low-rise FE (the Ford-Edsel engine family) big-block engine with a 4.2328-inch bore and 3.784-inch stroke. Ford's first-generation 427 FE was known as a top oiler (as opposed to the later 427 side oiler) and featured 11.5:1 compression pistons, a solid-lifter cam (at 324 degrees duration and 0.555 max valve lift), a set of 2.09-inch-diameter intake and 1.66-inch-diameter exhaust valve–equipped 427 low-rise cylinder heads with shaft rocker arm valvetrain, an 8-quart oil pan, an aluminum 2x4 Medium Riser/650 Holley–equipped dual-plane intake, Ford cast-iron headers, and Ford Autolite dual-point ignition.

Conservatively rated at 425 hp at 6,000 rpm and registering 480 ft-lbs of torque at 3,400 rpm, the 1963½ 427 Ford FE was backed by a BorgWarner T10 4-speed gearbox and 4.11-geared Ford 9-inch live rear axle. A 1963½ R-Code Ford Galaxie 500 featured a gross vehicle weight rating (GVWR) of 3,961 pounds due to extensive use of fiberglass and aluminum components. Those components included the front fenders, inner fender panels, hood, doors, decklid, front and rear aluminum bumpers, and an interior with the radio delete, heater delete, and Bostrum bucket seats. The R-Code Galaxie 500 rolled on 15x5.5-inch two-piece pressed steel wheels and 15x60 bias-ply tires. Like the Chevrolet Z11, actual production number data varies, but it is generally agreed that Ford subcontractor Holman & Moody produced 212 1963½ 427 R-Code Galaxie 500s. Elapsed times of 12.1 to 12.4 seconds in the quarter mile were published.

Only the cream of the Ford crop campaigned the 1963½ 427 R-Code Ford Galaxie 500, including Ford Performance Advisor Richard "Dick" Brannan, Bill Lawton, Phil Bonner, Gas Ronda, Les Ritchey, Ed Martin, Al Joniec, and many others. As was mentioned, expatriated Pontiac racer the late Mickey Thompson secured a last-minute and somewhat controversial Ford deal in August 1963 and was assigned one of the 1963½ R-Code 427 Ford Galaxie 500s to prepare for the 1963 NHRA Nationals at Indianapolis. Now being a "land speed record kind of guy," Thompson knew very little about running a stock-block 427 FE, so when Butch Leal (who admittedly knew even

Butch's midyear switch to Ford and the Mickey Thompson camp raised a lot of eyebrows. Could the Chevrolet star continue his winning ways driving Mickey Thompson's 1963½ 427 Ford Galaxie? Well, that's a silly question.

less about running one but was rapidly gaining a reputation as a 4-speed impresario) showed up for a job, Mickey Thompson screwed him into the driver's seat.

"Ford shipped the car by rail to Sepulveda, California's Galpin Ford about a week and a half before the 1963 NHRA Nationals at Indy," Butch said. "At the time, I didn't know anything about running an FE, so John Garrison built the motor, and I did the chassis. I installed a ladder-bar rear suspension setup, and we headed off to Indianapolis. Well, the car went like 114 mph. I could have walked faster. The other guys who had them, like Brannan and Bonner, were pretty fast and going like 116, 117 mph. Mickey came over to our pits at Indy. Les Ritchey had given him a pair of Holley carburetors to try, so we bolted those on, and the car and it went 115. [It was] just a little better but not enough to run with the big boys. Once I got the car back home, I took it to Lions, and the car didn't perform any better there either."

Like A Fly on the Wall

"Mickey said, 'You need to fly to Dearborn and get your new pickup!'" Butch said. "I flew to Dearborn and got the new Ford pickup they gave Mickey for me. Now, I was staying at the Dearborn Inn, and lo and behold, Dick Brannan and Phil Bonner happened to be there too. Well, I didn't know who Phil Bonner was, but I certainly knew who Dick Brannan was. I was 19 years old at the time, and Ford didn't know whether they wanted to hire me or not, so I was kind of maintaining a reasonably low profile.

"Bonner and Brannan were having a drink in their room, and they invited me in. Now, I was doing a lot of listening but not much talking. They were telling me what the deck heights were on the block, what the head CCs were, [and] they told me about what camshafts they used. So, I drove back to Long Beach and told John what I learned. He said, 'I'm not doing it!'

"Well, that got me all fired up. We went to Long Beach that night and the car went 115 [mph], which was the best it was going to run.

"Mickey came up to me and said, 'I've been talking to John, and he would like to put someone else in the car.'

"I said, 'Really?' I mean, it was his car, so what else could I say? At the time, Tom Sturm had a Mercury deal, so Tom went 113 mph. Well, John wasn't satisfied with that, so he went and got a guy named Larry to drive the car, and he went 113. I get back in the car and it went 115. Well, that ended that deal.

"But I'm like any other driver. My ego was so bruised and I was so pissed off that I went up to Mickey's office on Monday and told his secretary Felecia, 'Write me a

check, please. I'm out of here!'

"Felecia said, 'Wait a minute,' and she got on the squawk box and called Mickey.

"He said, 'What's going on?'

"I said, 'I've had enough of John. I've begged him to try this stuff I learned from Bonner and Brannan while I was in Detroit, and he won't listen to me. I mean, those guys are going almost 120 mph!'

"Mickey said, 'Really? Butch, could you ever build the engine yourself? Have you ever done it?'

"I said, 'Well, I know how, but I have a problem. I don't know how to run the Block Master [mill], and if I do it, I need to know how to operate the darned thing.

"Mickey said, 'I'll call Fritz [Mickey Thompson Chief Engine Builder Fritz Voigt], and he'll show you how to run it.'

"Next, Mickey called John and fired him, so it was all on me now.

"You can imagine how I felt. I pulled the engine out, got it all apart, and measured the deck height. It was 0.030, and those guys were running 0.010, so I took 0.020 off the block. Brannan and Bonner were running a No. 10 Holman & Moody cam. It was a big cam for big tracks. Bob Brooks made me a set of Mickey Thompson forged-aluminum pistons, and I bolted it all back together."

Heads Up!

"It took me an entire week to CC those 427 Medium Riser cylinder heads," Butch said. "I made every chamber exactly 74 cc. Fritz thought I was crazy and said, 'What are you doing?'

"He thought I was speaking Spanish when I was talking about CC'ing. Anyway, I got this thing together and dropped the engine back into the car. It was 5 p.m., and there was no telling what this thing's going to do, so I asked everybody to leave the shop. I mean, I was scared to death. I don't put a radiator in the car or anything. I just fired it up, set the timing, and made sure it had the correct oil pressure. After that, I installed the radiator. We didn't have a dyno at Mickey's, so I ran the engine in at 2,000 rpm three times, draining the water, and changing the oil each time. The thing sounded really healthy! The third time I did it, I whacked the throttle. Oh, my goodness! Right then and there, I knew that this thing was bad to the bone!"

"That night, we took the car to Fontana. Now, if you haven't driven a Ford, they sound a lot different on the top end than a Chevrolet. I whipped this thing into high gear, and it moaned out the headers. Now, that sound wasn't entirely foreign to me because my cousin's

This photo from November 1963 shows Butch setting the Fontana Drag City's top speed record at 121 mph with the Mickey Thompson 427 Ford Galaxie. (Photo Courtesy Donna Leal)

big-block Pontiac did the same thing on the big end. I pulled up to the time-slip booth, and wow, the thing ran 121 mph! Man, oh man, I felt like I was Keith Black, Ed Pink, and Sid Waterman all rolled into one!

"I end up beating Les Ritchey in the final. But as I pulled the car onto Hayden's old Pontiac-powered Dodge flatbed and was about to shut off the engine, it made a *ch, ch, ch, ch* sound. Well, I had turned it pretty hard running [against] Les and bent all the pushrods.

"I said, 'Les, I have to race in Bishop tomorrow, Sunday, and I don't have any spare pushrods with me. So, Les pulled all of the pushrods out of his motor and gave them to me. That's the kind of guy Les Ritchey was.

"I raced the Galaxie at Fontana, Bishop, and Lions and ran low 12s at 121 mph. Then, right about the time I got the car running really well, Mickey called [November 1963] and said, 'We're going to fly to Dearborn. Ford just built seven 1964 Fairlanes with 427 Hi Riser engines in them, and we're getting two of them.'"

After switching over to the 1964 427 Fairlane Thunderbolt, it was rumored that Mickey Thompson pulled the Leal-assembled 427 Medium Riser big-block out of the Galaxie and installed a standard 427 FE in its place. After that, the decommissioned factory hot rod was used for running errands around Mickey Thompson's Long Beach, California, shop prior to eventually being sold off. Furthermore, according to Butch Leal, it was also rumored that in its later life, one of the Galaxie owners outfitted the 1963½ lightweight with a 427 equipped with a set of Mickey Thompson's ultra-rare cast aluminum Hemi cylinder heads.

Clutching a *Cheetah*

The name Mike Jones may be familiar to many as the grand architect of Orange County International Raceway (OCIR). However, prior to designing and managing one of the nation's first "super tracks," Jones worked as an engineer/test driver at Anaheim, California's Bill Thomas Race Cars, and this was where the story below began.

"I remember Butch was just barely out of high school when he was racing his Bill Thomas–prepared 1963 427 Z11 Chevrolet Impala SS and was already making quite a name for himself as an up-and-coming Super Stock driver," Jones said. "At the time, we were developing the *Cheetah* race car [originally conceived by race car designer Don Edmunds], to go head-to-head against the Shelby Cobra in Sports Car Club of America (SCCA) road racing competition. Now, the *Cheetah* was anything but a drag car, but Bill wanted to generate as much publicity for the project as he could, so we took one up to Fresno, California's Raisin City Raceway.

"Launching the 90-inch-wheelbase *Cheetah* off the starting line initially proved to be a bit of a problem. Butch happened to be there with his Z11, and he showed me how to pre-load the clutch to maximize launch. Well, it worked, and I was able to produce a best [ET] of 10.50 at 140-plus mph."

CHAPTER 4

THUNDERBOLTS AND LIGHTWEIGHTS

"We walked into a huge building, and all eight of the Thunderbolts were parked down at the opposite end, but I could see them glimmering in the light."

In 1964, Ford Motor Company tore a page out of the hot rodder's handbook and created the 427 Ford Thunderbolt (a small car with a big engine), but Ford didn't do it entirely on its own. In early 1962, the Ford Special Vehicles Department and Andy Hotten from Dearborn Steel & Tubing Company teamed with New England Ford Dealer Bob Tasca to create the *Challenger 1* (a 1962 Ford Fairlane 500 in Rangoon Red with a 406 FE engine) to compete in the NHRA's emerging A/FX classes. Tasca's Bobby Price piloted the Fairlane to ETs in the 12.70s at 115 mph.

While Tasca's *Challenger 1* is considered the grand-daddy of the 1964 Ford Fairlane Thunderbolt, Tasca's *Zimmy-1* (a Mint Green 1963 Ford Fairlane 500 that was a joint project between Ford Special Vehicles Department, Dearborn Steel & Tubing, and Tasca) is considered the to be the father of the 1964 Ford Fairlane Thunderbolt and served as the virtual blueprint for the build. Like the *Challenger 1*, *Zimmy-1* was originally powered by a 406 Ford and Toploader 4-speed transmission. However, it quickly graduated to a 427 Ford Medium Riser engine. This car was driven by Bill Holbrook at the 1963 NHRA Nationals as well as by Bill Lawton (Tasca's resident hot shoe), who set the A/FX top speed record at 121.29 mph during an NHRA Division 1 Points Meet at Connecticut Dragway.

Zimmy-1, a 406- (and later 427-) engined 1963 Ford Fairlane envisioned by Tasca Ford and built by Dearborn Steel & Tubing, was the forerunner of the 1964 Ford Thunderbolt. Driven by Bill Holbrook, the car ran 121.29 mph, setting a record at Connecticut Dragway.

Members of the Ford Drag Council assembled on a cold wintry day in mid-November 1963 to drag test Ford's new 427 Fairlane Thunderbolts. Butch Leal, who posted the quickest time of the day, and mentor Mickey Thompson are to the far right. (Photo Courtesy Bill Holbrook)

If you conduct a side-by-side comparison of *Zimmy 1* and a production 1964 Ford Thunderbolt, there is no denying the 'Bolts lineage. The main difference between the two (other than sheet metal) is the Thunderbolt's late-1963-release, cast-iron R-Code 427 Hi Riser FE powerplant. Touted as the ultimate in 427 Ford Wedge head big-blocks at 11.6:1 compression, the Ford 427 Hi Riser included cross-drilled mains, a bore size of 4.232 inches, a stroke of 3.784 inches, and a solid-lifter camshaft at 2.185 inches of duration on the intake and 0.525-inch max valve lift. A set of Code 63 cast-iron 427 Hi Riser cylinder heads featured a 2.197-inch-diameter intake and 1.7.25-inch-diameter exhaust valves operated by a 1.76:1-ratio shaft rocker arm system.

Induction was handled by a Code XE aluminum 2x4 intake with a pair of C3 date-coded 780-cfm Holley 4160 carburetors. The 427 Ford Hi Riser utilized an 8-quart oil pan with a Rotunda oil filter. Ignition duties were handled by a Ford-Autolite dual-point ignition system. When dyno tested, the 2x4-equipped 427 Ford Hi Riser produced 425 hp at 6,000 rpm and delivered 476 ft-lbs of torque at 3,700 rpm.

An initial run of eight 427 Hi Rise Thunderbolts were built (all painted in Code X Vintage Burgundy) and debuted to Ford Drag Council members at Ford's Dearborn Proving Grounds in early November 1963.

At this juncture I'll let Butch tell the rest of the story.

"Right about the time I got the Galaxie running well (121 mph) Mickey called up in mid-November 1963 and said, 'Tomorrow, we're going to fly to Dearborn. Ford just built eight 427 Fairlanes with the new Hi Riser engine, and we're getting two of them.'

"I said, 'Really?'

"Mickey continued, 'The cars are designated for the members of the Ford Drag Council. Dick Brannan, Phil Bonner, Bill Lawton, Les Ritchey, and Gas Ronda, will also be there!'

"I said, 'Well, ok!'

"When we flew into Detroit the next day, Gas Ronda had already arrived. Naturally, we couldn't wait to see these cars, although we weren't supposed to do that until the following day.

"Gas said, 'Let's drive over to Ford, sneak in, and take a peek.'

"I said, 'Yeah, let's do it!'

"You know me. I wanted to see them too. But Gas said that the cars were being guarded.

"I said, 'Don't worry about it. We're going to get in. We'll put our business suits on and drive over there. I'll tell the guard at the gate that Henry Ford told us to go on in and take a look. Lo and behold, the guard lets us in!

"Gas said, 'That was easy!'

"We both laughed.

"We walked into a huge building, and all eight of the Thunderbolts were parked down at the opposite end, but I could see them glimmering in the light. They were maroon colored, and I thought that they were just about the most beautiful things I had ever seen. All eight cars had an aluminum front bumper and air-intake ducts where the inside headlights had been. I thought, 'That's kind of cool.'

"Of course, the Ford Special Vehicles Department's Performance Advisor Dick Brannan [who got the first one] and Danny Jones had a huge hand in all of that.

"Brannan wanted them light, and they were light with their fiberglass hoods, front fenders, and doors. I noticed that seven of them had a cloverleaf hood, which was probably the ugliest thing you ever laid your eyes on. It looked like an Irishman had designed it. Just think what an original one of those hoods would be worth today to a serious Thunderbolt memorabilia collector! Anyhow, the eighth car had the now-famous teardrop hood on it. I took one look at that hood and went, 'Whoa! I like that!'"

Teardrop Hood Lottery

"The cars were numbered 1 through 8 on the top of the windshield, and the teardrop-hood car was designated No. 7. That night we went to a nice banquet that Ford put on for us, and [it] gave the team members nice watches with our names engraved on the back. Henry Ford II was there, and we were all being nice and sociable. At that time, Ford thought I was a little too young [age 19] to be representing Ford Motor Company and Mickey Thompson Enterprises. Mickey stood up and said, 'He's a very nice young man, and pretty darned good with a 4-speed transmission. I think that he'll be okay!'

"So anyhow, Ford decided that team members would draw for car No. 1 through 7. I drew car No. 6, which was actually the third Thunderbolt built by Dearborn Steel & Tubing, and it was one of the cloverleaf hood cars.

"Well, Gas was sitting across from me. He immediately showed me that he had drawn No. 7, which was the teardrop-hood car. Well, Mickey was sitting next to me, so when I drew car No. 6, I kind of dropped my head a little in disappointment. When Mickey saw that, he asked me 'What's wrong?'

"I said, 'Gas and I snuck in to see the cars earlier, and there's only one car with the teardrop hood on it [car No. 7], and it's really a nice hood.'

"That's all I said to him.

"The next day, we went out to the Dearborn Proving Grounds to wring these cars out. Ford had set up an informal drag strip there with speed clocks only. Well, I went the fastest, and suddenly, Ford decided that [it] liked me a lot. When we got there, I was looking for my car number. I saw No. 7, and lo and behold, it had the teardrop hood! Mickey had talked to someone up high, and they had switched hoods overnight.

"Gas Ronda was so mad he couldn't see straight, and Bob Tasca, who drew car No. 8, didn't like it much, either. He and Gas had been with Ford quite a few years before Mickey and I ever became involved, so it was equally as much an affront to him as it was to Ronda.

"Anyhow, Gas, Les, and I towed the cars back to California. We got all the way from Dearborn to Oklahoma City, and they wanted to stop and sleep.

"I said, 'I'm not going to go to sleep. I want to get back home and run this thing!'

"When I got home, I took the Casler tires off my Galaxie and bolted them onto the Thunderbolt and ran Pomona that weekend. That was the first Ford Thunderbolt that NHRA Technical Inspector Bill "Farmer" Dismuke had ever seen!"

Butch relayed a funny story about when then-editor of *Hot Rod* magazine Ray Brock stopped by Mickey Thompson's shop for a visit.

"When I got back from Michigan, Ray Brock came by Mickey's shop for a visit," Butch said. [See the article *Draggin Bolt* by Ray Brock published in the February 1964 issue of *Hot Rod* magazine.] "At the time, he [Brock] was at the top of the heap at *Hot Rod*, so that was a pretty big deal.

"Brock got a big kick out of me because I was just 19 years old at the time. He just kept laughing and laughing and couldn't believe that a 19-year-old kid could handle a car this powerful, and I just kept saying, 'I can do this. You just watch. I can do this!'"

Brand spankin' new and un-lettered, Butch flexes the Thunderbolt's muscles at his home track, Lions Associated Drag Strip in Wilmington, California. "Being on the Lions board of directors [and with his shop located only a few miles away], Mickey Thompson had a key to the back gate at Lions, and we frequently used to test there," Butch said.

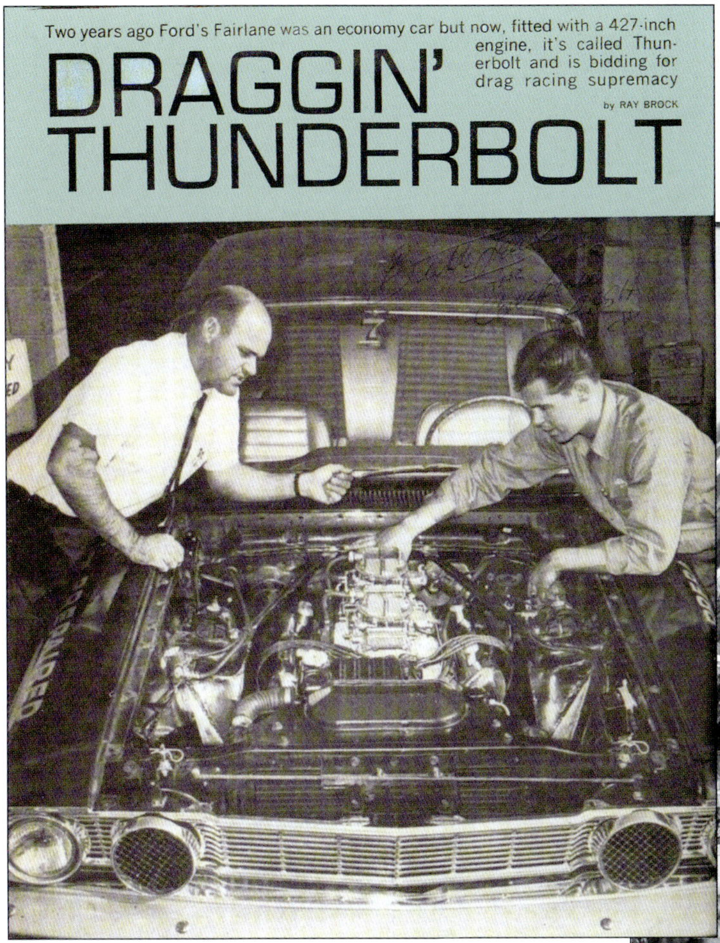
Two years ago Ford's Fairlane was an economy car but now, fitted with a 427-inch engine, it's called Thunderbolt and is bidding for drag racing supremacy

DRAGGIN' THUNDERBOLT

by RAY BROCK

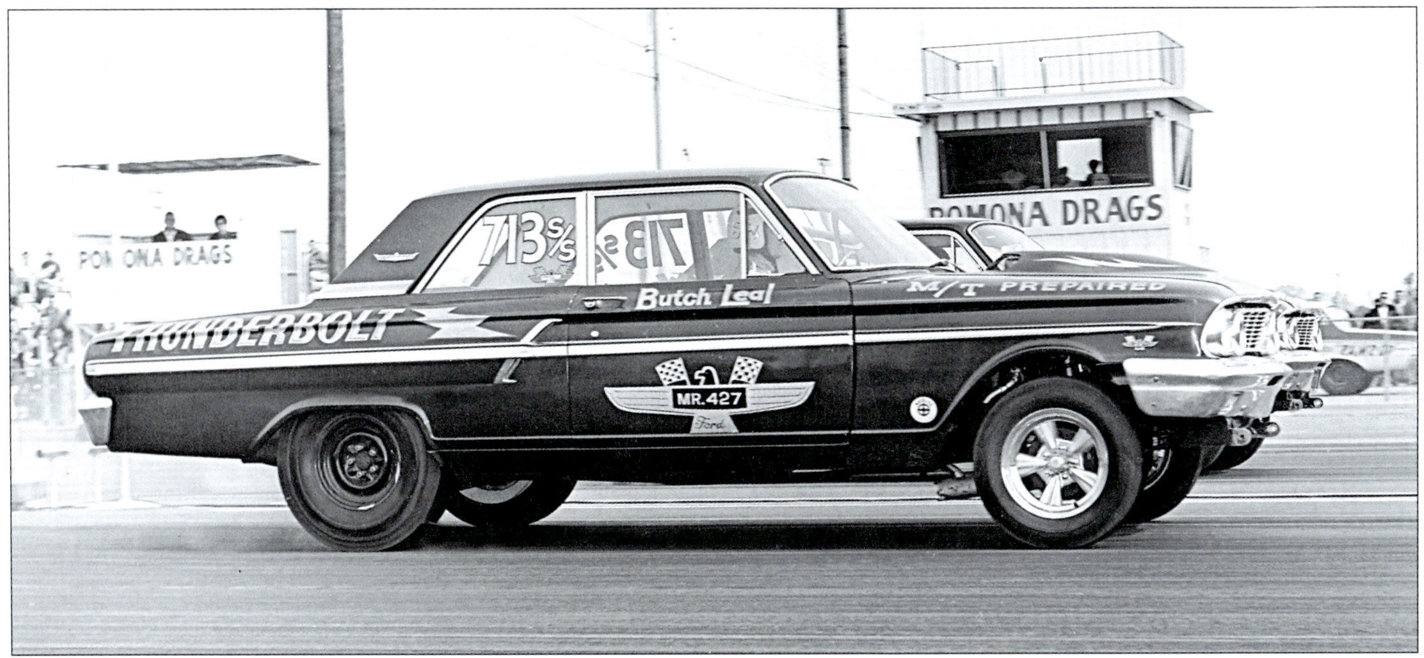

When Butch returned to the West Coast with his maroon Thunderbolt, he and Mickey were visited by Hot Rod *magazine Editor Ray Brock. "Ray kept laughing and voiced his doubts whether someone my age could actually handle such a potent machine," Butch said.*

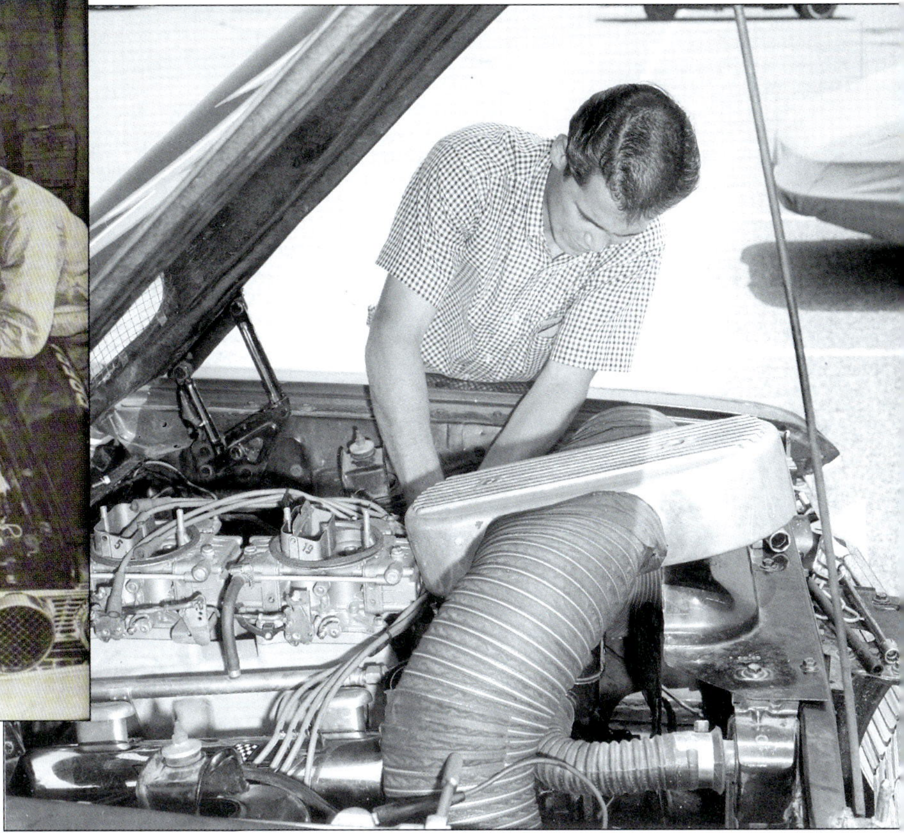

*I just kept telling him [*Hot Rod *Editor Ray Brock], "You just watch. I can do this!"*

When Butch and the Thunderbolt paid a first-time visit to the Pomona Drags, NHRA Technical Inspector Bill "Farmer" Dismuke couldn't believe what he was seeing.

Paybacks Are . . .

At the 1964 NHRA Winternationals, Gas Ronda sought retribution for the "teardrop hood scoop incident" by beating Butch and the Mickey Thompson Thunderbolt on Sunday in the Super Stock Eliminator finale. Gas continued to be Leal's final-round nemesis for the better part of the season. The two locked horns again at the inaugural *Hot Rod* magazine Championship Drag Races in June 1964 at Riverside International Raceway, and the results were the same.

For his efforts, Ronda won a 1964 Plymouth Barracuda as part of his prize booty, the first of two 'Cudas that the popular ex–Arthur Murray Dancing School instructor won. In addition, he won a second one later that year for winning the NHRA Top Stock World Championship.

"I was so mad," Butch said. "Ford had told us that [it] dyno tested all the engines and that they were all the same. Well, I should have known better. Plus, the NHRA rule book allowed an overbore of 0.060 inch. Well, that's about 11 more inches and probably 20 more hp. After losing in the final to Gas at Riverside, I pulled the engine out and bored it 0.060 over just like I did with the engine in the 1963½ lightweight. Bob Brooks made me a set of (0.060 over) Mickey Thompson pistons for it, I CC'd the heads, changed the camshaft, and never got outrun with the car again."

The 1964 NHRA Nationals served as the stage for Leal's breakout triumph, running an ET of 11.76 at 122.78 mph to capture class out of 54 cars entered, beating the Ed Martin Ford Thunderbolt on the final. However, Leal's first national event win almost didn't happen.

"Jenkins & Strickler's Dodge Polara was the only Chrysler car in the class. I had just gotten a call from home Saturday night telling me that I just became a first-time father, so I was feeling like I was on top of the world. Well, Sunday's race day. I talked to all the Thunderbolt guys and told them that I wanted Strickler [who's three cars ahead of me in line] in the first round.

"I said, 'Let me have that Dodge!'

"They all pulled over, and I drove right up alongside of him.

"Well, he did a little burnout and so did I. We pulled up to the starting line, and I'll be darned if he didn't red-light. Halfway through low gear, I broke the input shaft in the transmission. Fortunately, I had enough

Gas Ronda continued to be Butch's final-round nemesis into June 1964 when the two met with the same results in the Super Stock final at the inaugural Hot Rod Magazine Championship Drag Races at Riverside International Raceway.

Pat Patterson of Vaca Valley Drag Strip (Vacaville Dragway) holds out the bread. In the top row is "Dandy" Dick Landy (left), who made $250; Gas Ronda, (center) broke in the second round; Butch Leal (far right) made $500; Kneeling in the front, Ron Powers (left) came close but finished out of the money. (Photo Courtesy Greg Sharp Collection)

momentum to coast to the other end for the win. As I entered the return road, I looked up and there was a guy in a Ford pickup with huge push bar on the front. I hollered to him, 'Can you push me back to the staging lanes?' He was more than happy to oblige.

"Once there, I stopped and hollered to H.L. [Shahan], 'Go to my truck and fetch me the jack, some jack stands, and a spare transmission.' I jacked the car up and whipped out the broken transmission. [It was] lucky for me that the transmission broke the main shaft flush with the clutch disc. But whenever that happens, there's usually a 99-percent chance that it's going to be a major chore to get it out. I grabbed a pair of needle-nose pilers, and lo and behold, it came right out! What luck! I just couldn't believe it.

"I threw the new transmission in, got the shift linkage bolted back on, and climbed back into the car. I said to H.L., 'Man, this thing's [shifter's] tight!'

"He said, 'You won't notice it once you let the clutch out.'

"Well, he was right. I went through all those cars and won the race."

Filling A Seven-Pound Sack

"Back in the day the A/FX Comets were running 10-inch tires," Butch said. "Well, there's no way you could get 10-inch tires under a Ford Thunderbolt. I was thinking, 'What am I going to do?'

"I called Jess Tyree and went over to his shop in Fullerton [California] to use his rack. I made a cut across the bottom of the rear quarter panel inside the wheelhouse to the sub-frame and took a sledgehammer and beat that thing flat all the way across until I could get 10-inch tires under it.

"That night, I headed off to Six Flags Texas for a match race. I was there two weeks, and I ended up making $2,000 for two races. I also set the Super Stock class record and outran Joe Smith with the Fenner Tubbs Hemi Plymouth. That was the first race I ever ran a Christmas tree. Chrondek Timers had just come out with them, and at the time, they were a pretty big deal.

"Then, I got hooked up with Chevy racer Dick Harrell. He and I match raced each other all over the East Coast, and it was nothing but making money. We raced on Wednesday night, Saturday night, and Sunday afternoons. I was making over $3,000 a week, which in 1964 dollars was a lot of money.

"Here's an interesting side note to this story. In 1964, 'Wild Bill' Shrewsbury was driving Jack Chrisman's 427 A/FX Comet. We were both at a Super Stock meet they were having at Lions Drag Strip in Long Beach. There must have been 20 to 30 cars there, including all the heavy hitters. I had been beating old 'Wild Bill' like a drum almost everywhere we raced. We met again in the finals at Long Beach, and I beat him again.

"After the race, a very young Steve Chrisman ran up to me when I was loading the car onto my trailer, and he kicked me in the shins. Then, he ran off! Years later, I hired Steve as my crew chief, and we always had a good laugh about that."

That was also about that time that strip promoters and booking agents began calling Butch the "California Flash," a nickname given him by the wife of the Gold [Booking] Agency's Ben Crist. At the time, a number of racers were calling themselves "Mr. 427," and Leal needed something different, something fresh, and above all else something regional. The following quote was taken from the "How It Was" section of the July 9, 1971 issue of the NHRA's official house organ, *National Dragster*: "When Ford debuted [its] Thunderbolt in 1964, one of the most feared competitors in Super Stock racing on the West Coast made the switch. It was none other than Tulare, California's Butch Leal known throughout the racing world as the 'California Flash.' Leal enjoyed moderate success with the 427 engine Fairlane prepared by Mickey Thompson himself!"

Butch took his revenge on past NHRA National event disappointments when he outclassed and outran 54 Super Stock cars to win class at the 1964 NHRA Nationals. He beat the Ed Martin Ford Thunderbolt in the final with an ET of 11.76 at 122.76 mph.

Weekend Super Stock Shows (such as those at Lions Associated Drag Strip where Butch dominated for 20 weekends in a row) and match racing were Butch's bread and butter. He won anywhere from $650 to $2,000 per event.

It's a shame that only the front half of Butch's Thunderbolt was included in this color photo (the photographer must have been a Chevy fan) as he match races against the late, great Dick Harrell and his 427 Chevelle. Butch and Harrell teamed up in the summer of 1964 and made a lot of money match racing.

This static photo was taken in the pits sometime after Butch adopted the nickname, the "California Flash," which was given him by the wife of the Gold (Booking) Agency promoter Ben Crist.

Years later (circa 2020), Butch proudly holds up an October 23, 1963, letter written by speed king Mickey Thompson to parents Frank and Pansy Leal. The letter commended them on their fine son as a trackside ambassador for Mickey Thompson Enterprises while espousing his talents as an up-and-coming race car driver.

The Thunderbolt that Ford Couldn't Give Away

"While I was in Dearborn picking up a couple of new transmissions for Indy, Jacques Passano summoned me to the top floor of Ford's 'Big Glass House,' Butch said.

"Passano said, 'Butch, Ford would like to give you your Thunderbolt.'

"I looked at him and said, 'I don't want it.'

Passano looked puzzled and asked, 'Why don't you want it?'

"I said, 'Because the car belongs to Mickey [Thompson].'

"He looked at me kind of quizzical like and said, 'Well, let me call Mickey.'

"He got Mickey on the phone, and then Mickey asked to talk to me.

"'Yeah, Boss,' I said. (I always called him boss.)

"'What in the hell are they [Ford] doing?' he asked.

"'Well, they want to give me the car, and I told them that it belonged to you,' I said.

"'That-a-boy!' Mickey said. Those were his exact words.

"Once Passano hung up the phone, he said, 'I don't understand. Why don't you want the car?'

"I said, 'Because I have to live in Long Beach, and Mickey Thompson takes good care of me. It's not my car for the taking, and I don't want it.'

"That was the end of that. At the time, I felt that was the best move I ever made, but I sure wish I had that car now.

"After Ford found out about my Chrysler deal, Charlie Gray called and told me that I could keep the engine and transmission [out of the Fairlane] but that he wanted me to give the car to Jacques Passano's nephew Darryl Droke, who would pick the car up. I was so mad! By that time, Mickey had given me the car, and I figured it was mine to keep. So, I called Mickey and told him what Ford had said. However, I can't tell you what his actual reply was because your publisher wouldn't be able to print it. Man, was he ever hot!

"At the time I had that car set up perfectly: 10-inch slicks on the back, four rear shocks, ladder-bar rear suspension; I had everything right. I was so pissed off that I took everything off, put some old ragged-ass shocks on the back, and pulled the engine. Darryl threw an engine in the car, but he couldn't make the thing work.

"Believe it or not, Ford had enough nerve to call me and ask me to drive over to Darryl's Downey, California, shop and fix the car.

"I said, 'I'm not doing it!'

"Well, Ford ended up taking the car back from Droke, and they crushed it!

"Now, I knew what those cars were worth—especially that one. At the time [late 1990s] the prices on those cars were going sky high, and this one was worth twice [as much as the average car]. At the time, I had a little money and I wanted to get the car back no matter what. Just to be on the safe side, I got hold of Darryl, who wasn't doing too well health-wise, and he re-confirmed the fact that Ford had indeed crushed the car.

"In the meantime, I had found another Thunderbolt that was bone stock and would have made a perfect clone. For a while, I was going to build up the car and take it around to all the shows and tell everybody that it was my car. Then, I thought better of the idea and decided that it wouldn't have been kosher. It could have turned out to be a bad deal, so I just passed on the whole idea!"

CHAPTER 5

FUNNY LOOKING BUT FAST

"Well, it wasn't five minutes after Ford gave me the bad news when someone tapped me on the shoulder and said, 'Butch, can I speak with you outside?' "

"After I won Indy, Ford set up a tent with a buffet in the pits that was strictly for the winners," Butch Leal said. "I'm sitting with Ford Racing czar Charlie Gray. I had just won the Manufacturer's Cup for Ford, I was feeling pretty proud, and I was thinking this ought to be worth some good money to me for the following year.

"Off the cuff, I asked Charlie, 'How's my budget looking for next year?'

"He said, 'We don't have one for you Butch.'

"That was of course because of Mickey's Indianapolis 500 debacle. Well, my heart immediately dropped down into my stomach.

"I said, 'Well, Mr. Gray, I'm sorry to hear that, but right now I've got to go home. I'm a brand-new father [with the birth of his oldest daughter, Lory] and my family needs me."

"Now, that wasn't the end of the world, but it sure seemed like it. I already had a deal (a small one) for the upcoming season with the late Jack Chrisman. Jack was going to get one of the 427 SOHC A/FX Comets, and I was going to drive for him. I could make a decent living driving for Jack, but it [the car] wouldn't be mine; it would be his.

"Well, it wasn't five minutes after Ford gave me the bad news when someone tapped me on the shoulder and said, 'Butch, can I speak with you outside?'

"Chrysler held a sponsor meeting in Detroit and all the drivers and engine builders flew in to attend a tech seminar where Chrysler sat down and actually explained how to build a 426 Hemi engine. They covered cam timing, combustion chamber CC'ing, compression ratios, etc. In other words, they went through building the entire Hemi Super Stock engine so that you could make things perfect. This seminar was really beneficial to H.L. and me since we had zero experience running a late-model Hemi."

"When I turned around and looked, this guy was about 6-foot-2-inches tall, and with me being kind of a little guy, I said, 'Hell no!'

"He said, 'No, it's nothing like that. Let me introduce myself. My name is Bob Cahill, head of Chrysler Racing.'

"I jumped up like I had springs in my shoes. We walked out of the Ford tent, and Mr. Cahill told me that they [Chrysler Corporation] were building a fleet of 12 altered-wheelbase Dodges and Plymouths.

"He said, 'We're looking for 4-speed drivers. We already have Strickler-Jenkins and Ronnie Sox and Buddy Martin on the East Coast, and we would like to have you and Dick Landy on the West Coast.'

"Unbeknownst to me, Mr. Cahill had been standing right there in the staging lanes at Indy watching H.L. [Shahan] and I change the transmission in the Thunderbolt and whip 'em all. Mr. Cahill was also quite happy that I was a new father and very complimentary.

"He said, 'Go home, and think about the kind of deal you want on the way back. Call me, and we'll get a contract together and see what we can do.'

"It just so happened that that was the most money that Chrysler Corporation had ever spent on its racing programs outside of NASCAR. When I got home, I talked things over with my father, and he said, 'Just triple everything. Plus, you want a truck. You need a street car to drive, and you need someone to help you, and you've got to pay their salary. Once you include all of that into it, it sounds like it would be a great deal.'

"The next week I contacted Chrysler, and they said, 'Deal!'

"I thought, 'Oh my Gosh! Let me rob this train!'

"I still had the Thunderbolt, of course, and was winning Long Beach on both Saturday and Sunday afternoons [a total of 20-plus times] and making $750 a week. Then, I match raced Tommy Grove and his 1964 *Melrose Missile* A990 aluminum-fendered Hemi at Fremont. Tommy beat me on a flag start in the first round in spite of the fact that I ran a 10.90, which was pretty quick. In the second round, Tommy broke an axle. I won that one by default, so now I was 1-1.

"Well, Tommy couldn't get the axle out, so I jumped in my pickup, tied a chain around it [the axle], and yanked it out of there. Tommy threw in another axle, and we were ready for the third round. I have no idea why, but Tommy was taking off in second gear. I was about a car length in front of him. He missed third gear, then shifted it into fourth and drove around me.

"[That experience] made me so happy that I was getting a Hemi."

Chrysler Racing had the first five altered-wheelbase B-Body Dodge Coronets and the first five B-Body Plymouth Sport Furys modified by Detroit manufacturer Amble Wagon. The front wheels were forward a total of 10 inches, and the rear wheels were moved forward 15 inches. The result was a 110-inch-wheelbase race car that boasted 56 percent of its weight over its rear wheels, which was practically unheard of at the time.

Powered by the Chrysler-Plymouth-Dodge (CPD) Gen II Chrysler 426 Hemi that was less than a year old and had 12.5:1 compression, the altered-wheelbase

Mopars were originally equipped with cross-ram Holley carburetion and backed by either an A-727 TorqueFlite or an aluminum-cased A-833 4-speed manual transmission and 4.56:1-geared Dana 60 rear end. Chrysler completed the first altered-wheelbase Mopar on January 12, 1965, and summoned its factory teams back to Detroit to attend team Pentastar's drag racing version of a new car reveal.

"'Dandy Dick' Landy and I flew back to Detroit and got a good look," Butch said. "The front and back wheels on the mule car (which was a Plymouth) were moved around so darned much that I couldn't believe what we were seeing. Actually, when you looked at the car, it was pretty darned ugly. It's just that I had never seen anything like that before, but after a while, its looks kind of [grew] on you."

Chrysler Racing's new Hemi hybrids officially went something like this:
- "Dandy" Dick Landy, Dodge
- Bud "Honker" Faubel, Dodge
- Bob "Flying Carpet" Harrop, Dodge
- Dick Branster & Roger Lindamood, *Color Me Gone*, Dodge
- Dave Strickler & Bill Jenkins, Dodge
- Butch, the "California Flash" Leal, Plymouth
- Lee Smith, *Haulin' Hemi II*, Plymouth
- Al Eckstrand, *Golden Commandos,* Plymouth
- Ronnie Sox & Buddy Martin, *Paper Tiger*, Plymouth
- Dave Koffel, *Flintstone Flyer*, Plymouth

Two more Mopars, the *Ramchargers* Dodge (still in legal A/FX trim and runner-up in Top Stock Eliminator to Tasca Ford the following month at the 1965 NHRA Winternationals) and the Tommy Grove–driven *Melrose Missile* Plymouth were upgraded to altered-wheelbase status by Amblewagon after the AHRA and NHRA winter meets making it a total of 12 factory altered-wheelbase race cars. Grove defected to Ford shortly after Pomona, surrendering driving duties to Cecil Yother.

"The trip to Detroit to pick up the car in late January nearly killed us," Butch said. "Since Hayden Proffitt was now on contract to Lincoln-Mercury Division, we drove over to his shop [in Garden Grove, California] and picked up his old Dodge hauler. The next day, we left Tulare and got as far as Oklahoma City before the thermostat stuck, overheated the engine, and blew it up. We called Dale Reeker at Chrysler, and he shipped us a new 413-ci crate engine to the local Chrysler-Plymouth dealer who installed it in one day and had us back on the road again.

"About 100 miles south of St. Louis, we ran into black ice, which slowed us to a crawl. H.L. and I drove the truck across the metal bridge crossing the Mississippi River leading into Illinois, and the truck and [empty] trailer slid sideways on the ice and bumped the curb. Fortunately, there was no damage.

"After the bridge incident, we came upon a turnout and wisely pulled over to grab a little shut-eye. Hours later, we woke up, and there was about 3 feet of snow on the ground. Now, it's only a couple hundred miles between St. Louis and Indianapolis, but it took us all day to get there, as we fought snow every inch of the way.

"We pulled into the Holiday Inn Northwest in Indianapolis and immediately collapsed into bed from exhaustion. The next morning, we looked down from the second-floor balcony. It had snowed so hard that night that we couldn't even see the truck. It took us hours to dig it out, and we drove nonstop from Indianapolis to Detroit. When we got there, we called Dale Reeker at Chrysler to pick up the car.

"Sox & Martin had already been there, and since we were two days late and our car was first in line for delivery, Ronnie got my car, and I took their car. On the return trip home, we drove all the way from Detroit to Kingman, Arizona, before we finally got out of the snow. That trip took two years off my life. I was so worried that we were going to crash and almost did a couple of times.

"Anyhow, the minute we got home, H.L. started building our spare engine and I went and got the bodywork done. The sheet-metal work on those cars was so bad that they looked like they had been in a NASCAR short-track race. We had Doyce Ray Henderson (owner of Doyce's Body Shop in Tulare) straighten and paint the car in 'Leal Corporate Blue' [GM Royal Blue] with white lettering, but once it was finished, the thing looked butt ugly! To make matters worse, Chrysler hadn't gotten us the correct width [narrowed] rear end yet. What we had was a somewhat-wider Dana truck rear end. Somehow, H.L. came up with a set of vintage Chrysler Imperial wheels that had the correct offset, and we ran those."

The AHRA Winternationals traditionally took place at Beeline Dragway in Mesa, Arizona, one to two weeks prior to the NHRA's Big Go West event. Some racers considered Beeline a pre-Pomona tune-up meet. The more liberal AHRA welcomed the Chrysler team cars with open arms.

"We got to the AHRA Winternationals a day late, which turned out to be sort of a blessing in disguise, as Landy had already blown the back window out of his altered-wheelbase car in the lights, and both he and Sox & Martin had bent the rear quarter panels on their cars. I immediately slid underneath our car and installed a set of subframe connectors. I also installed a set of rear window tabs. Between the two modifications, those sorts of things never happened to us!

"We brought two engines with us: one spare and one in the car. We warmed the thing up to make a morning pass, and it fouled the plugs. Neither H.L. nor I knew a

Freshly painted in GM Regal Blue, Butch puts his new Hemi car through its paces at the 1965 AHRA Winternationals at Beeline Dragway in Mesa, Arizona. "The thing was butt-ass ugly," Butch said. However, the car was quick, running an ET of 10.20 out of the box.

danged thing about running a Hemi. The thing kept popping and banging, so when I drove it back to the pits, I asked H.L. if he thought we should change the engine?

"He said, 'Nah, let's just change the plugs and see what it sounds like.'

So, we did that, and the thing sounded good. I went to make the next run and let out the clutch, and the thing stood up pretty well and made a little move to the right. Well, I just stayed in it and I was 0.15 seconds quicker than anybody. But, just as I was getting to the lights, there was no oil pressure, and I shut it right off! What happened was that when we adjusted the valves and tightened the adjuster nut on the rocker arm. However, we forgot to tighten one. It backed off, pitched the lifter out of the lifter valley, and there went the oil pressure.

A week later, Chrysler's altered-wheelbase cars failed tech at the 1965 NHRA Winternationals at the L.A. County Fairgrounds in Pomona, California. This Lynn Wineland photo shows the Leal & Shahan altered-wheelbase Sport Fury being put through its paces on an exhibition run in front of a packed house on Saturday.

After the NHRA winter meets, Butch repainted the Leal & Shahan altered-wheelbase Mopar in Mustang Poppy Red and GM Refrigerator White following an artist's rendition conceptualized by Chrysler Corporation's Cliff Getty. "We used those colors because they were so easy to touch up," Butch said. He poses here with mechanic H.L. Shahan (right) after having a fresh set of Doug's Headers installed by longtime friend and racing buddy Doug Thorley.

That year, the team of Leal and Shahan also fielded an A990 Super Stock car driven by Shirley "the Drag-on Lady" Shahan, who went on to win Super Stock Eliminator at the 1966 NHRA Winternationals event.

CHRYSLER-PLYMOUTH DIVISION
Performance Publicity
Chrysler Motors Corporation
12200 E. Jefferson Avenue
Detroit, Michigan 48231
VAlley 2-4700

                              FOR IMMEDIATE USE

        Larry "Butch" Leal, the "California Flash," will be running

(where) ____ on

(date) ____

        Leal, driver of the quickest and fastest stock car in the West,

is undefeated at the wheel of his orange-and-white, 1965 altered wheel-

base Plymouth. Butch is out to better his last year's victory average of

85% of his match races. Thus far, he's had little problem in going for

a new record.

        Turning times in the low 10's (on carburetors), Leal is downing

dragdom's top guns, one after another. The list of vanquished includes

the factory-prepared Comets of Hayden Proffitt and Arnie Beswick;

Houston Platt's Chevelle "454," Tom Grove's "Melrose Missile,"

"Landy's Dodge," Les Ritchey's A/FX Mustang "427" hi-riser and Tom

Sturm's "396" Chevelle.

        Leal holds strip records at the following California dragways:

Lions; Long Beach, Pomona, Fontana, Carlsbad, Fremont, Fresno,

Sacramento, Palmdale and Madiera. In addition, he also

U.S. 30 Dragway, Gary, Ind. and San Antonio Dragway i

"Well, here came Tom Hoover, Dale Reeker, and all the other guys from Chrysler Racing, who were really happy with how quick the car ran [10.30s]. Luckily, we hadn't hurt anything, so we reinstalled the lifter back into the lifter bore, installed a new pushrod in it, adjusted everything, and we were good to go.

"While we were getting all of that done, Reeker told us that they had some new shifters coming in overnight. When we got the car, they had a funky long-throw shift lever that came out from under the dash, and the thing was really awkward. They brought this new shifter in at 9 a.m. on Sunday, and we started putting it in. We ended up cutting the floorboard to make everything fit, and we were still struggling with it by the time they called to run the class, so they ran it without me. Man, oh man, was I ever upset."

Apparently, Chrysler naively thought that it would elicit the same response from the NHRA that it had from the AHRA the following weekend at Pomona and these cars would be allowed to compete in A/FX. However, when Butch and H.L. rolled through the NHRA Winternationals

BOTTOM LEFT, TOP, AND RIGHT:
Things were much simpler in 1965. Chrysler Racing's idea of a press kit consisted of a few pages of copy along with a color postcard (this one is autographed) of Butch standing alongside his 1965 altered-wheelbase Plymouth and a black-and-white 8x10 photo.

Butch flexes the muscles of the altered-wheelbase Mopar at Pomona. Note NHRA starter Buster Couch to the right.

This photo was taken during a match-race Stocker show at Irwindale Raceway in Irwindale, California. Note Tommy McNeeley's insanely wild 1965 Ford Falcon match racer in the far lane. "My altered-wheelbase car ran a career best of 9.69 at 144.92 (mph) on gasoline," Butch said.

tech line, officials (including Wally Parks, Jack Hart, Bernie Partridge, Bill, "Farmer" Dismuke, etc.) took one look at the car and said, "Butch, this car looks kind a funny, and we don't have a class for you to run it in."

However, the NHRA graciously allowed the altered-wheelbase cars one exhibition run each on Saturday, and Leal ran something like a 10.20 at 136 mph in front of a packed (and approving) house.

Shortly after Pomona, Chrysler came to Butch and asked him to repaint the car. He complied. Chrysler employee Cliff Getty had come up with a two-tone red and white motif design painted in Mustang Poppy Red and GM Refrigerator White executed by Tulare, California's Doyce's Paint and Body Shop. This was the paint scheme that Leal adopted throughout his entire career.

"We painted the car these basic colors because if it ever got scratched (and it did) it was easy to touch up. Since we had no NHRA class to run, we extensively match raced these cars instead, drawing huge crowds wherever we raced. I mean the fans used to go wild over those wheelies!"

The novelty of Chrysler Corporation's altered-wheelbase cars certainly did not go unnoticed by the automotive press, either. In 1964, Alexandria, Virginia's Eastern Publishing Company, publishers of *Eastern Drag News*, launched a brand-new magazine called *Super Stock & Drag Illustrated*, which not only championed the altered-wheelbase cause but also bettered the lot of doorslammer racers as a whole.

Butch and his altered-wheelbase Plymouth made a guest appearance on Dick Clark's American Bandstand as part of the show's "Swinging Summertime" format. These photos were taken during rehearsal, as guest cameras were not allowed on set during actual taping.

Veteran *Super Stock & Drag Illustrated* editor Jim McCraw said, "When the Hemi-powered '65 Dodge and '65 Plymouth altered-wheelbase cars came along with huge power, that odd stance, and bumper-dragging wheel-stands, the game was changed permanently. I remember very well a match race between Sox & Martin and 'Dandy Dick' Landy at Cecil County Dragway where both teams brushed rosin into the track surface and both cars did enormous wheel-stands to the delight of the crowds. It only took a year for the flip-top Mercury Comets to upstage the altered-wheelbase Mopars, but those cars will never be forgotten."

Butch continued, "Early into the season, Chrysler also realized that the altered-wheelbase cars had more or less reached their performance peak with carburetors, so Hilborn came up with a new fuel injection system for the Hemi engine. We very quickly found out that the injector size with the first design was too small, but once Hilborn put a bigger butterfly in it, the thing really started to run.

"Then, there were the cylinder heads. Initially, Chrysler didn't want you to cut the intake port on the K-Race Hemi aluminum cylinder heads to no more than 180 cc. Well, the intake seat would chip and get in the bore and scratch it up. Chrysler made new hardened seats, so as I pulled the old ones and decided that since there was no class for these cars anyway, why be so cautious? I wanted to run more compression anyway, so I ground the seats and notched the block to pass the valve.

"After doing that, I called Gene Adams who worked for Hilborn. At the time, the 427 Chevrolet big-blocks had a larger-diameter butterfly than the injected Chryslers. So, I figured why not bore my injector manifold out and install the bigger [GM] butterfly? Gene measured it, and it barely fit. Well, I didn't tell anybody that we did that, and all of a sudden, I had times of 9.69 at 144 to 145 mph. People were going crazy because at the time my car was by far the fastest and quickest gas-burning [Funny Car] in the nation!"

Butch said the following when asked how the altered-wheelbase Plymouth was to drive.

"It was very nice to drive, but that car only had a single roll bar installed in it, and the floorboard was as thin as a beer can, so nobody ever drove that car but me," he said. "If I ever got on my head, it would have folded up like a tin can and killed me for sure, but I never had any trouble with it other than initially having handling problems.

"As I mentioned, it would stand up and go to the right. I told Chrysler about this, so we put the car up on a lift and measured everything. That thing was so fragile. We discovered that the rear end was cocked a little, so we straightened it out, and the car went straight.

"The second thing I had to fix was I noticed that with the larger-size butterflies, the car leaned out and start popping out the pipes in the lights. I had a 1-gallon fuel tank installed in the front grill. I would come back from a run, and the darned thing would be half full, but it felt like it was running out of fuel. Well, the Ramchargers were having a similar problem, and they figured out that under hard acceleration the fuel was swirling away from the pickup. What they did was build a 2-gallon tank that eliminated the swirling problem. After we installed the new tank, I went out to Detroit Dragway and ran a 9.85 at 144 mph.

"That year was so much fun. Ultimately, the car ran a 9.69 at 144.92 mph on gasoline. In fact, I ran five straight events in five consecutive weekends with that car [Spokane, Washington; Seattle, Washington; Fremont, California; Long Beach, California; and Phoenix, Arizona]. Other than blowing the hood off in the lights at Houston Dragway in Dickenson, Texas, I never had any problems!"

Back-to-Back Wins at Indy

"At the time, Dick Maxwell was one step down from Mr. Cahill at Chrysler Racing. He called me a week before Indy and said, 'Butch, would you like to defend your title at the NHRA Nationals?'

"I said, 'You bet I would!'

"Chrysler happened to have an A990 car sitting idle at Ashley-Dabbs Motors in Clarksville, Tennessee, and I happened to be at Sox & Martin's shop in Burlington, North Carolina, so I drove over and picked up

This was one of the last photos taken of Butch and his altered-wheelbase car. He squares off against "Dandy" Dick Landy's 1966 match-race Dodge Dart at Fremont Raceway. Shortly thereafter, Butch sold this car to Mr. Norm, and the car was eventually totaled in a freak street accident. (Photo Courtesy Steve Reyes)

At Chrysler's request, Butch quickly prepared an A990 Plymouth Hemi to defend his title at the 1965 NHRA Nationals at Indy, and he won Super Stock Stick for the second straight year in a row.

the hood from the altered-wheelbase car (it had a wider hood scoop) and painted it the same Mustang Poppy Red and GM Refrigerator White paint scheme.

"After H.L. and I parted ways, I hired Ray Sissener, who previously crewed for Dick Landy. Besides his mechanical abilities, Ray was also an accomplished body and paint man, and he painted my A990 Super Stock car.

"Well, I'll be darned if I didn't win Super Stock Stick at Indy for the second year in a row."

Hold Your Breath and Win

"When I got to Indy, I didn't run the car right away," Butch said. "My cousin was there with his Pontiac, and he came over and asked, 'Aren't you going to run the car? Vanke just went so fast and Strickler went so fast.'

"I said, 'It'll be alright, Ronnie.' I

the car. Next, I ordered a set of Cragar S/S wheels and Goodyear tires for the car. I installed the carbureted gasoline-burning Hemi out of my altered-wheelbase car (a legal Super Stock motor) and called Doug Thorley to order a set of headers for the car. Chrysler sent me a really trick aluminum-cased 4-speed that Chrysler of [Dagenham] England built, and I bolted it in. I also installed

could just tell that the car was going to run well. I had everything set just right.

"We started eliminations, and I beat Vanke in the second round and Strickler in the finals. Now this thing's running pretty darned well.

"At the time, I had no inkling about vapor lock. If you remember, Strickler red-lighted against me in 1964. This

When not competing in NHRA events, Butch extensively match raced his A990 Super Stocker. Note the A/FX-type modifications: no front brakes, lightweight mag front wheels, no headlights, a lightweight altered-wheelbase fiberglass hood, and 11-inch slicks. Butch reported that the car launched so hard that it buckled the rear quarter panels. This photo was taken at Fremont Raceway. (Photo Courtesy Steve Reyes)

It may say "California Flash" on the door, but that's gasser racer (and Butch's future injected Funny Car partner) Tommy Rogers racing Butch's NHRA Nationals-winning A990 Plymouth Belvedere at the 1966 NHRA Winternationals. Unfortunately, Tommy missed a gear in class eliminations.

June 1966: Butch wrapped up the Super Stock Eliminator title at the Hot Rod Magazine Championship Drag Races at Riverside Raceway. He defeated Harry Holton in the final. (Photo Courtesy G. K. Callaway)

time, he gave me a little head start, and I won the race, but just as I was about to cross the finish line, the darned thing vapor locked on me, and I slowed down about 3 to 5 mph. But, I held on for the win, and Mr. Cahill and Dick Maxwell were beside themselves with joy. I mean, a Chrysler car would have won the eliminator anyway, but I think they were secretly rooting for me.

"That car was pretty unbelievable. Back in California, they were going to run a five-car race. Well, Shirley [Shahan] wanted to go to Spokane, so I left the Super Stock car at home, and we took her car. She ran in the 3,400-pound class. Her car was running high 10.90s, and she and I both won our respective classes.

"Once I was back home, I decided to take both the altered-wheelbase car and my Super Stock car to Long Beach and Phoenix. What a really nice-looking rig that was with the two cars: the altered-wheelbase car on the truck and the Super Stock car being pulled along on an identically painted trailer. I took the front brakes off the Super Stock car, installed an altered-wheelbase fiberglass hood on the car, removed the front headlights, put some weight in the back, and installed a set of M&H 10-inch slicks on the back.

"At Lions, there were only three cars in that class: my car, Shirley's car, and Harry Holton's car. Shirley and Harry raced each other, and I drew the single. Harry beat Shirley with a 10.99 to an 11 flat. It was a great race. On the final, Harry ran an 11 flat and I ran a 10.50. I brought the car back home, and I was looking it over. The car hooked so hard that it bent both rear quarter panels. I've seen that happen with the altered-wheelbase cars but never an A990 car. Ultimately, my A990 race car ran a career best of 10.50 at 137 mph.

"The next week, I went to Phoenix and everybody was there. Since I was running both cars, I had my cousin Ronnie along with me. Between running the two classes I got so tired [that] my right arm felt like it was about to fall off. Finally, I asked Ronnie, 'How many more of these races have I got left?'

"He said, 'Well, Butch, it's you, and it's you in the final!'

"I said, 'Ronnie, do you want to drive the Super Stock car on the final?'

"He said, 'No!'

"Ronnie was kind of funny like that. He didn't mind me driving his car, but he didn't feel at all comfortable driving somebody else's car—kin or no kin.

"A friend of mine from Tulare named Tommy Rogers who owned a B/Gas car was there, and he drove the A990 car on the final. Tommy fumbled high gear, and I got around him with the altered-wheelbase car. You might say that was the day I outran myself."

A Bridge Too Close

"In early 1966, I ended up selling the altered-wheelbase car and the truck to Mr. Norm's Grand Spaulding Dodge in Chicago, Illinois, right before Norm was leaving for Hawaii on his honeymoon," Butch said. "Norm sent a kid who worked at the dealership as a mechanic to pick up the rig.

"The guy showed up at my house, handed me the money, and headed off for Chicago. He arrived in Chicago, unloaded the car, took it out on the street, hit a bridge, and—I kid you not—totaled it! The kid hit that bridge so hard that he was lucky the impact didn't kill him. Well, Norm came home from his honeymoon and went berserk!

"Years later, during the Mopars at Carlisle meet, he and I had lunch, and he told me what happened when he got back. 'I chained the guy to the car and made him salvage every part that was salvageable off it, which wasn't very much," Norm said. 'I should have killed him!'

"That was Norm; he was joking of course.

"I said, 'Well, that car's only worth about a million dollars in today's muscle car collector market!'"

CHAPTER 6

WHEN FUNNY BUSINESS BECOMES SERIOUS

"Let me explain to you what I have in mind. Build the car and put a [427 SOHC] Cammer [motor] plate in it just as if it were one of the cars you're building for Lincoln-Mercury. If Al Turner walks by it, he won't know the difference."

After taking a year off to concentrate on his other driving passion, namely golf, Butch built the first Logghe Stamping Company privateer Funny Car chassis. It was cloaked with a flip-top fiberglass 1967 Plymouth Barracuda body and had an injected 426 Hemi that was on doses of 100-percent nitro.

But first, Butch wheeled "Dandy" Dick Landy's blue with white vinyl top 1967 Dodge Hemi R/T clinic car to win the SS/DA class at the 1967 NHRA Winternationals. However, driving an automatic was definitely not his thing, and the Landy gig was merely a professional courtesy.

"In 1966, Don Nicholson had the first Logghe Chassis flip-top Mercury Comet I'd ever seen," Butch Leal said. "Don was my hero. He had helped me quite a lot with my '62 409, so when I heard that his new *Eliminator 1* Mercury Comet had a one-piece fiberglass body on it, I just had to see it. I drove to Irwindale Raceway the day Dyno tested the car for the first time. When I first laid eyes on that thing I said, 'Whoa!' I mean the car was unbelievable!

"That was the day Earl Wade forgot to lock the body down and it flew off in the lights. I mean, the thing launched itself into the stratosphere. I distinctly remember Al Turner from Lincoln-Mercury Division was so mad that he banned everybody from the wreck site and told his guys to burn what was left of the body right there on the spot!

"Anyhow, I was very impressed with the Logghe chassis on that car. I knew Ron Logghe when he, Maynard Rupp, Tom Marsh, and Roy Steffey came out to Bakersfield with the *Slot Car* injected Chevy streamlined

This is the car that got Butch's nitro juices flowing. You might say he was a curious onlooker the day that Lincoln-Mercury Division first tested "Dyno" Don Nicholson's Eliminator 1 Mercury Comet at Irwindale Raceway in January 1966. Butch said, "I took one look at that thing and went, 'Wow!' [I] knew right away that I had to have one." (Photo Courtesy Steve Reyes)

Butch started out the year on a much quieter note, winning the SS/DA class at the NHRA Winternationals driving *"Dandy Dick" Landy's 1967 Dodge Hemi R/T clinic car. Butch said, "It felt kind a weird driving an automatic, but when-ever you get a chance to drive anything with a Hemi in it, you take it."*

This is the first privateer Logghe-chassis injected Funny Car in drag racing that carried the name "California Flash" on its sides. The Leal & Rogers 1967 Plym-outh Barracuda A/Fuel Funny Car was completed sometime in March 1967 and nationally toured until November 1967 when Butch sold the 'Cuda and ordered a new blown car from Logghe Stamping Company.

dragster. So, after I saw the chassis on Nicholson's car I said, 'This is it!'

"I called Ron and said, 'I want a car like Nicholson's. Can you build me one?'

"He said, 'Yes I will, Butch, but I can't do it right now.'

"I said, 'Why is that?'

"He said, 'I have an exclusive con-tract with Lincoln-Mercury. We're going to build them a few more cars, so I can't do it until the contract's over.'

"I said, 'Well, when's it over?'

"He gave me a date, and I said, 'Ron, will you do this for me? Build me a car right now?

"He said, 'Butch, I can't do that.'

"I said, 'Yes you can. Let me explain to you what I have in mind. Build the car and put a [427 SOHC]

Cammer [motor] plate in it just as if it were one of the cars you're building for Lincoln-Mercury. If Al Turner walks by it, he won't know the difference. I also want you build me a 426 [Hemi] motor plate. When you get that done, put it under your work bench or hide it somewhere, and the day the Mercury contract is up, I'll come and pick up the car!"

Butch picked up his chassis the very day the Mercury contract with Logghe expired and took it to the local fiberglass shop in Dayton, Ohio, that already had a mold of a Gen II Plymouth Barracuda ready and waiting. Butch sprayed the fiberglass himself, and race car fabricator Don Mann, who had a shop right around the corner, did all the tinwork.

With that done, Leal took the car back to California and had Doyce Henderson spray both the chassis and the body in his traditional Mustang Poppy Red and GM Refrigerator White . . . or so he thought!

"When it was finished, I used a cotton hauler to bring the body back home," Butch said. "It was a gloomy day, I was about halfway there, and the sun was popping out and hitting the car. I looked at it out the side mirror and the darned thing was pink. It wasn't Poppy Red—it was pink! So, I turned around, took the car back to Doyce's, and he had to repaint it.

"It turned out that old Doyce grabbed the wrong can by mistake! Anyhow, we got the car back to Poppy Red. It looked really cool!"

Once back home, Butch and partner Tommy Rogers installed the Leal-assembled 12.1:1-compression Hilborn-injected 426 Hemi and Art Carr 727 Torque-Flite with 9-inch Art Carr torque convertor between the Logghe frame rails. Depending on track conditions, rear-end gearing in the M&H Racemaster–equipped Chrysler 8¾-inch pumpkin varied from 3.90:1 to 4.11:1.

Butch personally hand laid the Gen II Plymouth Barracuda body prior to having Ohioan Don Mann fabricate the interior aluminum. Then, Doyce Henderson painted the body shell in Butch's familiar Poppy Red and Refrigerator White racing team colors.

"When I started to set up the fuel injection system (using the same modified Hilborn intake used on the 1965 altered-wheelbase car as a starting point), I called Gene Adams at Fuel Injection Engineering for some tech tips.

"Gene asked, 'How much fuel [nitro] do you plan to run?'

"I answered, '100 percent!'

"The phone got quiet for a minute, and then he asked, 'Why 100 percent?'

"I said, 'Well, Gene, they [Funny Car racers] started out running 50 percent. Then, they went to 60 percent. Then, they went to 70 percent, and now they've jumped to 80, 85, and 90 percent. So, what's wrong with 100 percent? That way, I won't have to mess around with a hydrometer!'"

Fumes of 100-Percent Nitro

"The 'Cuda was kind of unique because I installed amber windows in it, which went along really well with the orange and white paint job," Butch said. "Those amber windows might look real pretty, but the way we had them mounted, there was no way to get out of the car in a hurry, as that was light years before escape hatches. I mean, I could get out, but it was going to be a struggle.

"So, here I am at San Diego, California's Carlsbad Raceway with a brand spanking new race car and I'm dressed to the nines in this brand spankin' new fire suit, but I know zero about running a nitro Funny Car. I drove up to the starting line for my first run, and my goggles started fogging up. I took them off, and the starter immediately shut me off.

"That sort of made me mad, and Jack Chrisman walked over and asked, 'What'd they shut you off for?'

"I said, 'Because my goggles fogged up, and I threw them on the floor.'

"He said, 'You were breathing so hard you fogged your goggles up? Cut a hole in your face mask so the air can escape from your breathers.'

"I did that and drove back up to the starting line again. I was breezing down the track and started feeling tire shake for the first time. Seems that I was so busy getting the car put together that I forgot to balance those M&Hs. Anyway, I got through there, pulled the chute, and everything was

Butch peers over his nitro-burning 426 Hemi engine. Ultimately, this car ran a best of 7.82 at 181 mph against "Dyno" Don Nicholson at Martin, Michigan.

cool. I was sitting at the big end waiting for my mother and father to come pick me up when I decided to take off my helmet and face mask.

"All of a sudden those [100 percent] nitro fumes hit me, and I couldn't breathe. Oh my God! My eyes were watering, and I couldn't see. I was gasping for air and fighting to get out of the car all the while hoping that my folks would be there any moment and lift up the darned body. But, nobody was coming—or at least not fast enough!

"Finally, I unsnapped the window on the driver's side and rolled out of the car onto the ground gasping for air. That was my first [and most memorable] trip down the quarter mile driving a Funny Car."

Road to Victory

"In either June or July 1967, I went to the Cars Magazine Championship Drag Races at Cecil County, Maryland," Butch said. "On Saturday night, Nicholson and I tied each other for Low ET of the meet at 8.03. We were starting eliminations [round-robin style] and up came a very pretty young lady with a beehive hairdo. It turned out she was "Fast Eddie" Schartman's wife, Fast Lynette.

"I was kidding her about her having bees in her hair and she said, 'Butch, you look like Pat Boone!'

"I said, 'Where's your old man?'

"She replied, 'He's up at the starting line!'

"So, I said, 'Tell him not to move, I'll be right there!'

Butch and partner Tommy Rogers pack the parachute prior to the Flash making another blast down the quarter mile. Rogers purchased and raced Butch's 1965 A990 car from him the previous year and provided the truck and trailer for the 1967 program. The duo went their separate ways midseason.

"Eddie had just beaten Nicholson, but I put him away pretty easy. We got down to the semifinals, and I raced Maynard Rupp in the STP Cougar and beat him. Nicholson beat the Ramchargers on his race, but he blew the cam plug out of the back of the engine. To fix those on an SOHC motor, you have to remove the entire engine from the car, and Dyno couldn't get that done between rounds, so strip promoter Ebby Procorpio and strip manager Chuck Lorah came over and said, 'We were hoping to see you and Nicholson in the final, but it looks like that's not going to happen, so how about you race Maynard Rupp again?'

"I said, 'Sure.' I hopped it up a little, ran an 8.03 at 177 mph, and won the race."

Taking Down the Champ

"Marvin [Rifchin] from M&H Tire Company had just come out with a 1½-inch-wider tire the week before Indy, and I found out about it. Up to that point, the injected cars more or less dominated the Funny Car class, but the blown cars like Jack Chrisman's Comet and Doug Thorley and his *Doug's Headers* Corvair were starting to come around. In fact, Doug was running Marvin's new tire when he won Indy. I could see the writing on the wall. The blown cars were starting to get hold of the ground, so I decided not to go.

"After Doug won Indy, C.J. "Pappy" Hart called me the following Tuesday and asked if I wanted to run a match race against him at Lions. The money was good, win, lose, or draw. So, I thought, 'Why not?'

"That next Saturday night we were at Lions, and I was trying to psyche Doug out, saying stuff like 'Make sure you don't leave in reverse.'

"On the first run, Doug smoked the tires, and I beat him. On the second run, he hazed the tires again and couldn't get around me. All I could hear was the whine of that supercharged Chevrolet big-block.

"Of course, I was running my mouth again saying, 'Your crown didn't last long, Indy champion.'

"Old Doug was so damn mad at me he couldn't even talk!"

Manufacturer's Memories

Lions General Manager C.J. Hart never really embraced the early Funny Car movement like many other strip promoters did. He

Butch said, "Two weeks after winning all the marbles at the Cars magazine meet at Cecil County, I raced Jack Chrisman's Comet at the NHRA Springnationals in Bristol, Tennessee. [It was] not one of my better races. The engine loaded up, wouldn't run, and I lost the race. I went back to the pits and pulled out the screens inside the injector nozzles and threw them away. That was the last race I ever lost to Jack or any other Team Mercury racer for that matter." (Photo Courtesy Steve Reyes)

Perhaps the highlight of Butch's entire 1967 racing season was when he beat Michigander Roger Lindamood (who had been bragging about being the quickest injected car in the nation) in a best of three match race at Lions Drag Strip. According to a press clipping published in Drag News, "In a battle to see who was the quickest injected [Funny Car] in the country, Butch raced Roger 'Color Me Gone' Lindamood. Both claimed the title, but it turned out that the California Flash was the quickest. Butch turned a fabulous [ET of 7.97 at 177.51 mph]." (Photo Courtesy Steve Reyes)

Butch and his 'Cuda were always a crowd favorite at Lions Drag Strip. Here, Butch prepares to dispose of the late Fred Goeske driving the famed rear-engine Hemi 'Cuda II." (Photo Courtesy Steve Reyes)

called them "circus acts," and played carousel music on the public announcement (PA) system whenever these cars appeared at the "Beach."

In November 1967, Lions hosted the *Drag Strip* magazine–sponsored East-West Funny Car Championships. Being 54 years ago, Butch's memory was a little hazy as to his first- and second-round opponents, but he distinctly remembered beating Gary Dyer driving Mr. Norm's *Super Charger* in the last round.

Ultimately, the overall Manufacturer's title at the Lions event for 1967 was won by Hayden Proffitt. His 427 Corvair roadster performed a bumper-dragging wheel-stand in the final when Gas Ronda failed to come to the line. Proffitt, who had been unceremoniously dropped from Team Mercury at the end of the previous season, got on the PA system and publicly dedicated his win to former Lincoln-Mercury bosses Al Turner and Fran Hernandez.

Meanwhile, in Orange County

Just 34 miles south of Lions Drag Strip off California Interstate 5 was Orange County International Raceway (OCIR), which was one of the nation's first super tracks. Dedicated on August 5, 1967, OCIR saw Butch and his 'Cuda and Doug Thorley's Corvair lay rubber to virgin asphalt during the super

track's grand opening press party held on August 2, 1967.

Three months later (November 23, 1967) OCIR hosted the first of many drag racing extravaganzas called the Manufacturer's Funny Car Team Championships. More than 64 injected and blown "floppers" from all over the country made the roll call, and Butch Leal's injected 'Cuda was one of them.

However, in spite of the fact that Leal won all of his races as part of Team Plymouth, it became readily apparent that the blown cars were the wave of the future. This was one of the last races Leal ran with the 'Cuda prior to selling it to Vernon Rowley, who was an injected Funny Car racer from Baltimore, Maryland.

"After I sold my injected car, I had Logghe Stamping build me a brand-new blown car," Butch said. "I went to Keith Black to order a new Keith Black Racing engine, and he [also] asked how much nitro I was going to run.

"I said, 'I want to run the can!'

"Now, not even some of Black's best clients were running 100 percent at the time.

This photo was taken on August 2, 1967, at Orange County International Raceway in Orange County, California. Butch and Doug Thorley lay rubber to virgin asphalt during the OCIR Grand Opening pre-event press party. Butch won the match.

This mid-season placard proudly proclaims Butch's 'Cuda as being "the World's Fastest Injected Chrysler" with an ET of 8.28 at 178 mph, although the Flash greatly improved on those numbers by season's end (7.97 at 177.51 mph).

Butch blasts off into the evening air during one of Irwindale Raceway's weekly Funny Car shows. Note the wheelie bars, which were a necessary mid-season addition. (Photo Courtesy Lou Hart)

High-Flying Flopper

"Keith looked at me quizzically and said, '100 percent? Really?'

"I said, 'That's what's coming, so why not?' Black built an engine for me with the right compression ratio. I picked it up and put it in the car. At the time, I was using an Art Carr transmission and got that installed. I had the car plumbed, and then I took it all apart again and painted the chassis.

"Basically, the car was ready to go, but I had one problem. I didn't know how to tune a blown motor. One of my dearest friends was Jack Chrisman who ran the *Kendall GT1* Mercury Comet with the blown Cammer in it.

"I asked Jack, 'Would you help me a little?'

"He said, 'No problem. Come down Saturday afternoon. I'm going to run Lions on Saturday night and Bakersfield on Sunday.'

"On Jack's first run at Lions, he hung up an intake valve and blew the roof right off!

"I was thinking, 'Wow! That must have been a real shocker!'

"It ended up not hurting the roof too badly, so we gathered all the pieces. When it came to running a race car, Jack could do just about anything, so he was busy fiberglassing the body back together and putting a new windshield in the car.

"Then, we repaired the engine and headed on out to Bakersfield early Sunday morning. On the first run there, he hung the same valve, and did it all over again. But this time, it burnt his hands pretty badly, as those were the days before onboard fire extinguishers."

"I had plenty of time to think about things that Sunday evening as I drove back home to Tulare," Butch said. "I woke up Monday morning and got ready to take the [Barracuda] body off the chassis and deliver it to Doyce's to be painted when the phone rang. My wife came out and said, 'Don Schumacher's on the line!'

"I had raced Don back in Chicago with my injected car [he raced the *Stardust* Dodge Charger A/FC], and I knew him pretty well.

"He said, 'Butch, I understand your car's for sale.

"Heck, I didn't even know my car was for sale!

"I said, 'Well, anything's for sale, Don—for the right price.'

"Don said, 'I'll be there tomorrow!'

Schumacher flew into Los Angeles with his mechanic "Col. John" Hogan and drove some 200 miles up to Tulare. He took a good look at the car and said, 'I want it!'

"We came to terms, and I made a little money on the deal, just enough to make me feel comfortable.

"Then, he said, 'Oh, by the way, I would like you to do me a favor.'

"I replied, 'What's that?'

"He said, 'Would you deliver it to Los Angeles International Airport for me? I'm flying it back to Chicago!'

"I thought, 'Wow—that's kind of cool!'

"A few days later, I delivered the car to the United Airlines Freight Terminal at LAX. I supervised them loading it onto a pallet, made sure that it was tied down well and had enough air in the tires, and off it went. Of course, Don was really successful with that car, and I'll never forget the day we loaded a blown nitro Funny Car into the cargo bay of a 747—darnedest thing I ever saw!"

Butch participated in the Supertrack's first-ever Manufacturer's Funny Car Team Championships on November 23, 1967, as a member of the Plymouth team and won all three of his races.

The Manufacturer's meet drove home one indisputable fact: blown cars were the wave of the future. Butch sold his 'Cuda to an injected Funny Car racer in Baltimore, Maryland, and ordered a brand-new blown car from Logghe Stamping Company.

This was the blown 1968 'Cuda that Butch built and eventually sold to Don "the Shoe" Schumacher, which thundered into the consciousness of the Funny Car racing public with its 200-plus-mph runs. It was tuned by "Col. John" Hogan. Butch said, "Every time I run across multicar team owner Don Schumacher at the drags these days, he laughs and says, 'See what you started?'"

CHAPTER 7

PUT A DODGE IN YOUR GARAGE

"I drove that thing down through there, and just before lights, the whole inside of the car lit up. I was on fire!"

"After I sold the Barracuda to Don Schumacher, I wasn't doing much," Butch Leal said. "I just played a little golf and spent time with my family. One day, a man named Dave Price called me. He was a nice man, and he and his partner happened to own Delano Dodge in Delano, California. Dave had a 1967 Dodge Coronet Street Hemi with a Dick Landy motor and a 4-speed. He was having trouble driving the car and asked me if I would be interested in taking over the wheel?

"I said, 'Sure!' I brought the car back to Tulare. Doyce painted the car my team colors, and I was off and running. The car ran pretty well for being a big tank. It competed in the SS/D class, and I ran in three or four races.

"Dave called me one afternoon and said, 'I can't get one of the new 1968½ Hurst Hemi Darts! Chrysler won't sell me one!'

"I said, 'Well, I can.'

"He said, 'How can you do that?'

"I said, 'Hold on, Dave, I'll get right back to you.'

"I called Mr. Cahill at Chrysler and told him that I was working with Delano Dodge, and the dealership wanted to purchase a Drag Pack Hemi Dart. I think they made 14 or 15 of the 4-speed cars. Then, Mr. Cahill asked, 'Are you going to drive it?'

"I said, 'I am.'

"He said, 'We have one left!'

"So, they shipped it to Delano Dodge, and Dave was absolutely flabbergasted.

"When the car arrived, I pulled it all apart, went

Butch bombs off the starting line at Fremont Raceway in California. Butch said, "At approximately 3,650 pounds, the R/T was a real tank to get moving. On 9-inch inch tires, you really had to bring up the RPM before dumping the clutch to achieve times in the 11.80s at 117 mph." (Photo Courtesy Steve Reyes)

through the engine and suspension, and had them paint the car my colors. I ran the Dart four or five times. After being runner-up at Irwindale one Saturday evening, I got back to the dealership about 2 a.m. Sunday morning, and Dave was in his office.

"He said, 'My partner and I got into a huge fight, and we're splitting up the dealership!'

"So, that was the end of the Delano Dodge drag racing program. Since that time, they [collectors] have found both the Dart and the Coronet, and both cars have been restored and painted back to my colors. In fact, just before Mr. Cahill passed away on November 14, 2011, he authenticated the Coronet. That's the only car I've ever driven [out of a total of 40] that's been authenticated by the former head of Chrysler Racing!"

Butch and Bob Cahill, the former manager of Chrysler Corporation's Vehicle Performance Planning Department, joined Butch as a special guest at the Midwest Mopars outdoor event in Farmington, Minnesota. It was there where Mr. Cahill signed authentication papers on the ex-Delano Dodge R/T Street Hemi, which Butch briefly drove in 1968. This is the only California Flash car to receive official Chrysler authentication.

Dave Price from Delano Dodge told Butch that he wasn't able to get one of the new 1968½ Hurst Hemi Darts at the dealership because Chrysler wouldn't sell him one. However, Price underestimated how well connected Butch was with Chrysler, as the dealership received the last 4-speed Hemi Dart built within a matter of weeks. Butch raced the Dart for three months, running a best ET of 10.80 at 124 mph before the agency partnership was dissolved.

Passing Gas

In the fall of 1968, Butch was approached by local Tulare, Califonia, BB/GS racer Joe Airoso to drive the Airoso brothers Chrysler-powered 1941 Willys coupe in a series of three Golden State–based blown gasser races. The Willys coupe had won the BB/GS class at Indy that year.

"Joe's wife didn't want him to drive anymore," Butch said. "In the meantime, the NHRA had come up with a mandate that you had to have a fire suit to drive a blown car anyway, and since I had one and Joe didn't, he asked me to drive. At the time, there were quite a few BB/GS races in the State of California, and the car was contracted to race at Raisin City, California, Lions, and OCIR at $1,000 to win at each race.

"I said, 'Yeah, I'll do it.'

"I won the race at Raisin City, won at Long Beach, and the next week, I went to Orange County and won there too!

"That car was really, really fast with its blown 354 Chrysler with a B&M Hydro. I just matted the throttle right off the starting line, and because it had a real low first gear, I pulled it into second just as soon as the car started to move. At OCIR, I remember racing Phil Lukens in the Marrs brothers BB/GS Corvette on the final.

"I drove that thing down through there, and just before lights, the whole inside of the car lit up. I was on fire! I had blown a head gasket, and all you could hear was the supercharger whining. That old Willys ran the best it ever ran, but I'm sure that Joe would have preferred that I had babied it a little. I'll never forget the fun I had driving that old Willys for a long as I live."

In the fall of 1968, Butch was approached by Joe Airoso, who was also from Tulare, California, about driving the Airoso brothers Chrysler-engine BB/GS 1941 Willys to fulfill a three-race contract. Butch jumped at the chance. "I'll never forget driving that car for as long as I live," Butch said. "That blown 354 Chrysler and that B&M Hydro–I was able to win all three races running in the low-9.70s at 140-plus mph." (Photo Courtesy Steve Reyes)

Circa 2020, Butch stopped by Jerry Enerline's shop and put the super tune on his ex-Delano Dodge Hemi Dart Super Stocker. "I just fixed the needles and seats on those Holleys, and the thing roared to life," Butch said. (Photo Courtesy Donna Leal)

CHAPTER 8

MATCH RACING MICKEY'S MUSTANG

"He [Mickey] called me one day and said, 'Ford's got a brand-new Boss 429 hemi motor. They're going to put them in the new Mustang fastback, and I'm getting one. Do you want to come back to work and drive the thing for me?'"

In the summer of 1964, Mickey Thompson, Butch Leal, and Ford figuratively harnessed lightning in a bottle when Butch won the Super Stock Stick class at the NHRA Nationals driving the Mickey Thompson–prepared 427 Ford Fairlane Thunderbolt.

In Chapter 5, I chronicled what happened to the 20-year-old Tulare, California, native shortly after that fabled Indy Nationals victory. Ford's loss was Chrysler Corporation's gain when, in 1965, Butch signed on as a member of its exclusive altered-wheelbase Mopar match race team. It was five more years before Leal rejoined the Blue Oval battalion in an attempt to repeat history after Mickey Thompson wisely asked him to drive his Boss 429 Mustang match racer.

"I really liked Mickey, and the feeling was mutual," Butch said. "In fact, he treated me like a son. I went back to work for him in March 1969. Backtracking slightly, in late 1968, Mickey was picked up by Ford for a second time. That was when former Pontiac Motor Division General Manager Semon E. 'Bunkie' Knudsen was appointed general manager at Ford Division, and he and Mickey were great friends.

"He [Mickey] called me one day and said, 'Ford's got a brand-new Boss 429 hemi motor. They're going to put them in the new Mustang fastback, and I'm getting one. Do you want to come back to work and drive the thing for me?'

"Well, naturally, I said, 'Yes!'"

At age 25, Butch Leal was riding on top of the world having won prestigious drag racing events for both Ford and Chrysler. In 1969, Butch returned to the Mickey Thompson camp to drive Thompson's Boss 429 Mustang match racer. (Photo Courtesy Danny Thompson)

With Mickey Thompson's new Boss 429 Mustang in the background, Thompson and Butch seal the deal with a handshake. (Photo Courtesy Danny Thompson)

But First, Do You Take This Woman?

"My future wife, Donna, and I had just started dating," Butch said. "We had gone out maybe two or three times when I broke the news to her that I had been re-hired by Mickey to drive this new Shotgun-motored Boss 429 Mustang and that I had to report for work in Long Beach the following Monday morning. Donna realized how important this was to me and my career and said, 'Go!'

"Right then and there, I knew that I had myself a 'keeper.'

"When Donna and I were married, Mickey actually loaned me $10,000 interest free and helped me get hooked up with a wholesale jeweler in downtown Los Angeles to get a good deal on our wedding rings. He even flew up to Tulare to attend our

Butch and his fiancée, Donna Harrison, were married on June 18, 1969. Pictured left to right are Frank and Pansy Butch, Butch and Donna Leal, and Lela and Leo Harrison.

Boss 429 Mustangs were all the rage at the time, but very few examples had been converted to full-on drag racing vehicles. Of course, Butch and Mickey Thompson were the notable exceptions, and big things were expected by Ford and Mickey Thompson/Butch Leal fans alike. (Photo Courtesy Danny Thompson)

June 18 wedding ceremony. Then, he paid for Donna and me to fly back to Dayton, Ohio, to pick up his new Ford F-250 ramp truck and drive it back to Long Beach. Some honeymoon, eh?"

Do You Take This Mustang?

Brighton, Michigan's Kar Kraft built the car. The Code M, Wimbledon White 1969 Mustang SportsRoof (KK 1206) was one of the earliest preproduction Boss 429 Mustang prototypes built. Also known as the Drag Test Car, it was assigned to Mickey Thompson Enterprises through Ford Drag Racing Manager Emil Loeffler (along with one Thunderbird and two Torino street cars), and it was the only Boss 9 built with two Holley 4-barrel carburetors.

"That Boss 429 was a pretty interesting engine, to say the least, with those massive intake ports, huge valve covers, and dual quads," Butch said. "When the car arrived at Galpin Ford, the thing was bone stock. I mean, there were no lightweight parts on it at all. It wasn't [acid] dipped or anything. I completely pulled the car apart and went through everything. By the time I was finished, I had pared the weight down to 3,120 pounds.

"Boss 302 and Boss 429 designer Larry Shinoda came up with the actual paint scheme.

"Then, I took the car over to Holman-Moody-Stroppe in Long Beach and had Dennis Erickson paint both car and ramp truck a custom mix we liked to call 'Mickey Thompson Blue.'

"The car ran 9.90s at 134 mph, which was about what the heads-up Super Stock Camaros, Darts, and Barracudas were all running. It was nothing earth shaking but still competitive."

After the wedding, Thompson flew the newlywed Leals to Dayton, Ohio, as a wedding present to pick up Mickey Thompson's new Ford F-250 ramp truck and drive it back home. (Photo Courtesy Danny Thompson)

Mickey Thompson's new Ford F-250 ramp truck was state of the art with its 429 Ford big-block, single man (or woman) sleeper, single car ramp, and lots of carrying capacity. This very truck has been fully restored and can be seen annually at the annual Fabulous Fords Forever event at Buena Park, California's Knott's Berry Farm, and Ghost Town. (Photo Courtesy Danny Thompson)

A Never-Ending Thrash

"Being that Mickey's shop was only 3 miles from Lions, I tried out several things," Butch said. "I would try stuff in the intake ports on the heads and try various camshafts, compression ratios, and carburetor setups. This thing wouldn't respond to anything. Finally, I grew tired and said, 'Mickey! This is getting really frustrating. Order me two [427] Cammers.'

"When they [the 427 SOHC engines] arrived, I uncrated the first one and bolted it to the engine stand. I was getting ready to change out the cams and all that kind of stuff when Mickey walked in and said, 'Butch! You got to stop!'

"I said, 'Why is that?'

"He said, 'I talked to Ford, and they want you to stay with the Boss 429.'

"I looked at him and said, 'Alright, boss, but I'm pretty upset about this. Do I have your permission to do anything [to the engine] I want to?'

"He said, 'You can do anything you want.'

"Well, that got me a little excited. So, I pulled the thing completely apart. Actually, the Boss 429 is not a full-hemi engine, as it had a quench area in the combustion chambers. I mean, they called it one, but it's really not.

"Joe Anahory was a great machinist, and he made a [cylinder] head cutter for me, and we converted the cylinder heads to a full hemi. I think the intake valve size was now 2.400 while the Chrysler Hemis were 2.220. I figured, well, that's got to be better than a 426.

"I had Bob Brooks make up a set of Mickey Thompson full-hemi pistons along with a set of Mickey's aluminum connecting rods. I got to talking to Racer Brown.

"I said, 'Racer, can you grind me either a Chevrolet or Chrysler firing order on my Ford cam?'

"He said, 'No, but if you can you get a Ford cam blank for me, I can.'

"I called Ford, and they sent me two cam blanks, and Racer ground each of them with a Chrysler firing order. I put everything back together, and when I fired the thing up on the engine stand, it sounded way different. I bolted it [the engine] back in the car and took it to Long Beach.

"When I let the clutch out the thing ran 9.67 at 136 mph! Right then and there, I knew I was on the right track. In later years, Bob Glidden did the same thing with his Boss 429 Shotgun motors and experienced tremendous success."

This Ford Motor Company photo was widely circulated among the automotive press and originally appeared in Car Craft *magazine.*

Butch prepares to climb behind the wheel of the Mickey Thompson Mustang at Long Beach as Mickey looks on. (Photo Courtesy Don Gillespie)

The Flash and Mickey Thompson's Boss 429 Mustang charge off the Lions Drag Strip starting line. The best ET for the blue Boss 429 was 9.67 at 136 mph. (Photo Courtesy Ford)

Butch lets out the clutch at he and Mickey Thompson's home track, Lions Associated Drag Strip. Actually, Mickey Thompson was the original strip manager at "the Beach," and had a key to the back gate, which made impromptu track testing a virtual snap.

LEFT: This photo was taken in late 1969 showing the Mickey Thompson–Ford lineup. Pictured (left to right) are Arnie Behling (Mickey Thompson Ford Maverick), Johnny Wright (Mickey Thompson Mach 1, formerly the red car), Mickey Thompson, Danny Ongais (Mickey Thompson blue Mustang and the seldom-driven Mickey Thompson Boss 429 Monocoque Mustang), and Butch Leal (Mickey Thompson Boss 429 Mustang match racer). (Photo Courtesy Danny Thompson)

It was discovered that someone at Holman-Moody had failed to final weld in the shock towers, and the front suspension was shifting around under hard acceleration. Once Holman-Moody fixed the problem, Pro Stock Maverick No. 1 was first offered to Butch, who declined the car, and Dick Brannan, who also declined it. In the end, the engineering mule was given to Ford Drag Team Eastern Captain Hubert "Hue Baby" Platt, who was quite successful with it.

The Coming of Pro Stock

"NHRA Division Director Bernie Partridge and I were great friends," Butch said. "I said, 'We need to get a new class going. We have all these guys with their Camaros and stuff, and they want to put tunnel rams on their engines, but there's no class for them.

"Bernie said, 'We'll have a race for them at Irwindale [Irwindale Raceway's Heads Up Super Stock Shootout] and see what happens.

"Well, everybody came: Bob Lambeck, Dick Landy, Bill Bagshaw, Jim Baker, and Ed Terry—all the heavy hitters. I ended up finishing in the runner-up spot to Bagshaw's *Red Light Bandit* 1968 Dodge Dart. However, it really wasn't 'heads-up,' as the NHRA was experimenting with the idea of instituting different weight breaks on certain makes of cars to make the show more equitable.

"When Bagshaw went through tech, his car came up in excess of 100 pounds light! I thought Bernie was going to choke him to death because he was trying to promote this Pro Stock thing with NHRA for 1970. Anyhow, we were declared the winner.

"Bagshaw told Bernie, 'Chrysler didn't like the idea of handicapping anybody. They wanted to maintain the same [heads-up] weight break across the board, so if I had to run Butch on the final, I was told to take the weight out and I did exactly what I was told to do!'

"That's how Pro Stock got started. So, here I am thinking we got our own class and we're off and running. Then, Ford pulled the plug on Mickey—again, which was largely based on the firing of Bunkie Knudsen as Ford's general manager. It was a real shame because Mickey had assembled the greatest group of people I had ever seen.

"We had fuel racer Don Ratican running the shop, and Joe Anahory was our chief machinist. Top Fuel racer Bob Skinner was running the flow bench, and championship motorcycle rider Al Gunner was working on my 429 cylinder heads. We had Danny Ongais and Pat Foster driving the blue car and the red car [Mickey Thompson's *Mach 1* Mustang] working there. We had Amos Satterlee tuning on the blue car, and John Kranenburg tuning on the red car. Steve Montrelli was assembling the engines and Funny Car driver Larry Fullerton was building the [Ford C-6] transmissions.

"It was *the* place to work. I was fortunate enough to watch them build the new land speed record car there [*Challenger II*] and all kinds of other interesting projects at Mickey Thompson Engineering. But, like they say, when it's over, it's over."

Mickey Thompson's Boss 429 Mustang match racer still lives and is owned by a serious collector living in Australia.

Drag Testing the Holman-Moody-Stroppe (Pro Stock) Maverick Prototype

"Toward the middle of the Mickey Thompson Boss 429 Mustang program, I received a call from Ford, and they asked me if I would mind taking the Boss 429 engine out of 'my' Mustang and take it over to Holman-Moody-Stroppe on Signal Hill in Long Beach," Butch said. "Ford said that they had a little Pro Stock Maverick engineering mule that Holman-Moody had built that they fitted with a Boss 429 dummy block for a mockup. But, they actually wanted to install a running Boss 429 engine and 4-speed and go out and test the car.

"Well, Mickey didn't mind, so I whipped the Boss 429 engine out of the Mustang and took it over to Stroppe's. When I got there, everything was [supposedly] ready. After some thrashing, we got it [the engine] installed, so now we head out to Long Beach and test the car. Gas Ronda and Ed Terry were also there.

"I was the first one to drive the thing. I whipped it down through there and came back and said, 'This thing's steering a little funny.'

"So, they (Holman-Moody-Stroppe) looked at the car and said, 'Maybe we forgot to set the toe in.'

"They set the toe in, and I made another run, but it was the same thing. Then, Gas got in the car. He made a few runs, and it was [still] doing the same thing.

"By that time, the thing [the Maverick] was really starting to rear up, so we all figured that's what was making the car do that. We put some air in the back tires and talked about hanging some weight on the front to keep the thing down on the ground, but Ford said no. They wanted to leave the car just the way it was.

"Then, Ed [Terry] climbed behind the wheel, and he made a couple of runs. At the end of the day, all three of us had made runs in the 9.80s to 9.90s with mine being the quickest.

"When Holman-Moody-Stroppe took [the Maverick] back to the shop, they noticed that the front spring towers were only tack welded in place, and they had been moving around under hard acceleration! Ford was so pissed off you just couldn't believe it. You can just imagine what might have happened had one of us turned the car over and crashed.

"They asked, 'Butch, how did you feel that?'

"I just said that it was obvious, especially when you drove the car back up the return road. Every time you hit a pothole (and there were many at L.A.D.S.), the car would go 'ka thunk' and dart from one side to the other.

"Ford kept the whole thing quiet and fixed the problem. I was asked if I wanted the car, but I said no because I felt it wasn't all that trick. In the end, that original Pro

Stock Maverick prototype was supposed to have gone to Ford Performance Advisor Dick Brannan, but Dick also passed, and Ford ended up giving the car to Hubert Platt instead."

Measured For Mickey's Maverick

"The whole time I was working on Mickey's Boss 429 Mustang project, 'Lil' John Buttera was there building Mickey's new 1970 Boss 429–engine Maverick Funny Car," Butch said. "Mickey and I had talked about my driving the Maverick, and 'Lil John' even fit the roll cage to my measurements.

"But, as the project was nearing completion, Mickey took me aside and said, 'Listen Butch, you're a nice kid. I run these cars real hard on heavy doses of nitro. Ford has insisted that I run these damned Boss 429s instead of the 427 SOHC engines that we're used to running, and I don't want to burn you up.'

"As usual, Mickey was right. Arnie Behling got the job as driver, and the life expectancy of the Mickey Thompson Boss 429 Maverick was short lived after the car went out in a blaze of glory."

According to Boss 429 expert Bob Perkins (Perkins Restoration in Juneau, Wisconsin), KK 1206 (the Emil Loeffler Drag Test Boss 429) vehicle identification number (VIN) 9F022117319 may be the car sent to Mickey Thompson. The only possible alternative Boss 429 (which could have

"Mickey and I were friends," Butch said, *"In fact, he treated me like a son."*

been mistaken for the Mickey Thompson/Butch Leal Boss 9 Mustang) is KK Engineering Mule 1207, which is VIN 9F022117320. Both cars were originally painted Code M Wimbledon White.

Butch was actually slated to drive Mickey Thompson's ill-fated 1970 Boss 429 Maverick AA/Funny Car, and builder "Lil" John Buttera actually configured the roll cage to fit around him. But in the end, Thompson had second thoughts and put driver Arnie Behling into the driver's seat instead.

BACK TO BOWTIES

"After word got out that Butch had gotten together with Chrysler Racing's Bob Cahill at the inaugural NHRA Hot Wheels Supernationals (sponsored by Mattel) at Ontario Motor Speedway and put together a deal to campaign a 1971 Plymouth Duster the following season, the Camaro's days were numbered."

"With the Mickey Thompson Boss 429 Mustang program ending so abruptly, I was going to call Mr. Cahill at Chrysler, but there wasn't enough time or budget to line up a deal for 1970," Butch Leal said. "The sad reality was that I knew how to make a 426 Hemi run (probably as good as anyone who ever touched one at the time), and the NHRA rule books for Pro Stock heavily favored the 426 Hemi engines.

"I found myself in a bit of a quandary. I did not want to go with an independent Mopar Pro Stock program and possibly embarrass Chrysler by turning in a subpar performance due to lack of proper technological support, funding, and/or dealing with outdated equipment.

"Finally, I figured the heck with it. If I couldn't score a Chrysler deal, I would do the next-best thing and build a Gen II 1970½ Pro Stock Chevrolet Camaro.

"I called Bill Thomas at Anaheim, California's Bill Thomas Race Cars Inc. and told him what I had in mind. Bill was happy to provide me with the work space and [some of] the technology I needed to build the car, but I had to pay for everything out of pocket.

"Tom Jacobsen, who had bought my '62 409, worked as a parts manager at Wilmington, California's Glendhill Chevrolet and really helped me out a lot. I bought a 2-ton Chevy C30 dually, a no-frills 6-cylinder 1970 Camaro coupe, and all the parts I needed, such as blocks, crankshafts, connecting rods, and even some parts like the 427 square-port cylinder heads, which I previously didn't know you could even get, all at dealer cost.

"The first thing I did was drive the Camaro to Bill's shop, and we started taking it apart. Then, I hauled the body shell over to Chem Tech in Cen-

tral Los Angeles and got it acid dipped. That was a chore in itself, being that I had broken my left collarbone in a dirt bike riding accident a few weeks earlier and I pretty much loaded and unloaded the car all by myself. In fact, I broke my collarbone for the second time when my foot slipped loading the body onto Tom Jacobsen's ramp truck to bring it back to Thomas' shop. What misery!

"Bill wasn't familiar with acid dipping at the time. He looked at it and said, 'Now, that's interesting.'

"He got a big kick out of the sheet metal being so thin.

"Anyhow, every day, Donna and I drove over to Bill's shop, and I made more progress. When it came time to install the four-point roll bar (which is all the NHRA required at the time), I called Darryl Droke at Mr. Roll Bar and got fixed up.

Fresh from the acid-dipping tank, Butch loads his chemically lightened 1970½ Camaro body shell onto the trailer. He broke his left collarbone a few weeks earlier and broke it again when he slipped while loading the body onto the ramp.

Shakedown runs were made at OCIR. Butch said that he liked to back up from his burnouts with the door open, which was something he learned while match racing Hubert Platt. The fans loved it.

"After that, I built a set of subframe connectors and tied both front and rear subframes together. I also set the engine back in the chassis 1½ inches per the NHRA rule book and lengthened the front spindles to increase suspension travel and transfer more weight. That took a little time.

"I also installed a narrowed 4.56/4.88 Schiefer-geared Summers axle-equipped Dana 60 rear end, which I had left over from my altered-wheelbase car, and it fit perfectly. Dennis Ereck and I installed an A&I Fiberglass hood and front fenders, which took some body work, as the fiberglass parts didn't fit very well.

"Then, Dennis painted the car in my traditional Mustang Poppy Red and Refrigerator White team colors, and it turned out beautifully. It was even featured on the cover of a couple car magazines."

These Parts are Butch's Parts

Throughout the 1960s and early 1970s, Ron Ogilvie served as parts manager at Bill Thomas Race Cars Incorporated (BTRC). Prior to Ogilvie's untimely passing in 2015, I sat down with him at his Las Vegas, Nevada, home and talked about working behind the counter at BTRC.

"I was used to logging in all kinds of high-performance parts coming across the counter at Bill Thomas Race Cars, Inc., but the stuff usually arrived in multiples and/or on pallets not in 'one-sie, two-sie' fashion," Ogilvie said. "So, when I started receiving boxes with parts addressed to Butch Leal c/o Bill Thomas Race Cars, Inc. Anaheim, California, I had to make sure that the help didn't mistakenly log them into inventory.

"Butch got his parts right away, and it could be safely said that in early 1970, Butch Leal's sponsors drop shipped enough parts to BTRC for him to build his 1970½ 427 Camaro Pro Stock car, box by box, and piece by piece."

That included all of the internals used to build the 427-ci (3.750x4.250) big-block Chevrolet powerplant

Wearing an outfit like this, perhaps Butch could have been called "the California Kid" instead of "the California Flash." (Photo Courtesy Steve Reyes)

that Butch jointly screwed together at Thomas's shop and his aunt's garage in Long Beach, California, where he was staying. He used the stock 427 Chevy crank, TRW engine bearings, stock 427 Chevrolet connecting rods, a set of 14:1-compression Venolia forged aluminum pistons, a set of big-block Chevrolet cylinder head gaskets, a General Kinetics cam and kit, and a set of 427 big-block cylinder heads prepared by Butch from Diamond Racing Engines in Detroit.

Induction was handled by an Edelbrock 2x4 tunnel-ram intake with twin Holley 850s. Ignition duties were handled by a Roto Faze ignition firing a set of Autolite spark plugs. Kendall GT-1 racing oil took care of lubrication duties, and Hedman Hedders took care of the exhaust. [Butch] banged gears using a Hurst-assisted aluminum-cased Chrysler-Dagenham 4-speed transmission bolted to a Lakewood Industries scattershield containing a Hays clutch, flywheel, and pressure plate, which more than stood up to Butch's brutal, signature-edition 7,000-rpm banzai starts.

"The Camaro was completed around May 1970," Butch said. "It wasn't quicker than the speed of sound or anything. It ran 10 to 9.80, which was about what all the West Coast Pro Stock cars were running at the time. Unfortunately, the fast guys like Sox, Booth, Jenkins, Carlton, Nicholson, and others had up to a tenth of a second on me so, whenever called upon, I had to try to compensate with my driving skills.

"Wins included two NHRA WCS points races, one at Irwindale and the other at Bakersfield, where I beat Bill Bagshaw's Dodge Dart and Darryl Droke's Maverick in the final. As far as national events were concerned, the Camaro just wasn't in the hunt. Sure, I would usually qualify well, but (despite my driving the wheels off the darned thing) the car just didn't possess final-round capabilities.

"To make matters worse, the NHRA outlawed the Nye Frank–fabricated 7-inch hood scoop I had built, saying that the cars didn't come that way. They had flat hoods, so I had to get an ugly black [fiberglass] hood and put an NHRA-approved (albeit flimsy looking) hood scoop on it to be legal for Pro Stock. To make sure the scoop didn't fall off or suck down on top of the carburetors, I installed an adjustable center bolt on both Holleys.

"When I got to the U.S. Nationals at Indy, I went to warm up the car, and I heared a clunk and immediately shut off the engine. One of the bolts had worked its way loose, fallen down through the carburetor, and dropped into the intake port of the cylinder head.

"Fortunately, Wally Booth had a friend who lived close by, and he had a shop that I could use. I worked all night on the engine. At about 4 a.m., my wife, Donna, fell asleep on the floor of the transporter.

"Thankfully, it hadn't done too much damage. It didn't hurt the block, but I had to replace two valves, which kind of put a damper on the rest of race week's activities. Until a few years ago, I kept that bolt as a reminder to check everything twice."

From "California Flash" to "Heavy Chevy"

After word got out that Butch had gotten together with Chrysler Racing's Bob Cahill at the inaugural NHRA Hot Wheels Supernationals (sponsored by Mattel) at Ontario Motor Speedway and put together a deal to campaign a 1971 Plymouth Duster the following season, the Camaro's days were numbered.

Butch said, "One day, Dick Harrell called.

"He said, 'Butch, I understand that your Camaro is for sale.'

"I said, 'It is!'

"Harrell said, 'Well, there's a guy in New York named Brooklyn Heavy who wants to buy the car.'

"I said, 'Have him bring [plenty of] money!'

"Within weeks, I had sold the Camaro to Brooklyn Heavy, and he paid me for the car with a brown paper bag stuffed full of cash."

With the Camaro, wins were few and far in between. Once such example was the 1970 Bakersfield WCS where Butch disposes of Darryl "Mr. Roll Bar" Droke's 427 SOHC Ford Maverick during the Pro Stock final. (Photo Courtesy Steve Reyes)

Butch and the Camaro tackle the 1970 U.S. Nationals at Indy with less-than-spectacular results.

The 1970 U.S Nationals was primarily an all-Chrysler show, or at least after the second round it was. Losing was not the Flash's style, and it got him to thinking.

In this photo taken during an October 3 Pro Stock race at OCIR, Butch and the Camaro compete against Ed Terry driving the Ford Drag Team Silver Bullet 427 SOHC Maverick. (Photo Courtesy Lou Hart)

Butch and the Camaro tackle a GT1 at the 1970 AHRA World Finals at Beeline Dragway, Mesa Arizona.

Off and running, the Flash drops the clutch at Beeline. Note the "S/S" designation on the window, which was the AHRA's idea of Pro Stock, which didn't become an official class until the following year.

A Sponsor Speaks

Industry veteran Tom Curnow is best known for his tenure as a public relations and advertising liaison at Culver City, California's Hedman Hedders. The company was a pioneering custom exhaust engineering house in the speed equipment and hot rod industry. In fact, CEO Bob Hedman was one of the founding fathers of SEMA.

"Butch and I worked together at Mickey's all the way though Mickey's Boss 429 Mustang program," said Bob Curnow. "In July 1969, I left Mickey's and went to work for Bob Hedman. At that time, Butch was still running Mickey's Boss 429 Mustang Pro Stocker without any great success. When that deal terminated, he went back to Chevrolet. That's when he contacted me wanting to know if he could come over to our Culver City, California, factory with a sponsorship proposal, and I said sure.

"That was the same time we were involved in doing exhaust work for Roger Penske, who had recently switched from the Traco-engine Chevrolets that propelled the team to the 1969 SCCA Trans Am Championship to AMC and Javelin in 1970. We applied much of the technology we learned working with Penske and Traco to Butch's program, including the Hedman 4-2-1 Collector, and Modulator Ninety designs, and it worked.

"Of course, Hedman remained with Butch as an associate sponsor all throughout much of his Mopar Pro Stock days, which proved to be mutually beneficial for all concerned. It was a great partnership."

Here's what Butch's Camaro looked like during its after-life under the care and feeding of New York street racer Brooklyn Heavy. Meanwhile, back in Southern California, a new Ron Butler-built 1971 Pro Stock Plymouth Duster was already in the works.

"HELLO CHRYSLER, THIS IS THE FLASH CALLING!"

"I was so excited. It was two tenths quicker than any of the other Chrysler cars that were there. At the time, I had drained all my resources finishing this car, and I really needed money."

"I had always gotten along with Chrysler Corporation's drag racing impresario Bob Cahill and he with me," Butch Leal said. "In fact, we were both born on the same day.

"Bob owed me a favor. So, after the 1965 altered-wheelbase program ended, I was owed a little money, but since Chrysler was so far over budget at the time and they had been so good to me, I light heartedly suggested that I would take a 'marker.' Well, after getting beaten by the Chryslers at the 1970 NHRA Hot Wheels Supernationals at Ontario Motor Speedway, I immediately looked up Bob at the track.

"We sat in the bleachers, and I said, 'Mr. Cahill, I would like to call in my marker. I would like to build an A-Body Plymouth Duster.'

"After Bob got done laughing, he tried to talk me out of that idea.

"He said, 'We think the Barracuda is a little slipperier.'

"At that time, I was right on top of my game and said, 'Well, the A-Bodies are 6 inches narrower.'

"Mr. Cahill replied, 'Yes, that's true, but the roof lines are 1½ inches higher.'

"I said, 'Mine won't be.'

"Bob said, 'When I get back to Detroit, I'll talk to my guys [including Manager of Performance Activities Dick Maxwell, and Engineer Dave Koffel], and we'll get back to you.'

"A few days later, Mr. Cahill called back and said, 'Okay, Butch. We have a deal.'"

Actually, it wasn't a full-blown deal like the one that Chrysler Super Car Performance Clinic super stars Sox & Martin and Don Grotheer had. Chrysler gave Butch a complete, running car. It provided him with the engines and driveline parts and provided technical support.

With his new Plymouth Duster still under construction, Butch jumped behind the wheel of Chrysler Super Car Performance Clinic star Don Grotheer's Hemi Road Runner after it was learned that original Grotheer team driver Bill Cooper couldn't drive a stick.

However, Chrysler didn't pay him a salary.

Leal was building the car out of pocket, but he had access to many of the highly classified drivetrain parts that others couldn't get. After seeing how Bill Bagshaw's Pro Stock Dodge Challenger turned out, Butch wisely decided to have Ron Butler build his new Duster. He had the car acid dipped in early January and delivered the body to Butler's Culver City, California, shop.

"In the meantime, my cousin Ronnie Broadhead was running an Oldsmobile, and he and engine-building wizard Joe Allread were good friends," Butch said. "Joe had built Bill Bagshaw's Hemi, and it was wicked fast. So, I said to Joe, 'It's been a long time since I put a gasoline-burning carbureted [426] Hemi together. Would you help me?'

"Joe said, 'Sure!'

"Every night, my wife, Donna, who was pregnant at the time, and I drove to the San Fernando Valley to work with Joe to build my engine. He had a little formula that I didn't know about called 'piston-to-head and piston-to-valve clearance.' He laid that [mechanical theory] on me and I went, 'Whoa!'

"We got this thing finished the same time Butler finished the car. I mean, we couldn't have timed it any better!

"Here's a funny story: Joe had a pool table at his home, and every night after we were done working on the engine, we played a few rounds of pool. I usually beat him out of enough gas money to drive back home again. I left my cue stick there for 20 years with some money on the eve.

"Many years later, Donna and I went back and visited Joe and his wife one evening.

"Joe said, 'Here, would you like your cue stick back? And, by the way, this is your money!'"

The Road Runner

"Unfortunately, the Duster was not done in time to compete at the NHRA Winternationals, and I had some spare time on my hands," Butch said. "In the meantime, Mr. Cahill had contacted Don Grotheer and asked him if he intended to run both clinic cars (his Pro Stock 1971

For beginners, Butch captured the GT-1 title at the 1971 AHRA Winternationals at Beeline Dragway in Mesa, Arizona, defeating Jerry Bickel's Camaro in the final.

A week later at Pomona, Butch continued to mow down the Modified Production competition only to lose a tight battle in the final against 1970 NHRA Modified Eliminator World Champ Carroll Caudle's G/MP '55 Chevy.

Plymouth Barracuda and his 1971 B/Modified Production Plymouth Road Runner) at the upcoming AHRA and NHRA winter meets. Don expressed concern that he might be spread a little too thin running the two cars all by himself. Mr. Cahill told Don that I was back on board with Chrysler and suggested that it might be a good idea if I drove the Road Runner, and Don agreed.

"Mr. Cahill remarked in sort of a tongue-in-cheek manner, 'It'll give the kid a little practice at driving a 4-speed!'"

Practice makes perfect—or nearly perfect. Butch and the Road Runner dominated the single 4-barrel GT1 class at the 1971 AHRA Winternationals on January 30, 1971, at Beeline Dragway in Mesa, Arizona. In the final, he ran an ET of 10.67 at 129.87 mph to defeat Jerry Bickel in the Bickel & Holthe's Camaro, who ran a 10.50 at 126.22 mph.

A week later, Butch and the Bird (now running a Pro Stock–style 2x4 intake) continued their romp through the Modified Production ranks at the NHRA Winternationals on February 7, 1971, at the Los Angeles County Fairgrounds in Pomona. However, he lost in the final with an ET of 10.46 to the 1970 NHRA Modified Production World Champion Carroll Caudle and his G/MP 1955 Chevrolet Bel Air, which ran an 11.79.

National Dragster magazine commented, "Leal was 0.05 under his index, while Caudle was 0.04 under his. However, Caudle more than made up for the difference at the lights, and Leal was never able to catch him."

Butch's first NHRA national event debut with the new Duster was the 1971 NHRA Springnationals in Grapevine (Dallas), Texas. Teething problems placed him in the 10th qualifying position, losing to Ronnie Sox in round two.

Early on, the Duster showed a strong propensity to rear up on its hind quarters. Too bad there wasn't anyone sitting in the stands at Sanair, Canada's 1971 NHRA Molson Grand National during Friday's Pro Stock qualifying session to fully appreciate the Flash's "auto aerobatics!"

When you go up this high, it's necessary to stay in the throttle. Note the bent rear bumper. Butch drove it almost halfway down the track before setting the car down, and the only appreciable damage was to the oil pan.

Fresh Out of the Box

"We got the Duster finished shortly after Pomona and took it to the NHRA points race at Irwindale Raceway for testing," Butch said. "I put a little air in the tires because I didn't know what the car was going to do. Joe wanted me to make a run with a set of hotter plugs in the engine to try and cycle it in because in those days, we had no other way of doing that. Then, we changed them out for a set of cooler plugs and made some horsepower.

"I'll never forget it. On its first run, the car went 10.13 at 139 mph, which wasn't too bad. We came back, we let some air out of the tires, changed plugs, rolled up to the starting line for the first round, red lit on a 0.05 tree, and went 9.82 at 142 mph. Forget the red light. A 9.82! I was so excited. It was two tenths quicker than any of the other Chrysler cars that were there. At the time, I had drained all my resources finishing this car, and I really needed money.

"The next week, I went to the WCS points meet at Bremerton, Washington. I called my dad and said, 'Dad I need some gas.'

"We had the trucking business, so I rolled into Pixley and filled up the truck. Then, Donna and I drove straight up to Seattle. Lambeck and Landy were there. In the first round, I let the clutch out, and if you were there taking

At the NHRA U.S. Nationals, Butch beat H.L. Shahan in round one, Don Grotheer in round two, and Bobby Yowell in round three before falling to Stuart McDade in the semifinals. (Photo Courtesy Steve Reyes)

photos, this was probably the prettiest run you've ever seen."

According to Bob Lambeck, Butch's Duster came up and it was almost on the bumper. Then, he shifted it into second and it didn't go left or right. It just kept going straight. When he shifted it into third, the car came down as smoothly as a hawk landing on a wire.

"Butch had that thing in the air all the way to half-track and still outran me," Lambeck said.

Cleared for Takeoff

While competing at the NHRA-Molson Grandnational Championship Drag Races in Sanair, Canada, Butch stood the Duster on the back bumper again. However, this time there were regrettable consequences.

"I was at Indianapolis testing tires for Goodyear, and I slid a set of test tires (that were better) into my truck," Butch said. "The rule was that you can't run a test tire in open competition because they are not certified for production and available for sale to everyone.

"Well, I mistakenly put them on the car at Sanair, and the car went straight up on the back bumper during qualifying. What a dumb move on my part. I split the oil pan upon landing and had to drive over to a Chrysler agency in Montreal and beat the pan back into shape, welding it back together using coat hangers.

"Luckily, I got enough points [he missed a gear in round one, gaining a total of only two] from the Molson Grand National fiasco while being given the long-distance award. The result of those high-flying auto aerobatics was that I had Ron Butler build me my first set of wheelie bars.

"Then, I ran Indy. After Indy, it was on to the second-annual NHRA Hot Wheels Supernationals at Ontario Motor Speedway."

With a new set of wheelie bars freshly installed, the Duster started to calm down and realize its true performance potential, qualifying fourth at the 1971 NHRA U.S. Nationals with an ET of 9.668 at 142.63 mph.

Butch stages at OMS, waiting for "Dyno" Don Nicholson to make his qualifying run of 9.607 at 143.08 mph to nail down the No. 3 qualifying spot at the 1971 NHRA Hot Wheels Supernationals. "Ever since my 409 days, 'Dyno' Don Nicholson has been my hero," Butch said.

Exactly one year to the day after Butch had his conversation in the stands at OMS with Chrysler's Bob Cahill, he qualified his 1971 Plymouth Duster Pro Stocker in the No. 1 spot at the 1971 Hot Wheels Supernationals with an ET of 9.53 at 143.76 mph. (Photo Courtesy Ed Justice Jr.)

In round two at the NHRA Hot Wheels Super-nationals, Stuart McDade in Billy "the Kid" Stepp's Pro Stock Dodge Challenger charges off the OMS starting line against the Flash. Stepp lost his clutch (note the death smoke) and ran an ET of 16.08 at 56.10 mph to Butch's hard-charging 9.69 at 137.40 mph.

Controversy at Ontario

"At Ontario, Ronnie and I met in the semifinals," Butch said. "I beat him in the lights by about 2 feet (9.553 to 9.558), and the crowd went absolutely crazy. Prior to the beginning of the race, Chrysler had told all its sponsored Pro Stock cars not to say anything about my car having a little more than 55-percent weight over the rear wheels. Well, after losing, Ronnie just couldn't stand it and had my car weighed at both ends. I got thrown out on the 55-percent weight rule and was pretty upset about it.

"I was going to get after Ronnie in the staging lanes when Mr. Cahill stopped me and said, 'Let me talk to you, Butch. There's no use in getting into this. I know what you're going to do. What I'm going to do for you is we have a brand-new [Dodge] truck with an Oleynik box on its way to North Carolina. I'll have it turned around and sent to you instead. And, next year, I'll cut their [Sox & Martin's] budget in half and give it to you instead.'

"I said, 'Well, Bob, guess I'm not mad anymore!'"

That afternoon, Butch also talked to Competition Director Jack Hart, arguing that if Pro Stock was truly supposed to be heads-up, then it should be heads-up! Jack agreed but said that they [NHRA] couldn't officially

Box Score: 1971

Statistics compiled by Bob Frey, an NHRA announcer, drag racing historian, and statistician

NHRA Division 7 Pro Stock Champion		
Event	**Location**	**Result**
Division 4 Points Meet	Amarillo, Texas*	Won: Defeated Don Grotheer
Division 7 Points Meet	Bremerton, Washington	Won: Defeated Ken Van Cleve
Division 7 Points Meet	Fremont, California**	Won: Defeated Dick Landy
Division 7 Points Meet	Sacramento, California	Won: Defeated Bill Bagshaw
Division 7 Points Meet	Orange County, California.	Won: Defeated Bob Lambeck

*No. 1 Qualifier at Amarillo with ET of 10.07
**Set the Pro Stock national record with ET of 9.57 at 144.92 mph

This was the beginning of the run that had fans on their feet when Butch defeated Ronnie Sox by half a fender length in the semifinal round.

Ronnie Sox (left) and Butch are in the lights during the semifinal round of Pro Stock Eliminator at Ontario. Butch won by about 2 feet with an ET of 9.553 to a 9.558. Sox & Martin protested Butch for having too much weight over the rear wheels, and Butch was disqualified.

reverse Chief Technical Inspector Bill "Farmer" Dismuke's decision during an event in progress. However, on the following Monday, the NHRA threw out that rule.

"At the last 1971 NHRA Division Seven Points Meet I ran at Orange County International Raceway, I ended up winning the Western Conference, beating Bill Bagshaw on the final by only two points," Butch said. "Remember those two points from Canada? Well, they paid off while Ronnie Sox simultaneously won the Eastern Conference."

Other noteworthy performances for 1971 included finishing as the runner-up match racing against Bill Bagshaw in Port Orford, Oregon, and then defeating Bag-

shaw the following week during a match race at Golden State Raceway in Santa Maria, California.

Small Models, Big Bucks

"In 1971, MPC Models called to discuss doing a 1/25-scale plastic model car kit of my Pro Stock Plymouth Duster, which I thought was pretty cool," Butch said. "MPC already had Bill 'Grumpy' Jenkins, Ronnie Sox, and 'Dyno' Don Nicholson signed up, and the contract called for a percentage of the sales. I kept getting sizeable royalty checks that were pretty nice.

Although Butch was tossed out after Sox & Martin protested, it was a profitable loss (in a manner of speaking) after Chrysler Racing's Bob Cahill compensated Butch by giving him this brand-new Olynik-bodied Dodge hauler, which was originally slated for Sox & Martin.

All Butch needed to do to update his 1971 Duster to a 1972 model was replace the taillight panel and front grille.

"One day, MPC called me and wanted to know why my model was outselling all three of the other guys' put together.

"They asked, 'Did you win more races than the other guys?'

"I said, 'Well, I've won a lot, but so have the rest of them.'

"About two weeks later, MPC called me back again and said, 'We think we know.'

"I said, 'And why is that?'

"They said, 'It's because the box says 'California' on it. It seems like when the kids come into the store and see the word 'California' on the box, they grab it.'

"That one word sold a lot of model car kits, *that* I can tell you."

Duster Do for '72

"The year 1972 was a pretty good one for me." Butch said. "With the car basically coming into its own, all I did

was change the rear taillight panel and put a new grill in the car, and now I've got a '72. That year, I also changed wheel sponsors [switching from Fenton to Cragar]. I tried a few other things, but not all of them were successful.

In 1972, Butch set top speed (at 144.69 mph) and low ET (9.58 seconds) of the meet for Pro Stocks at the 1972 NHRA Winternationals at Pomona but fell to "Akron" Arlen Vanke's 'Cuda in the third round. Butch said, "After the race, the NHRA told me to lose the rear-wheel discs, citing the fact that they could potentially fly off the car and seriously injure or kill a crewman or spectator."

These two starting-line photos show Butch's consistency. They were taken on two separate runs during the 1972 March Meet at Old Famoso Raceway outside of Bakersfield, California, where Butch met and defeated Bob Lambeck on the Pro Stock Eliminator final.

"One thing that didn't work was an air-shifted B&J 4-speed transmission. It was kind of like a Lenco, but the car went slower than with my Chrysler 4-speed, so that was the end of that. The rest of the year, I stuck with what I knew worked, and the car seemed to run quicker and faster with each ensuing pass."

OCIR Jackets

"Whenever I would set a record or win an event at Orange County International Raceway, the policy was that they awarded you with an OCIR jacket," Butch said. "I must have been given at least a couple of dozen of those distinctive blue windbreakers over the years. It seems like everyone I knew around Tulare had themselves an OCIR jacket."

Butch performed the very first Pro Stock fire burnout at OCIR for the cameras of Steve Reyes and me, which was much to the chagrin of OCIR Strip Manager Mike Jones, who claimed that "we" burned a hole in his asphalt. The image was featured on the cover of the June 1972 issue of *Drag Racing USA* magazine.

That year, Leal influentially served on the NHRA Division 7 Pro Stock Rules Committee. As the frosting on

Butch and Bill "Grumpy" Jenkins compete in what is believed to be the final round of the Pro Challenge race. In spite of the holeshot, Jenkins won. (Photo Courtesy Steve Reyes)

The following week (December 12, 1972) Holley Carburetor Company ran this full-page advertisement on the back cover of Drag News to congratulate the Flash on his Pro Stock Driver of the Year honor.

Box Score: 1972

Statistics compiled by Bob Frey

NHRA National Events

Event	Location	Qualifier	Result
NHRA Winternationals	Pomona, California	No. 2; 9.634 at 144.23 mph	Lost to Arlen Vanke (Rd. 3)
NHRA Gatornationals	Gainesville, Florida	No. 7; 9.649 at 144.00 mph	Broke against Melvin Yow (Rd. 1)
NHRA Springnationals	Columbus, Ohio	No. 7; 9.79, no top speed	Lost to Ronnie Sox (Rd. 2)
NHRA Summernationals	Englishtown, New Jersey	No. 4; 9.661 at 142.58 mph	Lost to Richie Zul (Rd. 1)

NHRA Points Meets

Event	Location	Result
Division 7 Points Meet	Irwindale, California	Runner-up to Bill Bagshaw
Division 7 Points Meet	Sacramento, California	Won; Defeated Larry Breaux*
Division 7 Points Meet	Long Beach, California	Runner-up to Bill Bagshaw
Division 7 Points Meet	Bonneville, Utah	Won; Defeated Bill Bagshaw
Division 7 Points Meet	Orange County, California	Won; Defeated Bill Bagshaw

*Set top speed and low ET of the meet in the final with a 9.58 ET at 144.01 mph

AHRA/IHRA Sanctioned Events

Event	Location	Result
AHRA Winternationals	Mesa, Arizona	Won (9.66 at 143 mph); Defeated Bill Bagshaw
AHRA Northern Nationals	Fremont, California	Runner-up to Bob Lambeck (no time available)
IHRA Springnationals	Bristol, Tennessee	Runner-up to Bill "Grumpy" Jenkins (no time available)

Non-National Events *January 1972*

Event	Location	Result
All Pro Series, Pro Stock Title	Orange County International Raceway	Won; defeated Bob Lambeck in the final with a 9.56 at 144.65 mph; Set top speed of the meet at 146.10 mph
Grand Premiere	Lions Associated Drag Strip	Runner-up; No. 1 Pro Stock qualifier (9.54); Set top speed of the meet at 143.54
Second OCIR All Pro Series	Orange County International Raceway	Won; Defeated Canadian Chrysler-Plymouth Super Car Performance Clinic star John Petrie with a 9.64 at 143 mph; Don Moody won Top Fuel; Gene Snow won Funny Car

Butch races "Dandy" Dick Landy's Dodge Demon at OCIR. The damage to the rear quarter panel was caused by the shearing of the axle studs during a race two weeks earlier at Phoenix.

"If a rooster can pull a freight train, you better hook him up." Butch's countrified axiom best describes the sheer power of his "Carburetor" John Baumann–blueprinted Holley 1,150-cfm 4500 Series 4-barrel carburetor-equipped Joe Allread-prepared 426 Hemi engine that Butch used in his 1971–1972 campaign.

February 1972

Event	Location	Result
Third OCIR All Pro Series	Orange County International Raceway	Won (9.58 at 144.46 mph); Defeated "Dandy Dick" Landy in the final
Las Vegas National Open	Las Vegas Speedrome	Won (9.44 at 138.88 mph); Defeated Don Lorentzen's Camaro

March 1972

In 1972-1973, Butch won Pro Stock Eliminator at the Popular Hot Rodding Magazine Championship Drag Races at Martin, Michigan. This photo shows Butch defeating "Dyno" Don Nicholson's Ford Pinto in the 1972 match, recording an ET of 9.51 to a 9.52 in the final. "That was one of the most memorable races I had all year," Butch said. (Photo Courtesy Steve Reyes)

Event	Location	Result
March Meet	Pro Stock Eliminator at the Bakersfield	Won (9.72 at 141.95 mph): Defeated Bob Lambeck in the final

April 1972

Butch drops the hammer in front of a packed house at the IHRA Springnationals in Bristol, Tennessee. Butch was less successful racing in IHRA, citing that the NHRA was where the real money was. (Photo Courtesy Steve Reyes)

Butch launches the Duster off the Fremont Raceway starting line on the way to facing Bob Lambeck in the final at the 1972 AHRA Northern Nationals. Lambeck won, but no times were given.

Event	Location	Result
West Coast Pro Stock Association event	Sacramento Raceway, Sacramento, California	Runner-up to Dick Landy's ET of 9.60 at 144.01 mph to Leal's (foul) 9.57 at 144.01 mph
Popular Hot Rodding Magazine Championship Drag Races	Martin, Michigan	Won for the first time. Butch Leal defeated No. 1 Qualifier "Dyno Don" Nicholson on the final with an ET of 9.54 at 144.92 mph to Nicholson's 13.03. (Nicholson missed a gear.) "That was one of the most memorable races I won that year," Leal said.
UDRA Pro Stock Showdown	Detroit Dragway	Won (9.29 at 148.20 mph) to take the Pro Stock title; defeated "Dyno" Don Nicholson in the final

With a new car on order, Butch and the Duster blast off the OCIR starting line into the dead of night for the last time!

September 1972

The lovely Miss Hurst Golden Shifter Linda Vaughn shares a private moment with Butch in the Popular Hot Rodding winner's circle. Vaughn later said, "From the look on Butch's face, I must have said something naughty!"

Butch set the Track Record at OCIR for Pro Stock at 145.86.

November 1972

The year 1972 was good for Butch. Drag News thought so too when it awarded Butch with Pro Stock Driver of the Year honors and featured the Flash on the cover of its December 2, 1972, issue.

Butch match raced Bill "Grumpy" Jenkins Vega as the featured attraction that was part of OCIR's West Coast Pro Stock Association–hosted southern-style "run what ya brung" feature on the Wednesday before the SEMA Show. Leal pulled all the weight out of his Plymouth Duster and won the best-of-three bout against Jenkins, recording a best ET of 9.11 at 150.50 mph to Jenkins's losing effort of 9.19 at 149.50 mph.

October 1972

Butch spreads the rosin during a "run what ya brung" southern-style match race at OCIR against Bill "Grumpy" Jenkins where he and the Duster unleashed an all-time-best performance of 9.11 at 150.50 mph.

OCIR East-West Pro Stock Championship	Won (9.45 at 147.29 mph); Defeated Ken Van Cleve (11.55 at 99.11); Leal set the ET and speed record with a 9.41 at 147.29 mph; "Big" John Mazmanian won Funny Car

In the spring of 1972, Butch was the very first (and possibly the only) Pro Stock driver to perform a fire burnout. Photographer Steve Reyes and author Bob McClurg took these shots for the June 1972 issue of Drag Racing USA *magazine and for the cover of the New York National Studios 1973 Automotive Encyclopedia.*

the cake, the Flash was voted as the *Drag News* 1972 Pro Stock Driver of the Year and was featured on the cover of its December 2, 1972, issue.

Not a California Flash in the Pan

"I had read much about Butch over the years, but up until the time I raced him, I just took it as 'big talk in the parking lot,' said Roy Hill, CEO of Roy Hill Drag Racing School.

"Now, Dick Landy was tough. Sonny Bryant was tough. Bob Lambeck was tough. and 'Dyno' Don Nicholson was definitely tough. But when it comes to Butch Leal, he's the toughest—head and shoulders above the rest of the West Coast bunch.

"I remember the first race I ran against him [1972] down in Spartanburg, South Carolina. I had been outrunning all the local competition [Hubert Platt, Reid Whisnant, etc.]. Then, Butch came along and qualified No. 1 while I qualified No. 2.

"In the final, it came down to him and me. Of course, it was common practice for the finalists to weigh in after the last race to make it official.

"I said, 'I can fix this.' Just before we ran, I removed all the bob weights and hid them in my truck. Then, I went and pulled 75 pounds out of the ex–Bobby Yowell [1972] Duster I was running. I looked over at Butch's pit, and he was pulling out weight bars that were at least 3 inches thick and 3 feet long! It didn't take me long to realize that he had removed in excess of 300 pounds from the car. When it came to the finals, it wasn't even a race.

"After that, Butch and I got to know each other pretty well, and we've had a laugh or two about the 'Spartanburg incident' over the years. I have come to regard Butch as the brother that I never had."

Butch's 1971/1972 Plymouth Duster is the only Butch Leal car that is currently listed as missing. All the other mounts either restored or crashed. However, Butch still has the discarded 1972 Plymouth Duster taillight panel left over from the 1971 to 1972 taillight and front grille panel upgrade and keeps it as a souvenir. (Photo Courtesy Donna Leal)

CHAPTER 11

DUSTER DO x 2

"On the first pass, I let the clutch out, and it was unbelievably fast. The car ran like a 9.32 at some ridiculous speed [148 mph], and that was the first time I had ever built a de-stroked 426 Hemi engine."

"In early 1973, Ron Butler built me a beautiful Pro Stock Plymouth Duster," Butch Leal said. "It was the very first all-tube-frame Chrysler Pro Stock car ever built with its adjustable coilover shock front A-arms, adjustable coilover rear shocks, and Lenco planetary 4-speed transmission. That car was at least two years ahead of its time."

"Butch called in January 1973 and asked if I was interested in building him an all-tube-frame Plymouth Duster Pro Stocker following the guidelines set forth in the latest NHRA rule book," Butler said. "Of course, I said yes."

While other cars followed in progression like the Butler-built *Mopar Missile* Plymouth Duster and Bill Bagshaw's Butler-built *Red Light Bandit* Dodge Demon, Leal's new Duster was the first tube-frame Chrysler Pro Stock car built from top to bottom using Ron's high-tech chassis jig.

"Several different thicknesses of 4130 normalized steel tubing were used on the Duster's 108-inch-wheelbase chassis," Butler said. "For example, I used 2x4-inch (1.20-inch wall thickness) rectangular tubing for the main rails. When it came to the 10-point roll cage, the main hoop required 1.75-inch round tubing with 0.120 wall thickness. The two tubes that ran from the main hoop down to the front windshield pillar through the floor to the main rails were also 1.75-inch outside diameter [OD] and were 0.095 inch thick.

New Zealand–born craftsman Ron Butler was called upon to build the first all-tube-chassis Mopar Pro Stocker in drag racing. (Photo Courtesy Steve Reyes Collection)

A total of three months' time was expended in the building of the lightest (at 2,560 pounds) high-tech Mopar Pro Stocker in the eliminator. (Photo by John Shanks, Courtesy Steve Reyes)

Butch's new 1973 Duster featured his first custom paint job done by Dennis Ercek and lettered by Kenny Youngblood. (Photo Courtesy Steve Reyes)

With the name "California Flash" emblazoned across its side flanks, Butch's 1973 Duster was not only the most high-tech Mopar Pro Stocker built to date but it was also undoubtedly the most expensive as well. It cost roughly $10,000 in 1973. According to Butch, it was well worth the investment. (Photo Courtesy Steve Reyes)

This artist's rendering of a dust devil was adapted by Chrysler Corporation to use on the new Duster side graphics as well as in its corporate advertising campaigns. Graphic artist Kenny Youngblood faithfully executed that artwork, clearly making the Flash's Plymouth his best-looking effort yet. (Photo Courtesy Steve Reyes)

"The two tubes that ran from the main hoop to the rear of the car were again 1.75-inch OD and were 0.065 inch in thickness. The bar that ran under the dash was 0.049 inch thick and had an OD of 1.75 inches. The bars that extended from the base of the windshield to above Butch's head [later christened as "Butler bars" by Chrysler's Tom Coddington] were again 1.75-inches OD with a wall thickness of 0.049 inch.

"The front suspension was converted to rack-and-pinion steering. I corrected the bump steer by either shortening or lengthening the tie-rod ends by heating and bending the steering arms on the uprights [in Chrysler speak] or spindles. I also utilized Koni coilover shocks and Wilwood Engineering front disc brakes on the suspension.

"The Duster's rear suspension consisted of a 4-inch-narrowed 5.38:1-geared Plymouth 8¾-inch rear end by Pepe that was equipped with Summers Brothers axles and Wilwood Engineering rear disc brakes, hooked up to a set of 36-inch ladder bars with a pair of Koni adjustable coilover rear shocks."

Cheating the Wind

"I cut 1½ inches out of the straight portion on each side of the Duster front bumper, welded it back together, and smoothed it off," Butler said. "Then, I took a mold off that and made a 0.100-inch-thick fiberglass front bumper. Next, I took that to the metal sprayer and had a thin

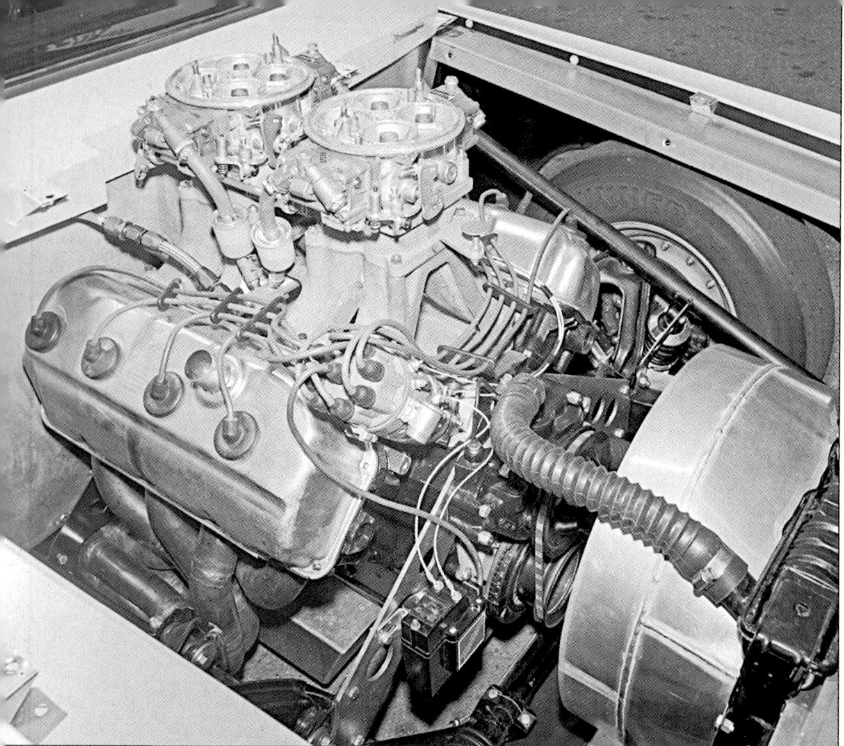

Powering the Duster was a Butch-built de-stroked 396-ci Mopar Hemi Little Oscar, which featured twin Dave Braswell-Purple People Eater Holley 1,100-cfm carburetors on a modified Weiand 2x4 tunnel ram intake. The horsepower was provided by Mullen cylinder heads, D&D pushrods, 14:1-compression Venolia pistons pressed onto Chrysler Hemi connecting rods, a General Kinetics cam, a Donovan Gear Drive, and a Milodon oiling system circulating Kendall GT1 racing oil through a Butch-designed, Butler-built 8-quart oil pan. Also along for the ride were Hedman Hedders and a Savage clutch. Early on, this car was one of the first Pro Stock Mopars to be converted to 16 spark plugs and a dual ignition. (Photo Courtesy Steve Reyes)

The Butler-built Koni coilover shock front suspension on the Duster featured rack-and-pinion steering and a pair of seriously lightened Wilwood Engineering front disc brakes. (Photo Courtesy Steve Reyes)

coating of powdered metal sprayed on the bumper to make it magnetic. Last, I took it to a friend of mine who worked at Mattel Toys, Inc. in El Segundo and had it flash chrome plated. What I ended up with was a 5-pound front bumper.

"I also narrowed the front grill 3 inches and moved the front edge of the fiberglass fenders in 1½ inches per side while moving the curled ends of the front bumper against the fenders to help reduce frontal area and reduce wind turbulence. This can be very helpful when you get up to the 100- to 150-mph range. All told, it took about three months for me to build that car."

From the get-go Butch was a fan of carrying a lot of weight over the rear wheels of his race cars to enhance traction. However, the purpose of these 33x6x35-inch lead bars was two-fold. First, they provided additional traction, being 2,650 pounds. Second, Butch needed the weight to make his Hemi Plymouth NHRA legal. (Photo Courtesy Steve Reyes)

"Ron [Butler] and I worked all day and all night to get the car finished and now we've got to weigh it," Butch said. "Would you believe the thing weighed 2,560 pounds? The car had to weigh 3,000 pounds to be NHRA legal, so I had lead stacked everywhere. Chrysler flew out and rented Orange County International Raceway for testing.

"On the first pass, I let the clutch out, and it was unbelievably fast. The car ran like a 9.32 at some ridiculous speed [148 mph], and that was the first time I had ever built a de-stroked 426 Hemi engine. On the second run, I blew the valve pocket out of the piston because I had it too thin. I'll never forget this.

"I got down to the other end, pulled it into high gear, and the car filled up with smoke. I shut it off, and I was just sitting there waiting for somebody to show up. Finally, I went to restarted the engine. Unbeknownst to me, the oil pan had filled up with race gas, and when it ignited, *ka-boom!* The percussion split the oil pan wide open! My plan was to debut the Duster at the 1973 March Meet. But now, I had to install new pistons in the engine.

"Ron Butler welded up my oil pan and fly-cut me a new set of pistons. Bill Bagshaw let me use his shop, which was located right next door to Butler's place. Steve Chrisman [son of drag racing icon Jack Chrisman] was working with me at the time, and we worked all night long to get this thing ready for Bakersfield. Now, Bill was a real neat freak, and I had stuff scattered everywhere."

The Mess Would Have Made Mr. Clean Cringe
by Steve Chrisman

If it wasn't for Bill Bagshaw loaning us the use of his shop, Butch wouldn't have attended, much less won, Bakersfield. After working all night long putting that engine back together, we didn't have time to clean up the place. We arrived at Old Famoso early the next morning with no sleep, and you know the rest of the story.

When Bagshaw came back to his shop the following Monday after the races and saw what a mess we had made of the place, he was furious and wouldn't speak to us for days. Of course, I went to work for Bagshaw in 1973, and one thing I learned from the experience was how to keep things clean.

"So, anyhow we got to Bakersfield," Butch said. "I let the clutch out, and the car tracked a little to the right, and it wouldn't run. I mean, the thing was just lying down. Don Rackemann was a friend of mine, and he got me a deal with Duke's [electric fuel] Pumps, but the pumps weren't producing enough volume to do the job on their own. So, I now had to not only fix that problem but also modify the front motor mount by hand to clearance a stock Chrysler manual fuel pump. Then, I had to readjust the ladder bars and barely made the show, qualifying 15th or 16th.

"However, in the first round, the car was quicker than greased lightning, probably 0.02 quicker than anybody there, and I beat Bob Lambeck on the final to win the race.

"I remember after the races, we were sitting with my family in a restaurant in McFarland, California, and I decided to lay down on the floor in the corner and fell soundly asleep while everyone else ate their dinner. True story."

The rear suspension on Butch's Plymouth shows a set of 36-inch-long Butler-built tubular ladder bars with Koni adjustable coilover rear shocks. Rear-end gearing in the Pepe-assembled 8.75-inch Mopar live rear axle was 5.38:1. The rear axles were from Summers Brothers, and once again, the brakes were from Wilwood Engineering.

Magnesium (Intake) Conflagration
by Ron Butler

Butch came into my shop one day with a Weiand 2x4 tunnel-ram intake under his arm and said, "I need to modify this manifold a little. Can I use one of your work benches?"

Normally, I like to work alone, but the guy was having me build him a car, so I certainly couldn't say no. I pointed him toward a 6x3-foot bench that butted up against some drywall in the back of my shop. Butch borrowed one of my Dot Co grinders and began grinding away. He must have been grinding on that thing for two hours.

At any rate, all of that magnesium dust was bouncing off the wall and settling between the bench and the wall. All of a sudden somebody yelled, "Fire!"

I looked over, and that pile of dust had ignited and caught the drywall on fire behind it! We always kept a 5-gallon bucket of water handy for heat treating, so I picked it up and threw it on the flames, not knowing that's the worst thing that you can do with magnesium. Then, we really had ourselves a blaze going!

Finally, someone ran over and grabbed one of the halon fire extinguishers we had in the shop and put the fire out. All things considered, we were lucky that it didn't burn the place down, much less ruin a very expensive intake manifold in the process.

Weight in the Rear
by Gil Kirk

Butch was a great drag racer and made a good living at it going from place-to-place. He basically walked out the door every spring with a race car dragging behind him and came back home at the end of the season just in time to build a new one. In 1973, Butch came to the shop and asked me if he could hang around for the summer. I'll never forget this. It was hilarious.

He had his Duster up on the rack and I was standing between him and the grille of the car, which had no engine installed, and it started to go up pretty high. Before the thing slid off the rack, I reached out, touched the front bumper, and said, "Got a little weight in the rear end, there Butch?"

That's when I learned about how Butch Leal set up his cars."

Get a Set of Stones, Man!

As part of his Chrysler contract, Butch performed testing during the week at Milan, Michigan, including complete engines, camshafts, fuel systems, gear ratios, suspensions, tires, etc.

"I tested several things with the Duster, including a Savage dual-disc clutch," Butch said. "Well, I should have never tried that. It just couldn't release quick enough. All told, I made almost 100 runs testing that year.

"That year, Don Carlton beat me at the NHRA Springnationals at Columbus with the *Missile* on Firestones. I was sponsored financially by Goodyear, and it supplied

Butch's "office" was fairly Spartan with its fiberglass bucket seats, Lenco shifter, Simpson Safety Equipment, 10-point roll cage, and "Butler bar" included. (Photo Courtesy Steve Reyes)

me with tires. I mean, it was a real sweet deal. The following week, we were testing again at Milan, and Dave Koffel told me to go and pick up a set of Firestones.

"I said, 'I can't do that, Dave.'

"He said, 'What are you talking about?'

"I said, 'I've got 50,000 reasons why I can't do that.'

"He looked at me and said, 'What kind of tires do you think we put on the cars we build?'

"I said, 'I don't have a clue.'

"He said, 'Goodyears! You let me worry about that. Go and get the Firestones!'

"I drove down to Penske Firestone, got a set of sixes and bolted them on the car. When I let the clutch out, it was smooth. I mean, the Goodyears jerked you real hard, but the Firestones were really smooth. So, I made this run, and when I drove back to the tower, Dave was up there going like this [thumbs-up sign]. I had just made the first Pro Stock run ever in the 8s: 8.90s at 154 mph.

"Well, I went up to Canada, and I was the No. 1 qualifier on the Firestones and beat Bob Glidden in the final with a 9.13 at 151 mph to his 9.40 at 135.74 mph. That was my first NHRA National Event Pro Stock title, and it was Chrysler's last NHRA National Event Pro Stock title win [1970s] for the 426 Hemi, and I was thoroughly delighted to be the one to give it to them!"

Box Score: 1973

Statistics compiled by Bob Frey

NHRA National Events

Event	Location	Qualifier	Result
Winternationals	Pomona, California	No. 7; 9.521 at 146.34 mph	Lost to "Dyno Don" Nicholson (Rd. 2)
Springnationals	Columbus, Ohio	No. 4; 9.378 at 147.05 mph	Lost to Don Carlton (final)
Summernationals	Englishtown, New Jersey	No. 3; 9.187 at 149.75 mph	Lost to Bill "Grumpy" Jenkins (final); set the NHRA National Pro Stock top speed record at 151.77 mph
Grandnationals	Sanair, Canada	No. 1; 9.062 (no top speed recorded)	Won; defeated Bob Glidden (final)
U.S. Nationals	Indianapolis, Indiana	No. 5; 9.147 at 150.50 mph	Lost to Bob Glidden (Rd. 3)

Additional stopping power for Butch's new Duster was provided by an 8-foot Simpson Safety Equipment Company parachute. (Photo Courtesy Steve Reyes)

Butch and car builder Ron Butler inspect the new Mopar's frontal clearance. "You could hardly fit a pack of cigarettes underneath the front bumper," Butch said. "It was that low." (Photo Courtesy Steve Reyes)

This head-on ground-level Hasselblad 500-mm photo was taken during Pro Stock qualifying at the 1973 NHRA U.S. Nationals at Indianapolis. It shows how car builder Ron Butler "tightened up" the front end of Butch's Duster by sectioning the front bumper a total of 4 inches and the grille a total of 3 inches. He also tucked in the front fenders 1½ inches per side while curling the ends of the front bumpers against the front fenders to reduce wind resistance and turbulence on the top end.

Non-National Event Wins
- Butch won Pro Stock Eliminator at OCIR's All Pro Series opener. He defeated Larry "Soapy Sales" Huff in the final.
- Butch won Pro Stock Eliminator at the second OCIR All Pro Series event. He again defeated Larry Huff in the final.
- As a personal record of sorts, Butch won his sixth straight OCIR All Pro race. He defeated "Dandy" Dick Landy in the final.
- Butch was runner-up at OCIR All Pro Series race. He lost to "Dandy" Dick Landy in the final. It was Butch's first loss in seven rounds in the series.
- Butch won the Las Vegas National Open. He defeated Larry Breaux in the final.
- Butch won the Wednesday night feature at Englishtown, New Jersey. He defeated "Dyno" Don Nicholson in a special match race with an ET of 8.98 at 151 mph to a 9.09 at 148.51 mph.

"Purple People Eater" Carburetors

"Whenever we (Butch and Mike Fons of the Rod Shop) went testing together, Fons always beat the hell out of Butch," Gil Kirk said. "But whenever we went to a national event, the guy would qualify low in the eliminator. I'm thinking, 'What the hell?'

"Well, all those years he carried a pair of trick carburetors (built by induction systems wizard Dave Braswell) with purple intakes in a briefcase. Then, when it came time to qualify, Butch had those purple carburetors on the car, and no one ever saw him make the switch."

Time to Re-Tire

"I called Bert Thomas at Firestone prior to the AHRA Grand American race at Orange County and they shipped me out a new set of [Firestones], but when I went to pick them up at the airport, they weren't there," Butch said. "I asked Bill Bagshaw if he had a spare set, and he said that

Box Score: 1973

"In 1973, I repeated my Martin, Michigan, win at the PHR Meet with the tube-chassis car but not without incident," Butch said. "Somewhere along the way, my wife and I had been drinking some of the local water and, oh man, did we ever get sick. Before heading back to the motel, I made a run Saturday afternoon and was the No. 1 qualifier at 9.20 When I came back Sunday morning, I was the No. 9 qualifier and drew "Dyno Don" Nicholson in the first round, Ronnie Sox in the second round, and Don Carlton in the *Missile* in the third round.

"In the final, I raced Wayne Gapp in the Gapp & Roush Pinto, running 9.15 and won the race. That was the most money [$26,200] I had won in one race all season, which, when taking into consideration all the problems we had that day, was absolutely incredible."

Butch was also runner-up to Bill "Grumpy" Jenkins at the PRA National Challenge at Tulsa International Raceway in Tulsa, Oklahoma.

"That's the only time ever that I broke a rocker arm," Butch said. "I qualified at that race with a 9.01 at 153 mph and was running dead even with Jenkins mid-track when the rocker arm (the No. 6 intake) on the passenger's side failed."

Furthermore, Butch won Pro Stock at the Irwindale Gran Prix, defeating "Dandy" Dick Landy in the final.

"Chrysler flew out and rented OCIR for testing," Butch said. "On the first pass, I let out the clutch, and it was unbelievably fast. The car went something like a 9.32 at 148.00 mph with a de-stroked 426 Hemi engine at 396 ci." (Photo Courtesy Steve Reyes)

Butch's competition was always keen to make certain that the Plymouth was 100-percent legal when it crossed the scales. Does that truck look familiar? It is the Olynik hauler that Chrysler Racing's Bob Cahill gave Butch at Ontario Motor Speedway after the previous year's dust up with Sox & Martin. (Photo Courtesy Steve Reyes)

> ## Box Score: AHRA National
>
> - In 1973, Butch won Pro Stock the AHRA Grand American West event at OCIR. He ran an ET of 8.88 at 154.10 mph to defeat Bill Bagshaw's 9.07 at 150.75 mph.
> - Butch also won the 1973 AHRA World Championship at Fremont Raceway. He defeated Bill Bagshaw with an ET of 8.95 at 151.26 mph and set the top speed (153.06) and low ET (8.91) of the meet.
>
> 
>
>
> *Butch warms up the Goodyears during Pro Stock qualifying at the 1973 NHRA Springnationals where the Flash was the No. 4 qualifier with an ET of 9.378 at 147.05. He lost in the final on a foul to Don Carlton with an ET of 9.446 at 146.81 mph to Carlton's winning 9.402 at 147.78 mph.*

he did but that he was going to use them. Then, I called Dick Landy and got the exact same story.

"So there I was stuck with no tires. I was the No. 1 qualifier at 9.00 with my old tires, but Bagshaw had run 9.01 on Saturday evening. I thought, 'That's okay. He did it at night, and since the race is on a Sunday afternoon when it's nice and hot, I'll be alright.'

"Then, I got to thinking, and Sunday morning I went over to M&H, which at the time, wasn't even in the hunt. We had this [M&H] compound that I had used years earlier on my 1967 'Cuda Funny Car that worked well. I asked Marvin [Rifchin] if he had that compound in a 32-inch tire and he said that he did. So, I bolted on a set of M&Hs, and in the heat of the day, the car went 8.94, 8.92, and 8.92. After I beat Bill Bagshaw in the final and ran 154.10 mph, the competition immediately beat a path to M&H western distributor Ernie Hashim's truck."

Not as Simple as It May Seem

Nothing ever is as simple as it may seem. Believe it or not, the *Drag News* returning 1973 Pro Stock Driver of the Year forgot to put gas in his car before racing Bill Bagshaw in the final.

"I did a really nice burnout, pushed in the clutch, and all I could hear was the rattling of the fuel pump," Butch said. "So, with just enough gas to back up, I shut off the car and motioned the kid who was helping me at the time to go over to Bill Bagshaw's car, step in front, and tell him to shut it off. That gave me enough time to get out of the car and run over to Bill and tell him that he would have to wait for me because I had run out of gas.

"Well, Bill didn't like that too much, but he waited long enough for me to gas up and beat him in the final with an 8.88 at 154.10 mph. While he was sitting there waiting for me to gas up, OCIR's General Manager Mike Jones walked out to the starting line and presented Bill with the Sportsmanship Trophy. However, that was little consolation for him losing the race."

Bill "the Red Light Bandit" Bagshaw, on the other hand, offered a slightly different version.

"Butch and I were the best of friends and the fiercest of competitors," Bagshaw said. "Butch has a personality that to this day ingratiates himself to his friends and fans.

"I remember an AHRA race at Orange County where we were in the final, and Butch ran out of gas after doing his burnout. His crewman Mike Browning had the presence of mind to come running over to me and look under my car as if there was something wrong and motioned to me to shut it off. So, I shut off my car knowing right from the beginning that I was being had. I knew there was nothing wrong with my car. So, anyway, I shut off the car, and we sat on the line waiting until Butch could run back, get some gas, and put it in his car. Then, he beat me."

Trust Not, Worry Not

"In the past, I had always transported my own race cars as a matter of personal preference," Butch said. "When I was running my '73 Duster, I had a young man working for me who seemed to be trustworthy. Due to certain time restraints with my [busy] schedule, it became necessary to have him drive the rig back to California from Indy while I went on ahead.

"It became known to me that on his way back to the Golden State, he stopped at his parents' home, unloaded the race car, and did some burnouts for family and friends. I was beyond horrified. He had never even warmed up the car.

"Of course, [I thought about] the likelihood of him having injured himself or someone else and the legal ramifications that went along with it, not to mention the fact that he might have wrecked my brand-new race car. Well, needless to say, I had to let him go."

Fresh off his Canadian NHRA Grand Nationals win, Butch qualified No. 5 at Indy with an ET of 9.147 at 150.50 mph.

At IHRA's version of the Springnationals in Bristol, Tennessee, Butch set the top speed and low ET of the meet with a 9.22 at 147.78 mph. However, when it came to Sunday's eliminations, Ronnie Sox beat Butch on a holeshot in the second round with an ET of 9.55 to Butch's 9.46. "After qualifying on Saturday, I drove to Richmond, Virginia, with my wife, Donna, and our 18-month-old son, Bret, and ran a match race against Bill Jenkins," Butch said. "Then, [we] drove overnight back to Bristol. That was a very long weekend." (Photo Courtesy Steve Reyes)

Duster With a Down-Home Drawl

"At the end of 1973, Bill Bagshaw and I were running one of our last races for the year at the NHRA Supernationals at Ontario Motor Speedway when Chrysler's Manager of Performance Activities Dick Maxwell came up and told us that we were not going to run.

"I said, 'Oh, really? Why can't we run?'

"Dick explained that Chrysler was through with NHRA Pro Stock, and it was going to boycott the race. For some reason, the NHRA and Chrysler came to a disagreement about recent rule book changes, and well, you can figure it out from there.

During the 1973 U.S. Nationals at Indy, Butch defeated Sonny Bryant (pictured) in the first round with an ET of 9.10 at 150.25 mph and Bobby Yowell in the second round (9.120 at 151 mph). Butch was looking good to win overall Pro Stock Eliminator honors. (Photo Courtesy Steve Reyes)

"I went up in the tower and talked Jack Hart into letting us run. Then, I came back and talked to Maxwell, and he said, 'No, you're not!'

"After that, Chrysler said that they were thinking that they would have Ronnie [Sox] run a '68 Hemi 'Cuda, have me duplicate my '65 A990 car that I won Indy with, and have Dick Landy build a '70 Dodge Challenger Street Hemi. So, basically, we would run SS/A, SS/B, and SS/D.

"In the meantime, Chrysler wanted me to put a 340 small-block in the Duster, reasoning that it was the lightest Pro Stock car [2,500 pounds] they knew of. Ron Butler made the motor mounts, and I went to Gainesville and tested their engine later that year. Unfortunately, that test didn't turn out very well.

"So, at the end of 1973, I was building a Chrysler A990 Super Stock car and I sold my '73 car. Roy Hill called me and asked if I would sell him the car, and I said that I would. Roy bought the car set up to run the Hemi in AHRA/IHRA/NHRA along with all the 340 small-block engine components, just in case Chrysler got that program worked out and he could make the switch.

Butch dry hops the Duster on his way to qualifying. That's the roof of Joe Satmary's Camaro in the tower lane.

Butch lost in the third round on Monday to eventual winner Bob Glidden with an ET of 9.090 at 150.75 mph to Glidden's 9.050 at 152.28 mph.

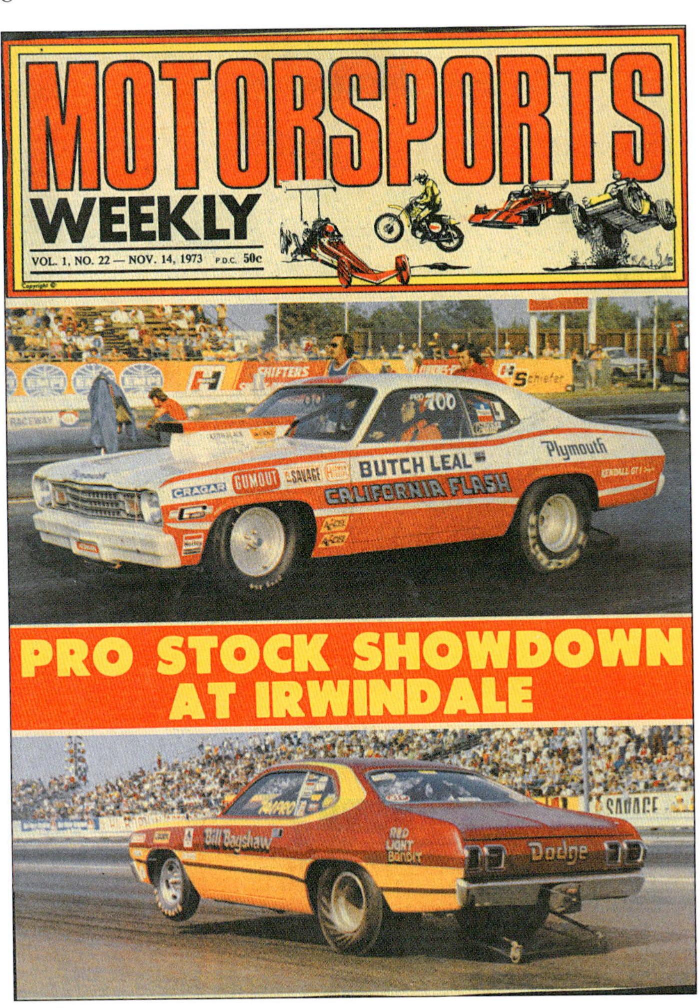

"The California Flash" versus Bill "the Red Light Bandit" Bagshaw rivalry always generated good press, as this November 14, 1973, cover of Motorsports Weekly *attests.*

Butch won the Pro Stock night race at Irwindale Raceway defeating "Dandy" Dick Landy's Dodge Dart in the final. (Photo by John Shanks, Courtesy Steve Reyes)

Butch won Pro Stock Eliminator at the Fremont, California-hosted 1973 AHRA World Championship. He beat Bill Bagshaw in the final. Here, Butch defeats Lee Hunter and his Pinto in the first round. (Photo by John Shanks, Courtesy Steve Reyes)

After Chrysler pulled the plug on Pro Stock, Butch sold his Duster to Roy Hill, who campaigned the Duster throughout the 1974 season. Here, Hill squares off against Bill "Grumpy" Jenkins's 1974 Chevrolet Vega during Pro Stock eliminations at the 1974 Professional Racer's Organization (PRO) National Challenge at New York National Speedway in Center Moriches, Long Island, New York.

Roy Hill competes at the 1974 NHRA U.S. Nationals. At the year's end, Roy parked the Duster and stepped behind the wheel of a Ron Butler-built Plymouth Arrow.

"Roy was running out of Richard Petty's shop at the time and those old NASCAR boys had never seen a car like that before. Over the years, we've often laughed about that. It was one of the first Pro Stockers that the front nose came off—much like the upper-echelon Gas-class cars.

"Anyhow, Roy ran the car in NHRA and IHRA and was quite successful with it. Of course, at the time I was working on my Super Stock car, and Chrysler told me, 'Do not work on the Pro Stocks!'

"At the end of the 1973 season, Roy called and asked me if I would freshen the car up. Since Roy was my dear friend, I said sure. He sent the car out to California, and we pulled the engine and put new pistons in it and did all the other trick stuff that I do. Then, I cut an inch off the runner on the magnesium intake manifold and added an inch to the plenum in an attempt to get the car to run over 154 mph.

"We put the car back together and took it out to Irwindale Raceway. I let the clutch out, and the thing went 8.70 at 158 mph. I called Roy and said, 'You're not going to believe this!'

"Of course, I couldn't tell Chrysler what I had done, so Roy made plans to fly out for the NHRA Winternationals. In the meantime, Roy's crewman Bill Basie decided he was going to clean up the car and scraped all the rubber out from under the rear fender wells. On Roy's first run, he made an immediate left turn off the starting line.

"I asked, 'What did you do? That rubber acts like a sponge after you do your burnout.'

"After that, Bill had to wipe out the water.

"Anyway, Roy made a second run [on dry tires], and the car went 158 mph, prompting NHRA announcer Bernie Partridge to comment, 'Oh my! Chrysler's back!'

"Eventually, that engine (which we affectionately called *Little Oscar*) kicked a rod out, and we both cried. That was one of the best 396 Hemis I had ever built."

CHAPTER 12

THE MOST-FEARED CAR IN SUPER STOCK

"On my second run, all I did was let the air out of the tires. I let the clutch out, and this thing was nearly 3 feet in the air and up on the wheelie bars. "

"As previously mentioned, Bill Bagshaw and I were out at Ontario Motor Speedway attending the 1973 NHRA Hot Wheels Supernationals when Chrysler's Dick Maxwell came up to us and told us that Chrysler was going to boycott the race and we're not going to run," Butch Leal said. "Chrysler was through with NHRA Pro Stock and basically threatened to pull my sponsorship if I defied them.

"Later, they got to talking to me and asked me if I would be willing to build a '65 A990 Super Stock car instead, just like the one I had won Indy with, and campaign it throughout the season. Well, naturally, I said yes."

Pro-Built Super Stocker

"Ron Butler built me the trickest NHRA-legal 1965 Plymouth Belvedere A990 Super Stock car that you could ever imagine," Butch said. "In fact, it was almost built like a Pro Stocker. I found the car in San Francisco. It was an automatic car minus engine, and it had been campaigned in 1965 by the team of Sutton & Walls. Being a factory A990 car, it already had all the trick factory parts I needed on it. I had Ron Butler tie the thing together and build me a really trick Pro Stock–style roll cage.

"Chrysler still had some original sheet-metal parts in stock for the '65, so [it] sent me new fenders, a new hood, and new doors. I acid dipped all that stuff, foamed the inside of the doors, and made them real light. I was building my own engines at the time and knew exactly what kind of horsepower I would be making, so I installed a set of wheelie bars on the car just as a precaution.

"The car turned out real nice, and it was fast right from the start. I took it out to Irwindale Raceway during the Winternationals warmups to test it even before it was lettered. Sox was there, and Landy was there. When I made my first pass, I had about 13 pounds of air in the tires and didn't know what the car was going to do. I let the clutch out, and the car ran a 10.13 at 139 mph, which was 0.27 seconds under the existing NHRA 10.40-second national record for class."

Up All Day and Up All Night

"I'll never forget this as long as I live," Butch said. "I had been up all day and night finishing the car. After the first run, Chrysler's Dave Koffel came up to me and said, 'You need to do something with the chassis.'

"I said, 'Dave, go back in the tower. I'll be up there in just a minute.'

"On my second run, all I did was let the air out of the tires. I let the clutch out, and this thing was nearly 3 feet in the air and up on the wheelie bars. The car went 9.80 at 142 mph. They [Chrysler's Tom Hoover and Dave Koffel] ran down from the tower hardly able to contain their enthusiasm. They put me on the scales; the car weighted 3,425 pounds, and the NHRA minimum weight requirement was 3,420. They said, 'Take it home and hide it.'

"I drove back to my shop in Van Nuys and had the sign painter letter the car, which included my new sponsor, Revell."

Getting Settled In

"I entered the SS/B car in the AHRA Winternationals at OCIR and won the eliminator, outrunning Harry Holton and his SS/AA Hemi 'Cuda in the final," Butch

Butch debuted his "new" 1965 Plymouth A990 SS/B Hemi at the NHRA Winternationals where it handily won class but found the going tough in Super Stock Eliminator. However, Butch didn't disappoint Winternationals spectators, pulling a huge wheelie in the second round.

The biggest news for 1974 (other than Butch changing from Pro Stock to Super Stock) was the signing of Revell models as a major sponsor. Over the years, Butch has been lucky to have signed a number of model-car manufacturers (either plastic or die cast) as sponsors, which is an honor that only a select handful of drag racing veterans can claim.

This overhead view of the "wolf in sheep's clothing" was taken at the NHRA Southern Nationals at Atlanta Dragway in Commerce, Georgia. Check out that sidewall flex.

Butch's Hemi was brutal off the starting line, as seen here taking out "Dandy" Dick Landy's 1970 Hemi Challenger at the 1974 NHRA Springnationals in Columbus, Ohio, where Butch finished as the runner-up to Bobby Warren's Chevy.

said. "I thought, 'Man, what a great start for a new car.'

"Lo and behold, I went to the NHRA Winternationals and won class.

"When it came to running in the eliminator, all I've got to say [is] those boys running Super Stock are some of the best drivers out there, and they spanked me pretty good. In AHRA racing, you didn't have to shut the car off. It was more or less balls to the wall. But in NHRA class racing, I couldn't go quicker than a 10.40. Chrysler kind of held me back. They didn't want me to bomb the record, full well knowing that I could at the drop of a hat.

"Leaving the line proved to be a problem. When I would see the last [amber] bulb being lit, I would leave and red light. So, I was trying to leave when it was going out, and that wasn't working, either. The competition would just kill me on the tree. Finally, halfway through the year, I moved the left wheel forward an inch and the passenger-side right front wheel back an inch so I could get more rollout and stay in the tree a little longer, and

it worked out perfectly. I could see the tree coming on, and I was cutting 4.0s and 4.teens, and I was right in the hunt.

"The first race I ran with the new setup was the NHRA Springnationals at Columbus, Ohio, where I was runner-up. Chrysler had sent me this new Dagenham 4-speed transmission, which they said was way better. I ran Bobby Warren in the final for Super Stock Eliminator, and I'll never forget this: Bobby came up to me and said, 'Every once in a while those straight shifts will break!' Well, I laughed because I had him. There was no question. I let the clutch out and I broke low gear. Oh, I was so mad I came back to the truck, pulled the transmission out, threw it as far as I could throw it, and it landed in the weeds.

"As I was putting my standby transmission back in getting ready for the next race, Dave Koeffel walked up and said, 'You want to go pick up that transmission?'

"I said, 'Hell No! So much for your fancy $3,500 transmission.'

Butch proudly hoists his first "Wally" for winning Super Stock Eliminator at the NHRA Summernationals at Raceway Park in Englishtown, New Jersey, defeating Garley Daniels' SS/O Chevy II in the final.

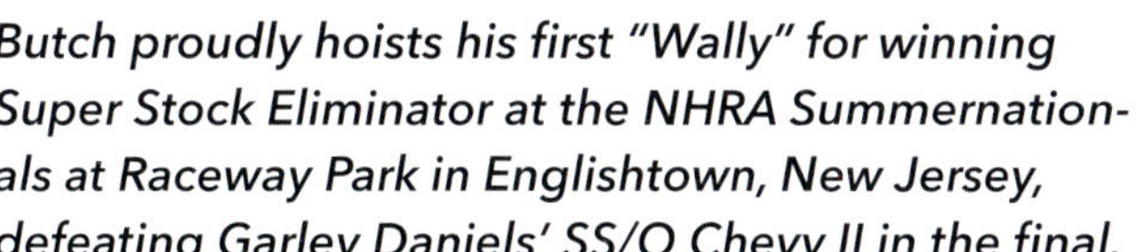

At the NHRA U.S. Nationals at Indy, Butch's Hemi again won class only to break out in round four (at 10.27) of the eliminator. "Those Super Stock Eliminator guys are so good," Butch said. "They can run within 0.500 of a second on each and every run."

This photo was taken from the berm at OCIR during the final at the AHRA Grand American. The outcome is fairly obvious, as Butch speeds through the finish-line lights ahead of SS/AA racer Harry Holton and his Hemi 'Cuda.

"Well, it all worked out. I won Super Stock Eliminator at the next race at Englishtown, which was my first NHRA Super Stock Eliminator title. Teething problems aside, that was a pretty amazing year. Those Super Stock guys are so good. They can run within 0.500 of a second on each and every run. A lot had changed in the eliminator since I won Indy in 1964, and it was a real learning experience. I'll admit I didn't want to do it at first, but after I got settled in, 1974 proved to be a lot of fun."

How the Car Got its Name

Where did the tagline the "Most Feared Car in Super Stock" come from? Credit former *Super Stock & Drag Illustrated* magazine Editor Steve Collison, who used it as the story title for an article he ran on the car in the magazine.

"I met Steve when he started out in the car magazine business while he was still working for *Car Craft*, and we became fast friends," Butch said. "Right before I was inducted into the 1997 Super Stock Reunion Hall of Fame in Rockingham, North Carolina, Steve said the reason why he chose that title was, 'You brought this car out for the NHRA Winternationals and you were at the Chrysler test session the week before at Irwindale Raceway, and the thing went 0.06 quicker than the national record on its first run. Nobody could believe it because there were other A990 4-speed cars out there that couldn't even come close to that, which was really amazing.'

"What's even more amazing was how much quicker the car got through the rumor mill. In between the time it had left there [Irwindale] and [when] I got through NHRA tech at Pomona the following week, the car had run a 9.65. To this day, there are people who still believe that.

"Steve knew how quick the car really was. He asked, 'How in the hell did you get that thing to run like that?'

"I said that I basically went from a 396 [in the 1973 Pro Stock car] back to a 434, which was an NHRA-legal 0.060 over 426. The car was running a single-carbureted Pro Stock engine under a Super Stock designation. In other words, it was a wolf in sheep's clothing.

"Steve replied, 'Yeah, but the car still had to weigh 3,400 pounds.'

"I said that I knew, but it was the way the car was set up.

"If you didn't tie the car together [unlike some of the other Hemi cars out there], the car would flex and it won't leave the line like this car did. Plus, the car was acid dipped, and it carried a lot of weight in the back. H.L. Shahan taught me that you can never have too much weight in the back. Of course, that all came about from our 409 days when we were running street tires and we needed all the traction we could get.

"I always liked to say that my cars carried so much weight in the back that they would stand up in a mud hole."

Epilogue

At the close of the 1974 NHRA drag racing season, Butch sold his A990 Hemi Belvedere to Atlanta, Georgia, Super Stock racer Steve "Rocket Man" Bagwell who converted the car back to an automatic, running it in SS/BA. Both he and driver Terry Earwood, the 1973 NHRA Super Stock Champion, jointly campaigned the Plymouth from 1975 to 1979 with great success. Highlights included Earwood winning Super Stock Eliminator at two NHRA National Open events and Bagwell winning

One of the last runs Butch made in the car was at the NHRA Hot Wheels Supernationals at Ontario Motor Speedway where he again won class but fell short in eliminator runoffs.

At season's end, Butch sold his storming Hemi Plymouth to Greater Atlanta, Georgia, resident Steve "Rocket Man" Bagwell who, together with 1973 NHRA Super Stock Eliminator champ Terry Earwood, shared driving duties. Bagwell won the Super Stock Eliminator title at the NHRA Cajun Nationals while Earwood won two of the NHRA National Open events.

the Super Stock Eliminator title at the NHRA Cajun Nationals. After that, the car changed hands a few times.

Then in 1996, the "Most Feared Car in Super Stock" was acquired from racer Bud "It's Hemi Time" Spears and restored back to "as raced" condition (à la Leal) by New Albany, Indiana, muscle car enthusiast Mike Kayrouz, where the car remains to this day.

This photo shows Earwood testing a new set of Hooker Headers on the recently acquired A990 Plymouth Hemi at Warner Robbins, Georgia, with spectacular results. (Photo by Marty Johnson, Courtesy Terry Earwood)

Where is the "most feared car in Super Stock" today? In 1996, the Hemi was acquired and restored by New Albany, Indiana's Mike Kayrouz and today lives in a climate-controlled garage. No, it's not for sale.

Another Fish to Fry

In the meantime, Chrysler also had Butch building a 360 small-block 1974 Plymouth Barracuda.

"That car was pretty simple," Butch said. "Most everything was already there. It wasn't a body in white; it was a genuine, bona fide 1974 Plymouth Barracuda street car, and you didn't have to do anything major to make it run. I built the 360 engine myself, and we also set up the chassis. However, I did have Ron Butler do a few things to the car but nothing major. The car turned out real nice.

"We tested the 'Cuda at Milan Dragway [in Milan, Michigan], and the car ran high 11s at 121 mph, which turned out to be one of the fastest cars in the SS/MA class."

As a side project, Chrysler also had Butch build this 1974 Plymouth Barracuda competing in the SS/MA and SS/NA classes with various-configuration 360-ci Mopar small-block engines. Performance numbers were ideally in the 11.70 to 11.80 zone at 121 mph. (Photo Courtesy Les Welch)

THE DIRECT CONNECTION ERA

"When CPD's [Chrysler-Plymouth Dodge's] Dave Koffel asked me in late 1974 if I would be interested in participating in the upcoming Direct Connection clinic program, he didn't have to ask twice."

"Like most things at Chrysler, nothing was assigned directly to one person," said Dave Koffel, an engineer (retired) with Chrysler Racing Group. "The man who I would say was the chief architect of the Direct Connection high-performance aftermarket parts program [in late 1974] was Bob Cahill, then-director of Chrysler Corporation's Vehicle Performance Planning Department who, after surveying the market to see what the competition was doing, envisioned the creation of the Direct Connection high-performance aftermarket parts program.

"At the time, Ford's Total Performance aftermarket parts program [administered in the early to mid-1960s through Holman-Moody and Shelby American] was practically nonexistent, while General Motors' high-performance aftermarket parts program maintained a low profile but was extremely active.

"Once a week, we used to have what you would call a 'cabal meeting' where the people who were immediately responsible to Cahill would get together in a room and go over what had happened that week [regarding Chrysler motorsports competition nationwide] and discuss new ideas."

Going Back in Time for a Moment

"In 1965, Chrysler built 50 Hemi Dodge and Hemi Plymouth A990 cars each for Super Stock Eliminator competition," Koffel said. "When they did that, there were some leftover parts. There was a skunk works type of warehouse, or executive garage, located across the street from the Lynch Road Assembly Plant where a guy named Frank Andrewczak was charged with warehousing those leftover Hemi parts. That's where the rudimentary beginnings of the Direct Connection high-performance aftermarket parts program began.

"As things progressed, it became necessary to move into a bigger and better building. Once that happened, Dick Maxwell was placed in charge of the Direct Connection high-performance aftermarket parts program and was charged with negotiating 'parts deals' with SEMA-member companies, such as Hooker Headers, Crane Cams, Holley, Edelbrock, and others. These brands were co-mingled with a laundry list of Direct Connection/Mopar High Performance Products to serve the drag racing, road racing, street rod/street machine, off-road, and recreational vehicle customer bases.

"Also highly instrumental in the success of the Direct Connection high-performance aftermarket parts program was Brian Schramm from the OEM parts division who was appointed the big boss of the performance parts warehouse. Three people who worked for Brian and were avidly involved in high performance included Ken Rutz, Dave Johnson, and Stan David. Parts pickers aside, these were the people who were responsible for looking after the Direct Connection high-performance aftermarket parts inventory, which at the height of the program occupied three separate buildings."

With Chrysler Corporation's newly launched Direct Connection aftermarket high-performance parts program sponsorship, Butch started the 1975 drag racing season campaigning his tried-and-true 1974 360 Plymouth Barracuda competing in the NHRA's SS/MA class.

Of course, an integral component in the overall success of Chrysler's Direct Connection high-performance aftermarket parts program was the publication of its yearly *Direct Connection Special Parts Catalogue*, which was distributed via magazine advertising and through participating Direct Connection retailers listing hundreds upon hundreds of Direct Connection aftermarket parts.

Chrysler sponsored high-profile drag racers, such as Butch Leal and Paul Rossi, who performed double duty, campaigning Direct Connection–sponsored Plymouth- and Dodge-bodied vehicles at the drags on the weekends while functioning as official mouthpieces at select Direct Connection retailers on weekdays.

A Word from the Flash

"In 1966, Chrysler had asked me to participate in its original Super Car Performance Clinic Program, but I turned them down flat," Butch said. "At the time, I was 21 years old and all I wanted to do was drag race.

"When CPD's [Chrysler-Plymouth Dodge's] Dave Koffel asked me in late 1974 if I would be interested in participating in the upcoming Direct Connection clinic program, he didn't have to ask twice. Of course, I said yes. I would have a second race car (a 1975 Plymouth Duster, which I ran in B/Modified Production), a second truck, more money to spend, and the extra personnel to make everything run. I mean, who wouldn't be interested?"

The Chrysler Direct Connection program sponsorship went like this: Koffel lined up the participating Direct Connection dealerships across the country, and Leal and company took their cars and displayed them (whenever possible, in close proximity to an NHRA event) and talked about the attributes of using Chrysler's Direct Connection high-performance parts.

"Although it was a lot of work, the real beauty of it was that we didn't have to lug all those heavy parts boards around like Sox & Martin, Dick Landy, Don Grotheer, and John Petrie did," Butch said. "That was the responsibility of the Direct Connection dealers themselves. We just showed up."

All told, Butch and company visited an estimated 25 to 30 Direct Connection retailers over a two-year period.

"Unlike the original Super Car Performance Clinics from the 1960s where they had an advance [public relations] guy to set up the clinics and publicize the events, we didn't have an advertising budget, so it was usually

The 'Cuda was only half of the California Flash's Direct Connection-sponsored one-two punch. Butch and company also built this 1975 Hemi Duster to race in the NHRA B/Modified Production class.

put on the shoulders of the Direct Connection dealers themselves, and it was kind of a hit-or-miss proposition. Some of those clinics were obviously more memorable than others."

The following story is one of Butch's favorites:

"We were holding a Direct Connection clinic at the Rice Lake, Wisconsin, Chrysler-Plymouth-Dodge dealer," he said. "Quite a few people showed up, and we were having a great time. After we finished our talk, we were loaded up and getting ready to leave when the owner's son said, 'Let's go down and have a drink at my favorite bar.'

"We drove about a half mile into town and we were sitting at the bar talking about how successful the clinic had been, and this guy walked through the door and he had a beard down to his chest. I mean, he was a *big* guy! He asked, 'Which one of you is Butch Leal?'

"I was sitting in the corner of the bar with my back to the wall and replied, 'That would be me!'

"He said, 'I need for you to come outside!'

"I looked at him and said, 'Have you lost your damned mind?'

"He said, 'No, I want to show you something!'

"We walked out, and I looked across the street, and there sat a 1965 Plymouth painted in my team colors with the words 'California Trash' lettered on its sides. This thing was so eaten up with body cancer. I mean, there were rust holes in it everywhere, and the guy raced it on the ice. It had a 318 small-block and ran on studded snow tires. It was the funniest damned thing I had ever seen. I just rolled on the ground laughing.

"I asked the guy, 'What are you doing during the weekend of the U.S. Nationals? Why don't you bring this thing down there, and maybe we can get it in a magazine? I told *Car Craft* Publisher John Dianna about it, and he had one of his staffers take a picture of it, and they ran it in the magazine."

Here's another memorable favorite:

"In the heat of the summer, we took both cars to a clinic held at a Direct Connection dealership in Brooklyn, New York," Butch said. "I was kind of nervous driving both clinic trucks into the heart of the city [which you're not allowed to do], and we had ourselves a police escort. Everybody was out in the street. The kids had the fire hydrants turned on and they were having a ball playing in the water. Even with the police escort it didn't stop them from running up, jumping on the back of our trucks, and riding them from block to block. It was the craziest thing.

"Anyway, we finally got there, and it turned out to be one of the largest crowds at a Direct Connection dealership we had anywhere on the East Coast, but the trip to and from is what I remember most."

Building Butch's B/MP Duster

"That car started out as a plain-Jane 1975 Plymouth Duster powered by a 318-ci engine," Butch said. "In fact, one of my guys flew back to Detroit and drove the car

Car Craft magazine originally put the Duster (without the 396 Hemi engine) on its April 1975 cover, and the same photo was used on the Direct Connection Special Parts Catalog cover released in July 1965.

Butch's "10-Day Wonder" rolled through the Pomona Raceway tech line a mere hour or so before closing. Then, the Hemi Plymouth proceeded to wade through a stellar field of cars to reach the final round of NHRA Winternationals Modified Eliminator.

cross country to my shop in Van Nuys, California. We called that car the *10 Day Wonder* because it took us exactly 10 days to build it from start to finish to have it ready for the 1975 NHRA Winternationals.

"Ron Butler built the [roll] cage and basically tied the unibody together. Then, I got the Duster painted and lettered because *Car Craft* magazine wanted to shoot the car for their April 1975 cover. We shot the cover at Petersen Publishing Company's drive-in studio on Sunset and La Cienega boulevards in West Los Angeles and had the front of the chassis weighted down because it didn't have an engine in it, but nobody seemed to notice.

The following month during the NHRA Gatornationals at Gainesville Raceway, Butch avenged his Pomona final-round loss by defeating Bob Riffle and his Rod Shop Dodge in the semifinals and Jerry Marquart's Corvette in the final to clinch Modified Eliminator honors registering a 9.67 at 142 mph on the money run.

Much to the chagrin of Butch Leal fans, Butch and his new Duster lost the Modified Eliminator finale after enduring what seemed like the world's longest handicap start given to overall winner Dave Andrews and his H/Gas Volkswagen.

Dave Andrews' H/Gas Volkswagen. Oh, I was madder than hell. I called up the NHRA the following Monday and asked, 'How many Volkswagens do you guys sell from one of your events?'

"Well, the guy with the Volkswagen wasn't very happy with me, either. They took over a tenth of a second off his index.

"The next race I ran was at Gainesville. He wasn't there, and I beat Jerry Marquart's Corvette in the final with a 9.67 at 142 mph and won the eliminator."

No sooner had Butch gotten the Modified Production car competitive when Chrysler Racing called and wanted to replace his out-of-production 1974 Plymouth Barracuda SS/MA Super Stocker with this Dart Sport, which used the same 360 small-block drivetrain as the 'Cuda.

"Anyway, after the *Car Craft* magazine photo shoot, we got the 396 Hemi (which I was simultaneously screwing together) fitted up and Hooker got the headers built. We got the car done just in time to go through the final hours of tech at Pomona. Lo and behold, I got to the final round of Modified Eliminator only to get beat by

Demon or Dart Sport

"So, now Chrysler wanted me to build a Dodge Demon Super Stock car to replace my out-of-production 1974 Plymouth Barracuda," Butch said. "Well, my wife, Donna, is the daughter of a Pentecostal minister, and she didn't like that idea in the least.

"She said, 'No, you're not going to build any car that's called a Demon.'

With various team drivers, the Dart Sport ran in the same class. Today, that car is owned by Steve Atwell of Walled Lake, Michigan, and the car has run a career-best ET of 10.38 at 135 mph.

Butch's finest hour with the Modified Production car was when he avenged himself at the 1976 NHRA Winston Winternationals.

Making a Beeline for Arizona, then Pomona

"About a week before the 1976 NHRA Winternationals at Pomona, the NHRA decided to have a race at Bee Line Dragway outside of Phoenix called the NHRA Winter Classic," Butch said. "It was a one-time deal, and I ended up beating Jim Steven's Maverick with a 9.78 at 142.18 mph in the final.

"The following weekend, I avenged my 1975 final-round loss and ended up winning Modified Eliminator against the Norm Mayerson–driven *Car Craft* Camaro at the NHRA Winternationals, running a 9.62 at 142.40 mph to Norm's 10.73 125.69 mph. That was a good two weeks."

"Fortunately, Chrysler also had what it called a Dart Sport, so we built one of those instead, running the same 360 small-block drivetrain that the Barracuda ran the year before."

Butch won Modified Eliminator at Pomona when he defeated Norm Mayerson and the Car Craft Camaro Super Modified with an ET of 9.62 at 142.40 to Norman's 10.73 at 125.69 mph. (Photo Courtesy Dave Kommel)

Duster Restoration Chronicles

Today, Butch's Modified Production Plymouth Duster has been authentically restored by Findlay, Ohioan Denny Laube.

Laube said, "When I was 20 years old, my friend Dan and I were building a big-block Plymouth Duster. On one of my many visits to the local Chrysler-Plymouth Dealer parts counter, I was handed a complimentary copy of the latest Direct Connection catalogue with Butch Leal, the California Flash, and his brand-new Hemi Duster gracing the cover. I was one of the gearheads that Chrysler's Direct Connection program was targeted at. I always told my friends that in our 20s, while they had copies of *Playboy* and *Penthouse* stashed underneath their mattresses, I had a copy of the Direct Connection parts catalogue with the California Flash on the cover under mine."

"Fast forward 40-plus years to 2016. I was having Saturday morning coffee at the kitchen table with my wife, Jodee, when my older brother John emailed a link advertising the sale of the Direct Connection B/MP Plymouth Duster with the heading 'Car for You!'

"I must have stared in disbelief at the ad for 15 minutes before finally racing upstairs, retrieving my original 1975 Direct Connection catalogue and copy of the April 1975 issue of *Car Craft* magazine for additional photo comparison.

"Although the race car in the ad had a Plexiglas windshield, fiberglass doors, a close but not accurate California Flash Direct Connection paint job, and was no longer powered by the twin-plug Hemi but was now powered by a big-inch wedge engine, I was more convinced than ever that it was the former Butch Leal B/MP race car.

"Once I got my head out of the computer screen, Jodee simply asked me, 'Why don't you buy it?'

"Well, not one to let an opportunity pass by, I immediately got my brother involved and cut a deal with Iowan Alex Polwik within the hour. The only thing Jodee insisted on was finishing our rental house and new shop before I started tearing into the restoration. [It was] easier said than done. I didn't have the Duster a week when I showed up to pick my wife up from work covered head-to-toe in 40-year-old race car grease and grime. She took one look at me and asked, 'Are you working on that car?'

"I sheepishly replied, 'A little.' Needless to say, the rest of the ride home was a bit on the cool side.

"For the actual restoration, I had immeasurable help from Thomas Voehringer from the Petersen Publishing

A beaming Butch poses with his freshly restored B/MP Plymouth Duster during the 2018 Mopar Nationals in Columbus, Ohio, where he was a featured guest. (Photo by Tim Costello, Courtesy Denny Laube)

Company Photo Archives. Thomas provided me with 8x10 proofs from the original 1975 *Car Craft* photo shoot that documented the race car fresh from Butler's shop taken from every angle. I wanted to ask Butch about some small details that the photos couldn't resolve, but more important to me, I wanted to ask him if he had any interest in building a brand-new period-correct 396-ci.

"A Butch Leal Hemi for his former race car? Since I didn't know Butch, I needed some help from an insider and got to talking to Joe Pappas from the Mopar Missile team. Joe gave me Butch Leal's telephone number. When I first called Butch, he didn't seem very interested, saying that he's constantly getting calls from guys saying that they have one of his old race cars and blah, blah, blah. But I called him for two reasons: 1) could he provide me with any information about the car, and 2)

Today, Butch's Modified Production Duster is owned and was restored by Denny Laube of Findlay, Ohio. (Photo by Tim Costello, Courtesy Denny Laube)

would he be interested in building me a 396 Hemi? He wasn't interested in building me a 396 Hemi.

"With the new paint from Boutwell Customs in Findlay, Ohio, still drying on the Duster's shell and a good six months from completion, Butch got wind of how well the restoration was progressing, and we started talking more and more about his former race car. During one of our conversations, Butch asked if the car would be ready to debut at the upcoming Mopar Nationals at Columbus, Ohio, a mere 60 days away.

"At first I thought, 'No way!' All I had was a painted shell and parts scattered everywhere with no idea when I would be seeing the show car Hemi being assembled by Steve Atwell some 100 miles away up near Detroit.

"Butch laughed at my excuses and reminded me that the car was originally built in 10 days. With less than two months to go, surely I could make it. After a quick call to the engine builder, I called Butch back and told him that I would have the car ready. To me, this was the chance of a lifetime. We completed the Duster just in time to debut the car at Columbus where an obviously pleased and beaming Butch Leal posed with the car, signing autographs and talking to the fans. Ever since then Butch Leal and I have been tight."

When Laube was asked what it meant to him to own the Butch Leal B/MP Plymouth Duster, he said, "I love it! I would rather have it than money."

In 1976, Butch commissioned Ron Butler to build this Plymouth Arrow, which was capable of running either as an Altered, a Gasser, or a Pro Stocker depending on weight and engine size. Butch's Direct Connection Arrow promptly set the NHRA B/Gas record with an ET of 8.80 at 156 mph at Warner Robbins, Georgia, running a 396-ci Hemi.

My Arrow

"I don't know exactly how it came about, but I made it known that I wanted to run a Mopar-bodied heads-up match racer," Butch said. "Well, Chrysler went and built me a tube-frame Dodge Dart, but when I got the car back home from Detroit, I started looking at the thing and it didn't even come close to comparing to the safety, quality, and engineering of a Butler-built car, so I never even took it out of the box.

"When Dave Koffel called me and wanted to know why, I just said that I would feel more comfortable having Ron Butler build me a Plymouth Arrow instead.

"Chrysler sent the Rod Shop's Gil Kirk out to pick up the Dart, and I ordered a brand-new 91-inch-wheelbase Plymouth Arrow, which was the first Pro Stock Plymouth

The Chrysler-Plymouth sales slogan "Me and My Arrow" proudly rode into battle with Butch on each and every run. Seen here in the pits at OCIR, Butch was a fan favorite with the locals.

Cooking Outside the Kitchen

"Butch's Arrow was initially a very scary car to me," Donna Leal said. "If you zoomed up on my face in that [color] picture, you can see that I was extremely focused. Until Butch got the car sorted out, you never knew what it was going to do in the bleach box because it had such a short wheelbase, and with those huge Firestone [drag] slicks sitting in all that water, you never knew if it was going to go sideways or straight. You had to hold on to the back of the spoiler and guide its movement side-to-side while paying close attention to what was going on all around you.

"Then there was all that deafening noise from that Hemi reaching peak RPM, which could be very, very distracting not to mention all that choking rubber smoke and water flying through the air. Overall, I would say my experience working [in] the burnout box was pretty darned intense."

Donna said that Butch's Arrow was very scary to be around at the beginning. Until Butch sorted things out, it was hard to tell what the car was going to do in the bleach box. Donna would hold onto the back of the spoiler to guide it side to side while paying attention to what was going on around her.

Butch's lovely wife, Donna, pours the water during one of Butch's many appearances at OCIR, the famed Southern California Supertrack.

Running a 454-ci Hemi, Butch burns through the rosin at OCIR probably during that same Pro Stock meet. (Photo Courtesy Steve Reyes)

This photo that shows Wayne Gapp slightly in front of Butch underscores the problem that Butch was having early on getting the Arrow to leave properly due to the incorrect-length ladder bars. "I would have to kind of idle the car off the line and then hammer the throttle," Butch said. "Once that happened, all hell would break loose." In this race, Butch, running an 8.19, defeated Gapp & Roush's Pinto.

Arrow ever built. It was a beautiful car—my kind of car. [It was] super light, and it ran a manual 4-speed transmission. I ended up setting the NHRA B/Gas record with it at 8.80 at 156 mph or something like that. I mean the car was really, really fast."

Butch said, "In the meantime, there was all this heads-up match racing going on with Jenkins, Nicholson, Sox, and all the others, so I decided that I would build up a 454 Hemi and get in on the action.

"I took all the weight out and got the car as light as a feather. But the chassis was not right for that big of an engine. It wouldn't hook up off the starting line; I would kind of have to idle the car off the line then hammer the throttle. The best run I ever made with it set up that way was an 8.19 against Gapp & Roush's Pinto at OCIR.

"After Ron Butler fixed the chassis and built a new set of shorter-length ladder bars, the car turned into a real rocket. That summer, I ran a match race against Larry Lombardo driving Bill Jenkins's 500-inch Chevy Monza at Englishtown, New Jersey, and it went 7.98

Butch's Arrow was so popular that Chrysler used an artist's rendering of the car as part of a montage of Direct Connection-sponsored race cars in its 1976 catalogue.

You could call this a "National Dragster sandwich," as staffers Theresa Long and Richard Brady capture Butch and his Arrow at speed, racing a Camaro mid-track during Gas class eliminations during the 1976 NHRA U.S. Nationals at Indianapolis Raceway Park.

at 171 mph, which was the quickest and fastest that car ever ran. Afterward, I went back to running B/Gas and let Roy [Hill] borrow the 454 motor to run in his Arrow to compete in the IHRA Mountain Motor class."

that size engine, they would be afforded a huge weight break. On the other hand, I wanted to stay running the [de-stroked] 396-inch Hemi in the class because I could

Well, It's Been a Real Gas, But . . .

"In 1977, I tried to put together a program with Chrysler's Dave Koffel, Tom Hoover, Ted Spehar, and Don Carlton," Butch said. "We all met at the *Missile* shop in Detroit and got Chrysler Vehicle Performance Racing Manager Dick Maxwell over there, and were trying to give him an idea of what we wanted to do for the following season.

"They [the Mopar Missile team] had developed a 340 small-block prototype, which showed great promise, and wanted to run that engine in NHRA Pro Stock. With

Unfortunately, by 1977, Chrysler's anti-Pro Stock national event policy was starting to wear thin. After Chrysler Racing's Dick Maxwell refused to entertain what seemed to be a logical and equitable proposal for ending Chrysler's ban of NHRA Pro Stock, Butch decided to call it quits and run as an independent.

make it run really well.

"Maxwell said 'No, absolutely not! We're not racing NHRA Pro Stock.'

"Well, I got really upset and said, 'Dick, are you going to be busy in the morning?'

"Maxwell replied, 'No, what's up?'

"I shot back, 'I need to talk to you!'

"The next morning, I was upstairs at Chrysler Racing's headquarters located on Woodward Avenue in Detroit and didn't mince any words. I said, 'I'm done!'

"Maxwell said, 'What do you mean you're done?'

"I said, 'I'm going to race NHRA Pro Stock. Figure out where our [Direct Connection] deal is, and let's settle up; I'm out of here!'"

Put a Direct Connection Dodge in Your Garage

Michigander Paul Rossi has had a long and colorful history racing Mopar Super Stock cars since 1963 and was chosen as Butch Leal's teammate to race a Direct Connection–sponsored 440 Magnum–engine 1970 Dodge Challenger in the NHRA's SS/FA class.

Rossi said, "In 1975 Dave Koffel called me and said, 'Paul, we want you to do our Direct Connection high-performance aftermarket parts program with Butch Leal. We're going to supply you with a 1970 AAR 'Cuda and the engine you'll be using is going to be a 440.'

"I said, 'Whoa! Wait a minute, Dave. What do you mean a 440? I'm a Hemi guy and have been from the beginning.

"Dave said, 'Paul, I need to have you do a 440,' but I still refused.

"Well, thank God that Dave didn't give up on me. In the end, Chrysler paid to have Ron Butler build the car, Butch paid me a salary, and Chrysler gave me all the technical support I needed, so now I was running a 440 Magnum—like it, or not.

"One day, Dave called me and said, 'Paul, stop!'

"I said, 'Stop what, Dave?'

"He said, 'Stop working on the 'Cuda. You've got to get that car out of Butler's shop.'

"I asked, 'Are you firing me, Dave?'

"He said, 'No, no. We're doing the Direct Connection clinics at Dodge and Plymouth dealers, right?'

"I said, 'Yeah, I know we are, but . . .'

"Dave said, 'You can't have a Plymouth. Butch has a Plymouth. We're sending you a Dodge Challenger instead. Have Ron [Butler] take the 'Cuda off the chassis jig and start on the Challenger instead.'

"So, that was how I ended up racing a Dodge Challenger.

Chosen as Butch Leal's Direct Connection teammate was veteran Mopar Super Stock racer Paul Rossi who toured the country putting on Direct Connection clinics with the Flash and ran this 440 Wedge-engine Direct Connection-sponsored 1970 Dodge Challenger in the SS/FA class at NHRA events.

"That car turned out beautifully. I think the car ran 10.50s at 127 mph, and it won a couple of NHRA points meets. Moreover, the car was really popular with Dodge fans at the Direct Connection aftermarket high-performance clinics for its jaw-dropping starting-line antics. The Direct Connection program lasted for two years and was extremely successful, and I believe that we raised the bar on how to do high-performance parts from the factory.

"After the Direct Connection program ended, I ran the Challenger for a few more seasons under the 'Team Dodge' banner. Then, in the 1980s, I became involved in Chrysler's IMSA road-racing programs and fielded a team of front-wheel-drive Dodge Chargers in conjunction with the late Carroll Shelby. So, Chrysler Corporation has always been good to me."

Butch brought the Arrow back home to Tulare, painted it back to his familiar Poppy Red and Refrigerator White team colors and competed in NHRA Pro Stock. Unfortunately, the Arrow didn't turn out to be nearly as fast and quick as he thought it would be. At the time, Bob Glidden's Ford Fairmont was lightning fast, and the big-block Chevrolets were [also] starting to hit their strides. The long and short of it was that Butch ended up running the Arrow throughout the remainder of the season with very little to show for it.

"At the end of the year I sold the entire rig (car, truck, and trailer) to Raymond Beadle of *Blue Max* fame who in turn sold the car to Cork 'Obsession' Bliss who successfully ran the Arrow in the NHRA Competition Eliminator class," Butch said. "I was done with NHRA's handicap Pro Stock racing format. It was like driving with a pair of handcuffs on."

Here's an interesting note: between 1974 and 1977, *Car Craft* magazine's All Star Drag Racing Team awarded Butch Leal either Super Stock or Modified Driver of the Year honors each and every year.

Sage Advice

"Butch and I were getting ready to go test for Chrysler in Detroit," Rossi said. "Between races, we tested a laundry list of parts, including clutches, headers, camshafts, cylinder heads, intake manifolds, carburetors, ignition systems, and other hard parts carried in the Direct Connection aftermarket parts catalogue.

"I was out there loading my truck with enough spare parts to last for two months on the road and making a laundry list to be sure that I had got everything I needed when Butch walked over and said, 'Paul, come over here for a minute.'

"Then, he asked, 'Where we going?'

"I said, 'We're going to Detroit to test for Chrysler!'

"Then, he said, 'Well, what are you doing?'

"I said, 'I'm loading my truck up with all the spare parts that I need to go test at Milan, aren't you?'

"He said, 'No! Where do they make those parts, Paul? In Detroit, right? We don't take parts *to* Detroit, we get parts *from* Detroit!'

"Having been constructively taken to task, the only logical thing for me to do was, you guessed it, unload the truck."

While attending the 2020 edition of Chryslers at Carlisle, Butch takes a break to hang out at the Mopar Pavilion with longtime Butch Leal fan Tom "McMopar" McClurg, who is author Bob McClurg's cousin. Note the enlarged copy of the April 1975 issue of Car Craft *magazine on the right. (Photo Courtesy Dean Herron)*

CHAPTER 14

THE FLASH GETS HOOKED ON GOLF

"I practiced every day and got to where I could hit lightning in a bottle and shoot low-65s and -66s, but I couldn't do it every day. Those guys out there are just unbelievably good."

"In 1965, I played golf for the first time in my life," Butch Leal said. "I was up in Spokane, Washington, at a race with Hayden Proffitt, Ronnie Sox, and Dave Strickler, and couldn't have been any more than 21 years old at the time. Ronnie could play well, Dave could play well, but like myself, Hayden had never played golf before.

"'These are just sticks,' Hayden would laughingly call the golf clubs.

"The long and short of it was we really had a ball that day, and I even managed to make one par for the round we played. I was hooked.

"I had a real good friend in Tulare named Ray Philpot who was an excellent golfer. Ray would often say, 'Let's go out and play us some golf,' to which I would reply, 'Man, it's over 100 degrees out there. I'm not going to go chasing some little white ball around in that kind of heat.' But, Ray kept after me and I finally decided to go.

"Ray scrounged up a set of golf clubs for me, and I went and played a round with him and two other guys named Wayne Hanson and Tinker Morris who turned out to be the local pro and assistant pro at the Tulare Golf Course, so I was playing with the best of the best. These guys were shooting a 75, 74, 72. Man, was I ever outclassed, and wish I could forget my score. I shot a 111. I came home that afternoon absolutely mortified. I thought about it for a while and said, 'This doesn't work with me!' I knew that I could do this, so I went back out the next day and talked to the local pro.

"You know me, when I'm in, I'm *all* in. I needed to buy a set of golf clubs, a golf bag, a putter, extra balls, a pair of golf shoes, and a pull cart. Just as Wayne was figuring all this up, the UPS truck pulled up and brought him a brand-new set of personalized Ben Hogan irons, drivers, and woods—in other words, the whole enchilada.

"I said, 'I want those!'

"Wayne said, 'Well, you can have 'em for a price. I really like the set of Hogans I'm using from last year and want to keep playing with them.'

"I said, 'So how much will it cost me for the whole enchilada?'

"He said '$600.'

"That was a lot of money back in those days, so I said that I didn't want to play golf *that* badly. Then, I reached in my pocket, and pulled out four crisp $100 bills and laid 'em down on the counter.

"Wayne said, 'Nah, that won't get it done,'

"I said, 'Wayne, I'm not through yet, for that $400, I also want you to give me golf lessons every day, and I can hit all the balls I want!'

"Wayne thought about it for a minute, smiled, and said, 'I like that. Deal!'

Very few professional drag racers successfully step out of one occupational pastime and into another with ease. Butch Leal is one of those select few. He is just as formidable on the links as he is behind the wheel of one of his race cars.

"Golf is a real good gambling game," said Butch. "There's no telling how much money I've made playing the game over the years. It's also great for honing in on your concentration skills. It helps me focus much like the same way I have to when I'm driving one of my race cars."

"I'll never forget the time Castrol had all of its employees come down to Florida for its annual corporate meeting," Butch said. "Larry Morgan and I were flown in as their guests. Afterward, Castrol held a golf tournament and awarded $1,000 to the Castrol rep who got the closest to my top golf score, which was a 66. I played with the Florida State Gold Association [FSGA] Champion Hank Byrd, and there was no way that any of those guys could even come close."

"For the next two years, I hit over 1,000 balls a day. In fact, I hit so many golf balls that when I would come home at the end of the day, my hands would be bleeding, and I would have to soak them in corn huskers [lotion]. The next morning, I would get up, soak them in hot water to soften them back up, slather on some more corn huskers, and go back out and hit some more golf balls.

"Ray [Philpot] bet me $100 that it would take me six months for me to break 80. On the sixth week, I rolled in about a 50-foot putt and shot a 79, and it cost him the hundred bucks. So, I ended up paying about $300 for everything."

The Can's Still There

"One day, Dave Koffel called me at my shop in Van Nuys, California, and asked me if I would do him a favor," Butch said. "He and his wife, Susie, owned a vacation home on one of the lakes just outside Detroit, and they were very interested in buying a new jet boat. Dave found one that he liked for sale in Southern California, and he wanted to know if I would be interested in bringing it back [to Detroit] with me on my next road trip.

"Of course, I said yes. I picked up the boat, brought it

back to my shop, and had it lettered 'Fat Albert' [Koffel's nickname] along with a cartoon on the back. We hitched it to one of our race rigs and delivered it to Dave's home in Detroit.

"In the meantime, I was working on the Direct Connection program and stayed with Dave and his wife in Detroit for a few weeks. One day, I had some spare time on my hands, so I asked Dave if he would mind if I mowed their lawn. They had a small strip of grass on the side of their house, which looked like a great place for a putting green, so I asked them, 'Would you mind if I dug a hole and installed a metal can in the ground to make a makeshift putting green?'

"They said, 'Sure.'

"An empty peach can proved to be the right size, and I putted away to my heart's content.

"After all those years, I was talking to Susie during the

2018 Mopar Nationals at Columbus, and she said, '[Do you remember] that old can you buried in the back yard?'

"I said, 'Yeah.'

"She said, 'Well, it's still there.'"

Motorcycle Daredevil Meets the California Flash

"In the mid-1970s, I joined a group of golfers informally called the Rat Pack, and we played for money almost every day," Butch said. "I was a member of the Lakeside Golf Club in Toluca Lake [a high-end neighborhood in Greater Burbank, California], which is located directly across the L.A. River from Universal Studios.

Butch said that he was known to bounce a golf ball or two off the roofs of the Universal Studios sound stages, prompting studio security to come over to the club wanting to know who was to blame.

"We had Gordon McRea, Forest Tucker, Frankie Avalon, Bruce McKeagen, Mac Davis, and Glenn Campbell as part of our entourage," Butch said. "We would not only play golf but we would also play cards when it got late in the day. Anyway, one day I happened to drive into the Lakeside parking lot, and I saw a Cadillac El Dorado pickup truck that immediately caught my eye. It had a custom Harley Davidson loaded in the back. I walked inside the club house, and there stood Evel Knievel. I remember he tipped two of the porters $100 apiece as he walked through the door.

"I said, 'Man, don't be doing that. Makes the rest of us look bad, and you don't want to spoil them.'

"Evel let out a hardy laugh and asked if I wanted a game.

"Of course, I said, 'Sure!' I told him that we played for $100 a unit, but he wanted to jack it up.

"He asked, 'How about a thousand a unit?'

"Well, I wasn't backing down, and neither were a couple of the other guys in our group, so we agreed, but we had to give him a couple of strokes. He was like a 16 handicap. I gave it some thought. I think I was about a 2 [handicap] then. I could play better, but I wanted to stay around a 2 handicap and make the rest of the group happy because I played with them every day. I think I gave him 14 shots, which he agreed to.

"We went out and teed up. Now, I was beating him up pretty bad, and my caddy told me to lay up to a par 4

Butch (far left), Miss Winston (middle), and Frankie Avalon (second from right), who was a 1950s teen recording idol turned actor, pose with others at the 1978 NHRA Winston World Finals Golf Tournament at the Red Hill Country Club in Rancho Cucamonga, California. "I won almost every NHRA Winston Golf Tournament they had," said Butch. "I must have won a half dozen golf bags full of golf clubs, and we have a shelf full of trophies sitting at home. It was a fun time."

with a 6 iron off the tee and not to try to knock it on the green. Just hit an iron off the tee and then lay it up.

"He said, 'Smother it and knock it into the left bunker.' So, I did.

"I remember Evel walked over and looked at it and he said, 'Do or don't for a thousand!'

"I said, 'You got it.'

"Then, I hit it about 4 inches from the hole out of the bunker, and all he said to me was, 'That will be enough of that!'

"I made two grand on that one shot. Knievel came back the next day, and I gave him a couple more shots, and I ended up being $12,600 to the good. That was a nice piece of change for two days' work."

In the early 1990s, Butch seriously contemplated retiring from drag racing as a whole and becoming a full-time golf pro.

"In 1992 Donna and I moved to Southern Pines, North Carolina, and I started playing golf every day," Butch said. "I had a golfing partner named Bobby Schmitz, and we quite often gambled on the outcome. Bobby and I were the same age, and we played in a lot of amateur tournaments around Ohio and in Florida and we did okay. Then, when I turned 49, I wanted to play on the PGA Senior Tour, but you had to play in the Senior Tour PGA Series first, which was a series of warm-up events prior to becoming eligible [at age 50] to qualify for the PGA Senior Tour.

"I practiced every day and got to where I could hit lightning in a bottle and shoot low-65s and -66s, but I couldn't do it every day. Those guys out there are just unbelievably good, but they started out in the game when they were just kids, while I didn't start playing until I was 21 or 22 years old. At the time, Mark Montgomery was my golf caddy, and we went to PGA Senior Series Qualifying School in Florida where we both qualified. Out of 420 players and 4 different golf courses, they took 20 players, and Bobby and I both made the cut. Somehow, when the bell rang to qualify, I think that [the discipline of] racing helped me a ton because I played my best golf in the qualifier."

Meeting His Hero

Mark "Willie Boy" Wilson said, "I was working at the Grove Fort, Ohio, golf club [outside Columbus, Ohio] where, unbeknown to me, Butch was a member. One day, I was standing there with a friend waiting to tee off, and there were a bunch of guys ahead of us who routinely played an 11 o'clock money game.

"So, I was just standing there waiting our turn and our caddie said, 'Do you know who that guy is over there?

That's Butch Leal, the California Flash.'

"I had been reading *Hot Rod* magazines ever since I was a kid [1966] and definitely knew who Butch Leal was, so I turned around and hollered out, 'California Flash!'

"He [Butch] spun around and said, 'Who said that?'

"The caddie said, 'He did.'

"Butch said, 'Boy, nobody's called me that in years!'

"He said, 'What do you know about the California Flash?'

"I said, 'I know everything about you!'

"He laughed, and we started talking. I told him that I had every car magazine article ever written about him and told him that I had done grunt work for [original Rod Shop member] Ray Noltmeyer. In fact, I also knew Bob Riffle, Bob Stickel, Jim Thompson, and all those guys.

"Later that night, I sat down with him at the bar, and we just talked about all kinds of stuff having to do with drag racing, and he and I became fast friends."

Teeing off with the Pros

Wilson said, "In the spring of 1994, I was hanging around the house and not working because of a construction-related back injury, so I tried to spend time with Butch every chance I had because we had so much in common. At the time, Gil Kirk from the Rod Shop was starting to sell off stuff because at the end of the year they would be getting out of racing. That was it. They were going to call it a day.

"In the meantime, we started playing golf together. Butch began working hard on his game, and I mean really hard. We would go to a golf course somewhere and we would spend the afternoon hitting golf balls. Because of my experience working at some of the better known golf courses around the Ohio Valley, I got to where I became more of a coach than a fellow player.

"I would tell Butch, 'You're doing this, you're doing that, you're laying off the top or whatever,' and he would immediately correct it.

"Then, he would say, 'Boy, you really know what you're doing.'

"One day he called me up and said, "Willis, I just won the qualifier in Blue Ash, which is a PGA golf course located in a suburb outside of Cincinnati. They gave me my card to go and play the Kroger Senior Classic.

"I mean, he was so excited. Then he asked if I wanted to go with him. Of course, I said yes.

"The next day, he picked me up, and we drove to Cincinnati. We walk out on the driving range and standing there was every big name in professional golf that you could imagine. There was Arnold Palmer and Lee Trevino, and we were standing there between Orville Moody

Butch and his wife, Donna, proudly display a copy of the 1998 PGA United States Senior Open Championships entry list in their Tulare, California, home. Note Butch's name in the first column, 27th signature down.

This is a scan of Butch's 1994 Kroger Senior Classic badge provided by Mark Wilson. The Kroger Senior Classic was a qualifying event on the PGA Tour at the Blue Ash Golf Course located outside Cincinnati, Ohio, where Butch won the qualifier and became automatically eligible to quality for the PGA Senior Tour. "No one in drag racing had ever done anything like that ever before," Wilson said. (Photo Courtesy Mark Wilson)

and Gay Brewer. I mean, Butch was like a kid in a candy store. We were out there hitting balls and these guys were joking with him trying to make him feel comfortable because they knew he was a little nervous.

"At the end of the day, Butch gave me his badge, and there's not many of those around. It's one of my favorite keepsakes."

U.S. Open Aspirations

"I came back to California in 1998 and went to the U.S. Open Qualifier at the Lodi Country Club," Butch said. "There were two or three qualifiers in California that you could choose from, and Lodi happened to be the closest course to us. At Lodi, I tied for medalist, and they took two players out of 144. The closest thing to our qualifier was a 76 or 77, and we shot 70. What a nice feeling. I was just unbelievably happy.

"As it turned out, I double bogeyed the first hole and, if it hadn't been for my wife, Donna, being there with me, I would have probably given up. She looked at me and said, 'There are 17 more holes. Let's go and get 'em!' I rose to the occasion, and away we went.

"Things turned out great; I qualified about three weeks before the U.S. Open, which was at the Riviera Country Club outside of L.A. Now, I was just riding around in the golf kart at the beginning. I decided that I would walk and try to build my legs up because the Riviera is a tough course to walk. Wrong move!

Former Butch Leal crewman (1989-1991) and golfing partner Mark "Willie Boy" Wilson (third from left) provided this photo of Butch (far left) and 1998 Senior Open Champ Clayton Waites watching former Winston Racing Chief T. Wayne Robertson's swing. (Photo Courtesy Mark Wilson)

"What's really interesting about the Riviera is that you first sign in. After you've signed in, you go about three blocks and they've got new Cadillacs lined up a block long. They give you a free Cadillac [Cadillac was a U.S. Open Sponsor] to drive for the week, which I thought was pretty cool. You also go and see select movies premieres coming out at that time. The wives were treated to all kinds of social amenities and special gifts, and there were all kinds of other special perks. I mean, it was wonderful!

"I decided that I wanted to play a practice round. Now, a friend of mine from North Carolina named Bobby Strobel and I went out, and instead of playing 9 holes like everyone else out there practicing, we played all 18 holes.

"I could hardly walk the next morning. I went out and hit a few balls, and all of a sudden, I started shanking the darned ball. I went and got wraps on my legs and did anything else we could to help my knees and, obviously, that didn't work. The bell rang and away we went.

"The first day, I played awful. Then, I played a little better the second day, but I missed the cut, and I was really disappointed. If I had to do it over again, I would have ridden that kart until the minute we teed up. It was really disappointing, and still I think about it a lot, even to this day.

"About a week after the U.S. Open, my knees all of a sudden started really hurting. I would soak them and try to get them to feel better. I didn't know at that time that I had bad circulation in my legs. Still, I played a few more tournaments, and I did pretty well. I managed to work on my legs and had balloons and stints put in them and got them to feeling a little better.

"Now-a-days, I don't play as much golf as I used to because it's much harder to practice. I may hit 20 balls and can barely shoot par, although I did shoot my age, 68, 70, 71, three or four times. But I haven't seriously gotten after it and played hard for two years."

It's a Generational Thing

Butch's 19-year-old grandson Harrison "Butch" Leal said, "I started golfing with my grandfather when I was 7 or 8 years old. He taught me everything I know about golf. He also taught me how to fish, and together, we've done a lot of both.

"The times we actually played a full round [of golf], I would occasionally become a little exasperated. My grandfather would simply tell me that I was thinking too much and to slow it down and focus on the game much like the same way he does when he's driving one of his race cars. It was a great bonding time together."

A proud Grandpa Butch proudly poses with grandson Harrison "Butch" Leal prior to hitting a few golf balls at the local driving range.

"My grandfather taught me everything I know about golf," Harrison Leal said. "He also taught me how to fish, and together, we've done a lot of both."

Harrison Leal said, "Whenever we would play a full round of golf and I would become a little exasperated, my grandfather would simply tell me to slow down and focus on the game, much like the same way he does when he's driving one of his race cars."

THE HORIZON

"I stayed with them all throughout the building of the Horizon. In fact, I stayed so long that we started making jokes about them declaring me as a dependent on their income tax schedule."

"After taking a couple of years off, I decided to go Pro Stock racing again in late 1982," Butch Leal said. "I was originally going to have Ron Butler build me a brand-new Pro Stock Plymouth Horizon, but he had retired from building race car chassis and was now building 427 Cobra replicas instead, so I looked around and decided to have Willie Rells build my chassis."

Rells said, "Back in the day, I operated a small fabrication shop out of my mother's garage in San Diego, California. One day, Butch Leal walked through the door and said, 'Hey Willie, I want to build a new car but I ain't got any money.'"

Fresh out of paint and ready to run, Butch's new Willie Rells-constructed Plymouth Horizon Pro Stocker weighed 2,300 pounds and ran 8-flat ETs at 169 mph using a 500-ci Leal-built 426 Hemi for power.

This photo was taken of Butch shaking out the car at OCIR racing against Maskin & Moreno's M&M Boys Pro Stock Pontiac Firebird. Note the tire smoke still in the interior of the Horizon, as Butch was apparently eager to get with the program.

"He just blurted it right out. Obviously, I knew Butch's name from racing, but I had never met him personally."

"Willie and his wife, Marilyn, are wonderful people," said Butch. "I stayed with them all throughout the building of the Horizon. In fact, I stayed so long that we started making jokes about them declaring me as a dependent on their income tax schedule. By the time we completed the Horizon, I was so busted that I didn't have two nickels to rub together.

"I remember, once completed, we rolled the car down

Butch runs the Horizon at Pomona. Quite often, Butch qualified the Plymouth in the middle of the field and usually had to race the No. 1 qualifier, which was usually Bob Glidden, Warren Johnson, or Lee Shepherd in the first round.

Butch has his best finish of the year against a red-lighting Warren Johnson at Indy. Butch said that he kicked out a connecting rod and didn't have a replacement engine, so he was done for the time being. (Photo Courtesy Gary Nastase)

to the bottom of the hill from Willie's shop. We both looked at each other and I asked, 'You got any money, Willie?'

"He said, 'I've got exactly 15 cents in my pocket.'

"I said, 'Well, hell, I've got a nickel in mine, so I guess we're still doing okay.'

"That's the reason why I hadn't quite gotten around to building the big-inch Hemi I had planned to run in the car yet, so I borrowed a small cubic-inch motor from Bob Lambeck instead to test the Horizon with."

Willie said, "I remember we were just finishing up the car when Butch took the Horizon over to nearby Carlsbad Raceway to test it. Would you believe, going over 150 mph without any floor panels? That was Butch!"

Butch said, "The car ran well, but I remember I dropped an intake valve and had to fix the engine before I gave the thing back to Bob. Once I finished up my 500-inch motor, I ran the thing again, and it was fast. At 2,350 pounds, it ran 8.0s at 169 mph, but by then, the Chevrolets were running 7.90s, so I was a little behind the curve.

"I took the Horizon to every NHRA national event that year where I was the No. 9 qualifier and the only Chrysler car in the field. Usually, I had to run the No. 1 qualifier in the first round, which was either Warren Johnson, Bob Glidden, or Lee Shepherd, and they spanked me every time. Well, I was getting plenty tired of that. The only race I was successful at was the U.S. Nationals at Indy. I was the No. 9 qualifier [at 7.919] and ran Warren Johnson in the first round. He red-lighted, and I kicked out a rod. I didn't have a replacement engine to put back in, so that was the end of that.

"I had been talking to the Rod Shop's Gil Kirk, who wasn't racing at the time, and sort of coaxed him back into it. I loaded the Horizon into the back of a U-Haul truck and drove back to Columbus, Ohio, unloaded it, lettered 'Rod Shop' on the rear quarter panels, and finished the year out with that."

However, the writing was on the wall and Butch knew it.

"The big-block Chevrolets were out-running everybody at the time, and it became a matter of "if you can't beat 'em, join 'em.' Butch sold the Plymouth to Doug Kirk who converted the car over to run in Super Gas.

"Prior to selling the Horizon, I pulled the 500-inch Hemi out, and Doug installed a regular 426 Hemi with a 4-barrel on it so that the car could run on a 9.90 index.

"Doug asked me, 'Should I put an automatic in it?'

"I said, 'Just run the Lenco. Hell, what's the difference? You can let the clutch out on time, can't you?'

"So, that's what he did, and Kirk won a ton of races with the car. Then, he started running the car in the IHRA Mountain Motor class, and I never knew what happened after that.

"In 2019, I was at the Chrysler Show at Columbus, Ohio. I was sitting there signing autographs. Two of my

This photo was featured on the November 11, 1983, issue of National Dragster and was taken during the NHRA Winston World Finals. Butch was the No. 6 qualifier with a 7.723 at 178.18 mph and lost to Lee Shepherd driving the Rehr, Morrison, & Shepard Camaro. (Photo Courtesy Leslie Lovett)

older cars were there [my 1975 A990 Plymouth Super Stocker and 1973 Pro Stock Plymouth Duster] when a guy drove up in a golf cart and said, 'Butch! Do you know that your old Horizon is sitting back there in the swap meet area?'

"I said, 'No way!'

"Sure enough. I went and took a look, and it was my old Horizon. The car was painted black, but I immediately knew that it was my old car. It had the same gold anodized tin and the same wheels on it that I ran. It also had a Hemi in it with a 4-barrel just like the way it was

After recording another run in the high 7s, Butch drops the laundry in the lights at OCIR and prepares to exit the turn-off road.

set up when Doug Kirk raced it. Only the car now had a TorqueFlite in it.

"The seller also had a ton of spare Hemi parts that he was selling along with the car but didn't have a clue what they were. I looked over and there was a 426 Hemi sitting on an engine stand and it had 'Rod Shop' stamped on the valve covers. I took a closer look, and it was a Kramer block. Chrysler had a few blocks lightened in 1973 for drag racing. They took about 20 pounds or more off each block.

"I said to myself, 'Boy, that's a nice piece!' I got to talking to the fellow who owned everything, and he asked me if I could help him sell some of the stuff and I said that I would try.

"In the meantime, I spoke with Denny Laube, the man who restored my 1975 B/MP Plymouth Duster. Denny wanted me to come back to his shop the following summer and build him a 396 Hemi to put in my old M/P car, which was the only thing the car lacked to complete the restoration. Denny's friend Steve Atwell bought the Horizon, and Denny bought the engine from Steve.

"So, I flew back this past year and began pulling the motor apart. Lo and behold, it was my [500-ci] engine! I thought, 'You've got to be kidding me!' This engine had sat idle for 37 years! I pulled the valve cover off, and it had the first set of Dick Landy Hemi roller rocker arms ever made. I pulled the head off the engine, and, well, nobody fly cut pistons like I did.

"I said, 'Denny, we've got a problem!'

"He said, 'What's that?'

"I said, 'This isn't just any old 396 Hemi. It's my old 500-ci motor. This thing's a real thumper. It's got 16:1 compression, a General Kinetics cam, and all the trick stuff. Back in the day, I always ran this thing on freaking kill! When we get this thing screwed back together, it will be the best-sounding 396 Hemi you ever heard!'

Long story short, Denny's Duster ended up having Butch's 500-ci engine in it, if only momentarily, so that Laube could get the car ready for Columbus. However, Butch cautioned Denny that the big-inch Hemi was such a monster that it made no sense running it in the M/P car because (with only subframe connectors and an eight-point cage in it per the 1975 NHRA rule book) it would have twisted that thing up like a pretzel.

Steve Atwell of Walled Lake, Michigan, still owns Butch's Horizon and restored it back to "as raced" condition. Unfortunately, Steve had a run-in with the Bowling Green, Kentucky, Beech Bend Raceway Park guardrail in the summer of 2020, and is currently in the process of rebuilding the car.

My Father, the (Professional) Drag Racer
By Lisa Leal-Voss

I'm Butch Leal's youngest daughter, Lisa, and I was born in November 1966. When I was born, I was so tiny. Somewhere in the family scrapbook are pictures of Dad holding a pillow with me lying on it. Naturally, I grew up around cars. My mom used to tell me that when I was barely one year old whenever my dad would start up his race car out in the garage, I would become so excited.

I just loved going to the races. The smell of nitro and the rubber in my face. I have fond memories of going to Orange County International Raceway to see Dad race his Pro Stock Plymouth Horizon. Between qualifying on Saturday, we'd take off and go to nearby Lion Country Safari, which is one of the best memories I have of Dad doing something with me other than racing!

I remember I would call my father during Winternationals week and have him pick me up. I would say, "Dad, I want to go to the [drag] races," and I would go with him all four days. Pushing his car up through the staging lanes, I became fast friends with all the racers. Those were amazing memories.

As a child, I had always known the tender side of Butch Leal. However, I got to see another side of Dad at the races, that I had never seen before. I'm sure you've heard how intense a racer Butch Leal can be. When I would go with him to the track, sometimes he wouldn't talk to me. Later, he explained to me that I shouldn't take it person-

ally because being in the moment was just his job.

He would often say that when it came to his racing, it was strictly business.

"I'm working," he would often say. But just to be there and to be with him was worth the world to me.

I am so much like him. He's got a way to make things work and make them work easier. I often come up with solutions to make my life easier too. When my dad was inducted into the Don Garlits International Drag Racing Hall of Fame in March 2015, my husband, Phil, my son, Brock, and I flew out. When Erica Anders started talking about Dad, I had no idea that he had done all those things. It was truly amazing. Dad was the first stock-bodied drag racer in the 9s, then in the 8s, and then in the 7s.

Today, my family and I live near Bandimere Speedway, and we go to the races quite often. In fact, we're good friends with the Bandimere family. To this day, I'm still in awe by the number of people who know him. They say, "Butch Leal's your father? Oh wow!"

This March 3, 2015, photo was taken of Butch and his youngest daughter, Lisa Leal-Voss, just as they were about to enter the Don Garlits International Drag Racing Hall of Fame Gala where Butch received a lifetime achievement award. Lisa said, "When Erica Anders started talking about Dad, I had no idea that he had done all those things. It was truly amazing."

CHAPTER 16

THE ROD SHOP YEARS

"I liked Pontiac's Trans Am because style-wise, they were a much better looking car than the Camaros," said Butch. "They had that certain look to them that made them appear as though they were going 200 mph just standing still."

As Butch mentioned in Chapter 15, when it came to his future as a competitive force in NHRA Pro Stock, the writing was on the wall. The big-block Chevrolets were out-running everyone at the time, and it became a matter of, "if you can't beat 'em, join 'em."

Gil Kirk said, "Butch had a lot to do with the reemergence of the Rod Shop in the early 1980s. In 1983, Butch pushed me and prodded me until he finally convinced me to go Pro Stock racing again. It had been six long years since my [politically charged] contract with Dodge Division of Chrysler Corporation had expired, and I had mixed emotions about jumping back into the fray."

Why a Pontiac and Not a Chevrolet?

"I liked Pontiac's Trans Am because style-wise, they were a much better looking car than the Camaros," said Butch. "They had that certain look to them that made them appear as though they were going 200 mph just standing still."

Kirk said, "It went something like this: I called up my buddy John Zwerner with whom I had attended Duke University. John had recently come over from Chevrolet Motor Division where he was running the Advanced Engineering staff at General Motors. I said, 'John, we want to do this car, but I need some help.'

"He and I walked from his executive office over to the racing department, and there was a bunch of NASCAR memorabilia in it. The guy who was running it (who shall remain nameless) made us wait for 30 minutes while he had his feet up on his desk and casually talked to someone on the telephone!

"Finally, John said, 'That's it!'

"The next thing I knew, the guy was fired.

"Zwerner put a guy in there named John Callies, who had been working on the Pontiac Fiero Indy 500 Pace Car program. Up to that point, the Pontiac Motor Division of General Motors had never officially raced in NHRA Pro Stock before. So, John said, 'Let's go and see Callies, and we'll see what he can do!'"

John Callies

John Callies graduated from Oregon State University with a degree in automotive engineering, and his first job was at General Electric working on computers well before IBM debuted its first computer chip. In 1968, Callies signed on with Pontiac Motor Division in its engineering department. When the 1984 Pontiac Fiero was selected as the Indianapolis 500 Pace Car, Pontiac Chief Engineer Bob Dorn selected Callies to develop the Pontiac Fiero Indy 500 pace car package, which was nothing short of all encompassing, as the United States Auto Club (USAC), the sanctioning body for the Indianapolis 500, had a requirement that a pace car reach a terminal speed of 125 mph and stop in 500 feet.

However, according to Callies, "You couldn't get 125 mph out of the OEM Pontiac Fiero powertrain even if you dropped it out of a 747. We had to design a new cylinder block, new cylinder heads, and a new braking and suspension system other words. Once we were done with the Pontiac Fiero Indy 500 Pace Car Program, Bob Dorn named me to launch Pontiac's Motorsports Program at the behest of John Zwerner, and the rest is history."

Off and Running

Callies said, "We [Zwerner, Callies, and Kirk] met at GM's Mesa, Arizona, Proving Grounds where Callies was headquartered, and we [Pontiac Motor Division] decided to go NHRA Pro Stock racing. Then, the following week [SEMA Week], we signed a contract with Butch Leal as our driver.

Kirk said, "We had Willie Rells build us a stealth-looking big-block Chevrolet-powered Pro Stock Trans Am Firebird, and we painted it black and gold to honor the late Don Carlton. Once completed, we took the car to the SEMA Show, and Pontiac displayed it on a turnstile.

"I was standing there, and there was a great big, tall guy (as tall as I was) standing there looking at the car, and he went, 'Phew! How much did this cost us?'

Car owner Gil Kirk said that it cost $357,000 (including car, truck, travel, upkeep, and crew) to campaign the first of a long line of Butch Leal–driven Rod Shop Pontiac Trans Am Firebirds in NHRA Pro Stock Eliminator that first year (1983) prior to picking up any sponsors. (Photo Courtesy Gina's Photos)

"It turned out that his name was Bill Hoglund, and he was the President of Pontiac Motor Division. Little did he know that it cost me $357,000 to build and campaign that car in NHRA Pro Stock that first season, which included car, truck, travel, upkeep, and crew, and not one dollar came from Pontiac Motor Division."

Since there was no big-block Pontiac engine suitable for adaptation to NHRA Pro Stock, power came from a Butch Leal–built, Bob Ingils aftermarket 427 Chevrolet race block, which featured thicker cylinder walls so that you could overbore it to 4.50 ci to attain 500 ci, which at the time was the maximum allowable bore size for NHRA Pro Stock competition.

Butch selected a Sonny Bryant stroker crank and a set of Bill Miller Enterprises [BME] billet-aluminum connecting rods pressed onto a set of 15.7:1 compression Venolia Pistons to complete the rotating assembly. Cam choice varied between a Cam Dynamics or Comp Cam with a Jesel belt drive taking care of cam timing. Down below, Leal selected a Weaver dry-sump lubrication system circulating 10-30 Kendall GT1 racing oil through an Ed Hamburger oil pan. Nicknamed "Red," that was your basic Butch Leal–built Pro Stock Chevrolet short-block.

As with most engines, it's all in the cylinder heads, and, in this case, cylinder-head porting wizard John Eicke "rolled" the Diamond Racing aluminum alloy big-block cylinder heads by welding extra aluminum to the deck of the head and angle milled them while subsequently relocating the intake and combustion chambers. All told, it was about a 2½-month endeavor. Internally, Eicke installed a set of 2.300-inch-diameter Manley titanium intake and 1.880-inch-diameter Manley titanium exhaust valves using Comp Cams springs and titanium retainers along with a set of 1.8-ratio Crane Cams roller rocker arms.

Induction was handled by a modified Edelbrock tunnel-ram 2x4 intake manifold sporting a pair of Dave Braswell–blueprinted 1,150-cfm Holley Dominator carburetors. Setting things into motion was an MSD ignition system, while the exhaust duties were handled by a set of Black Jack Headers.

"Most people automatically think of Butch Leal as a great race car driver, but the truth be known, Butch's mechanical expertise is absolutely nothing short of incredible," Callies said. "His knowledge on engines, compression ratios, camshafts, induction systems, etc., is very, very good. In fact, I would put Butch Leal's engine building ability up against anybody."

New-Car Teething Problems

"That first Rod Shop Pontiac Trans Am Firebird was (next to my 1973 Pro Stock Plymouth Duster) one of my all-time-favorite built cars," said Butch. "The car had an up-to-date roll cage in it, which resembled one from a Funny Car. We started out with a four-link rear suspension with a short top bar, thinking that it was the hot setup. However, no matter what I did, I couldn't get the darned thing to stop shaking the tires.

"So, I drove from Columbus, Ohio, back to Willie's shop in San Diego, California, and had Rells install a set of equal-length four-link bars. Then, Gary Hansen and I took the car out to Orange County International Raceway. The car shook a little bit on the first run, so we adjusted the coilover shocks, and boom—it went right down the track!

"I loaded 'er into the back of the truck, and 32 hours later, I was back in Columbus. At that time, we did not have a single decal on the car. We built that thing entirely out of our own pockets and bought everything."

1984: A Car with No Sponsor
by Gil Kirk

We had a car and a deal with Pontiac but no sponsorship money as of yet. I had been working on Nationwise Auto Parts for what seemed like an eternity. Larry Skolnick,

Box Score: 1983
Statistics compiled by Bob Frey

Overall record: 1-3
Points: 15th place

Event	Qualifier	Result
NHRA Winternationals	No. 11; 7.944 at 176.81 mph	Lost to Roy Hill (Rd. 1)
NHRA Gatornationals	Did not qualify	N/A
NHRA Springnationals	No. 9; 7.913 at 174.08 mph	Defeated John Brumley (Rd. 1); Defeated Alan March (Rd. 2); Lost to Bob Glidden (Rd. 3)
NHRA Summernationals	No. 7; 7.888 at 173.41 mph	Defeated Reid Whisnant (Rd. 1); Defeated Bob Glidden (Rd. 2); Lost to Frank Iaconio (Rd. 3)
NHRA U.S. Nationals	No. 10; 7.860 at 174.41 mph	Lost to Lee Shepherd (Rd. 1)
NHRA Golden Gate Nationals	No. 5; 7.723 at 177.16 mph	Lost to Frank Iaconio (Rd. 1)
NHRA World Finals	No. 6; 7.723 at 178.18 mph	Defeated Fred Taylor (Rd. 1); Lost to Lee Shepherd (Rd. 2)

This photo is from 1984 (season two). Carrying sponsorship from Nationwise and Castrol motor oil, Butch charges off the Pomona Raceway starting line where he qualified No. 1 at 7.684 only to fall to Frank Iaconio in round two, but things were looking up. (Photo Courtesy Richard Shute, Auto Imagery)

The Rod Shop's next stop on the national event trail was the NHRA Gatornationals at Gainesville Raceway where the Flash qualified sixth at 7.695 and made it to round three prior to falling to Warren Johnson. (Photo Courtesy Richard Shute, Auto Imagery)

The Rod Shop's next stop on the national event trail was the NHRA Gatornationals at Gainesville Raceway where the Flash qualified sixth at 7.695 and made it to round three prior to falling to Warren Johnson. (Photo Courtesy Richard Shute, Auto Imagery)

Butch leaves the starting line in wheels-up fashion during the NHRA Southern Nationals where he qualified fourth with a 7.76, falling to Kenny Dondero in the second round. (Photo Courtesy Richard Shute, Auto Imagery)

who was running Nationwise, became so frustrated. Every time they went to the SEMA Show or any place else like that with this 222-store chain (about the biggest in the country I think), people would say, 'Oh, you're from Columbus, Ohio, home of the Rod Shop?' Every time, I swear to God!

I had one sales pitch to get Skolnick to sponsor me, and I knew that he wanted to. I was up all night, and this was a make-or-break situation. My hands started sweating on the way to go over to meet him, and I remembered my dad (who was a doctor) telling me that when he would give verbal medical exams, he would shake hands with his students and their palms would always sweat. So, I got some powder and put it on my hands.

I walked into Skolnick's office at 10 o'clock and started talking. By the time I got done, he said okay, and within a few weeks, I had signed a contract for a million-and-some dollars using my system of getting Nationwise to take and sell high-performance parts from the Rod Shop's participating sponsoring manufacturers.

I said, "Look, you need to set up special Rod Shop kiosks in your stores, and you stock those kiosks with only the top-of-the-line brand-name high-performance Rod Shop–sponsored parts. It's a win/win situation for everyone."

Of course, that put some pressure on across the street at JEGS because it [Nationwise] was now selling major-brand speed equipment throughout its 222 locations at a substantial discount. After the Nationwise deal was signed, I put together the deal with Castrol Motor Oil Company who, up until that point, had by and large only been involved in SCCA sports car racing. So, with both Nationwise and Castrol sponsorships on the car (and later Mr. Gasket), we were off and running."

Breaking 180-Plus MPH in a Flash

"I took the black car to Indianapolis, and it was running mid-7.60s at 179 mph," Butch said. "In the meantime, Albert Clark and Don Coonce had their Don Ness cars there, and Wayne County Speed Shop was there running the twin to my black car. They took the engine out of the Wayne County car and put it in Coonce's car, and the thing went 180 mph. I was thinking, 'Wait a minute.'

"I walked over and took a look at Coonce's car, and the only thing different that I could find was the fuel cell. Both of our cars [Butch's and Wayne County's] had flat fuel cells in them while Coonce's car had a Harwood stand-up fuel cell in it, and that made the difference.

"With the flat fuel cell, I was thinking, 'Wow, this thing could be running out of gas under extreme

Butch and the Firebird square off against Brad Yuill driving the Yuill Brothers Camaro during nighttime qualifying at the NHRA Summernationals at Raceway Park in Old Bridge Township, New Jersey. (Photo Courtesy Richard Shute, Auto Imagery)

However, "E-Town" wasn't one of Butch's better races, as he qualified No. 7 at the event with a 7.735 and lost to Sam Carroll in the first round.

Butch and the Black Bird charge off the U.S. Nationals starting line where the Flash qualified No. 3 with a 7.69 but lost to Ken Dondero in the opening round. (Photo Courtesy Richard Shute, Auto Imagery)

Butch qualifies at the 1984 NHRA World Finals with an ET of 7.691 against Bob Ingles of Carmel, New York. Butch beat Ronnie Manchester in round one while Ingles lost to Don Coonce. From there, the Flash proceeded to beat Reid Whisnant (round two) and Coonce (round three) prior to losing to Bob Glidden in the final. It was Butch's best showing of the year. (Photo Courtesy Richard Shute/Auto Imagery)

Butch and his brand-new Willie Rells Firebird compete at Pomona. Once again Butch looked as though he would sweep Pro Stock Eliminator at the 1985 NHRA Winternationals at Pomona, qualifying well with a 7.671 ET for the No. 6 spot. He took down "Dyno" Don Nicholson in the first round and Lee Shepherd in the second, but he fouled to Warren Johnson in the third round. (Photo Courtesy Richard Shute, Auto Imagery)

acceleration and I wouldn't even feel it.' So, once I got back to Willie Rells's shop, the first thing we changed was the tin work a little and then installed a new stand-up Harwood fuel tank.

"That weekend, I took the car to Fremont Raceway, let the clutch out, and on the first run, the car went 181 mph. I immediately knew I was back in business, and I felt pretty darned good about it."

An Aversion to The Color Green

"Initially, the folks at Castrol wanted me to paint the first Pontiac Trans Am green like a Castrol oil can," Butch said. "Well, I don't do green at all [an old racer's superstition], and we proceeded to have the biggest argument you had ever seen. I just kept insisting, 'I'm not doing it. I'm not doing it. *I'm not doing it!'*

Box Score: 1984 *Statistics compiled by Bob Frey*

Overall record: 13-11

Points: 5th place

Event	Qualifier	Result
NHRA Winternationals	No. 1; 7.684 at 177.86 mph	Defeated Ken Dondero (Rd. 1); Lost to Frank Iaconio (Rd. 2)
NHRA Gatornationals	No. 6; 7.695 at 180.36 mph	Defeated John Brumley (Rd. 1); Defeated Roy Hill (Rd. 2); Lost to Warren Johnson (Rd. 3)
NHRA Southern Nationals	No. 4; 7.764 at 178.57 mph	Defeated Jerry Eckman (Rd. 1); Lost to Ken Dondero (Rd. 2)
NHRA Cajun Nationals	No. 4; 7.703 at 179.28 mph	Defeated Don Campanello (Rd. 1); Defeated "Dyno" Don Nicholson (Rd. 2); Defeated Frank Iaconio (Rd. 3); Fouled to Lee Shepherd (final)
NHRA Springnationals	No. 7; 7.817 at 177.86 mph	Fouled to Sam Gianino (Rd. 1)
NHRA Grandnationals	No. 6; 7.752 at 177.86 mph	Defeated Don Campanello (Rd. 1); Lost to Lee Shepherd (Rd. 2)
NHRA Summernationals	No. 7; 7.735 at 178.21 mph	Lost to Sam Carroll (Rd. 1)
NHRA Mile High Nationals	No. 5; 8.167 at 168.53 mph	Defeated Roy Hill (Rd. 1); Fouled to Warren Johnson (Rd. 2)
NHRA Northstar Nationals	No. 6; 7.805 at 177.86 mph	Defeated Roy Hill (Rd. 1); Fouled to Lee Shepherd (Rd. 2)
NHRA U.S. Nationals	No. 3; 7.695 at 179.64 mph	Lost to Ken Dondero (Rd. 1)
NHRA Finals	No. 2; 7.691 at 179.64 mph	Defeated Ronnie Manchester (Rd. 1); Defeated Reid Whisnant (Rd. 2); Defeated Don Coonce (Rd. 3); Lost to Bob Glidden (final)

The Team Concept Revisited

Butch Leal

Few argue with how when it came to running a successful (and winning) multi-car drag racing team, the concept was executed to perfection by Columbus, Ohio's Gil Kirk and his Rod Shop racers. Kirk not only did it once with his factory-backed Rod Shop Dodges from 1970 to 1977 but also did it twice with the Rod Shop Pontiac drag racing team from 1984 to 1988.

"Approaching potential sponsors like Pontiac, Nationwise, and Castrol with a proven track record was crucial in 'floating' the multi-car team concept," said Kirk. "And having racers like Butch Leal [Pro Stock Trans Am Firebird], Larry Morgan [S/S Trans Am Firebird and later H/GT Pontiac Fiero], and David Nickens [Comp Class Trans Am Firebird] in our stable proved that we were *very* serious about winning races."

In retrospect, the Nationwise and Castrol sponsorship funds were well spent. History recorded that Gil Kirk Racing Cars, the parent organization behind the Rod Shop, did "walk that walk and talk that talk."

While Leal and second-season recruit Dave Boertman (winner of the NHRA S/S World Championship for the Rod Shop in 1985) were wreaking havoc in the Pro Stock and Super Stock ranks, David Nickens' small-block Trans Am and Larry Morgan's fearsome Super Duty Pontiac Fiero 4-banger were absolute terrors in Comp. In fact, Morgan's Fiero celebrated its first (of many) major event wins at the *Popular Hot Rodding* Championships at Martin, Michigan, where the little Fiero 4-banger ran under its 10.50 index and ultimately clocked a career best of 9.80 at 144 mph. Other team members also included Greg Stansfield and Doc Dixon.

When speaking of the Nationwise Rod Shop Pontiac drag racing team as a whole, Kirk said, "It was like managing a rock band, and Butch was the lead singer."

Larry Morgan

David Nickens

Dave Boertman

Doc Dixon

"That was a pretty big deal, and I almost lost the Castrol contract over that.

"Anyhow, I got my way, and we ended up running the same black car for the 1984 season. As our performances improved, Pontiac and Castrol began to show increased interest."

No Time to Sweat

"About midway through the season, I called Willie [Rells] and ordered a brand-new car," Butch said. "When it arrived, we painted it all white. Why white? I really liked the look of the black and gold car. It was sort of stealth looking and maybe even a bit intimidating. After all, that look had worked out really well for Dale, 'the Intimidator' Earnheart, so why not us?

"The truth of the matter was, though, that white was a much cooler color. With the black and gold car, I sat in the staging lanes and just cooked. By the time I got up to the line, I was thoroughly drenched and half wrung out. It's not a good situation to be in when you're trying to concentrate on the tree and win a national event."

Car Crazy

Willie Rells said, "From 1983 to 1991, I think I built Butch at least one or two Rod Shop Trans Am Firebirds a year. While the suspension systems on these cars all pretty much remained the same, the trick was to make the chassis as light as we can."

Butch elaborated, "The reason why we [the Rod Shop] built so many cars over the years [1983 to 1991] was because they [Pro Stock chassis] work just fine when they are new. Then, over time, you make run after run testing and racing them in competition until you find that you're just holding your own. So, then you go out and build a new chassis. You install the drivetrain, etc. out of the old car into the new one, and all of a sudden, it picks up two or three hundredths of a second, and you're going, 'Wow, what's the difference?'

"Well, there is a difference because of all the flexing that's going on in the composition of the chassis. [As you repeatedly make run after run] the tubing loses some of its tensile strength and elasticity, and it fatigues. It's the same thing with Top Fuel and Funny Cars. You'll see a brand-new digger or Funny Car go out there and really lay down a sub–record-breaking run, but the car never quite lives up to those expectations again. It's the same thing with a Pro Stock car. You build a new chassis, and oh, man, this car's the greatest.

"For example, take Greg Anderson. He builds a new car every six months or so. Every once in a while, he'll go back to his old car, but most of the time, he does nothing but move forward, and that requires continuously updating and/or replacing the chassis. That's why I had Willie Rells build me at least a couple of cars a year. He would build me one to start the season with and one in the middle of the summer that I would race through the end of the season. Back then [at approximately $20,000 a copy], that was the least expensive and most productive thing to do.

"With Willie, we discussed my goal then worked together all day to achieve it. We would go home in the evening and be so tired that we could hardly move. Then, we would continue to talk about what we were doing over dinner. Should we try this? Should we try that? We'd do anything to pick up another couple hundredths of a second.

"Our Southern Nationals win came just at the right time. Castrol was getting a little nervous, and it was a real thrill to be able stand in the winner's circle with them. Personally, it was always a thrill for me to be able to beat Bob [Glidden], who at the time was at the top of his game."

This was the race that Butch, Gil Kirk, Nationwise, and Castrol had been waiting for. Butch qualified No. 2 at the NHRA Southern Nationals with an ET of 7.675 and had a top speed of the meet honors (181.45 mph) en route to capturing top honors against Bob Glidden in the final. (Photo Courtesy Richard Shute, Auto Imagery)

"Jubilation" is the term that best expresses Butch and company after defeating Bob Glidden for the team's first NHRA Pro Stock Eliminator victory at the 1985 Southern Nationals. (Photo Courtesy Richard Shute, Auto Imagery)

Box Score: 1985
Statistics compiled by Bob Frey

Overall record: 24-12
Points: 4th place

Event	Qualifier	Result
NHRA Winternationals	No. 6; 7.671 at 179.35 mph	Defeated Don Nicholson (Rd. 1); Defeated Lee Shepherd (Rd. 2); Fouled to Warren Johnson (Rd. 3)
NHRA Gatornationals	No. 3; 7.647 at 180.36 mph	Defeated Rickie Smith, (Rd. 1); Lost to Dempsey Hardy (Rd. 2)
NHRA Southern Nationals	No. 2; 7.675 at 181.45 mph*	Defeated Rickie Smith (Rd. 1), Defeated Ken Dondero (Rd. 2); Defeated David Hutchens (Rd. 3); Defeated Bob Glidden (final)
NHRA Cajun Nationals	No. 4; 7.635 at 185.10 mph*	Lost to Tony Christian (Rd. 1)
NHRA Springnationals	No. 5; 7.672 at 180.94 mph	Defeated Dempsey Hardy (Rd. 1); Defeated Bob Glidden (Rd. 2); Lost to Warren Johnson (Rd. 3)
NHRA Grandnationals	No. 6; 7.606 at 183 mph	Defeated San Gianino (Rd. 1); Defeated Gordie Rivera (Rd. 2); Defeated Bob Glidden (Rd. 3); Lost to Bruce Allen (final)
NHRA Summernationals	No. 6; 7.623 at 180.36 mph	Defeated San Gianino (Rd. 1); Defeated Warren Johnson (Rd. 2); Defeated Gordie Rivera (Rd. 3); Lost to Bruce Allen (final)
NHRA Mile High Nationals	No. 4; 8.029 at 171.75 mph	Defeated Pete Smith (Rd. 1); Defeated Dempsey Hardy (Rd. 2); Defeated Warren Johnson (Rd. 3); Lost to Bob Glidden (final)
NHRA Northstar Nationals	No. 5; 7.715 at 182.18 mph	Defeated San Gianino (Rd. 1); Lost to Bob Glidden (Rd. 2)
NHRA U.S. Nationals	No. 6; 7.676 at 184.35 mph	Defeated Pat Musi (Rd. 1); Lost to Bruce Allen (Rd. 2)
NHRA Keystone Nationals	No. 5; 7.575 at 182.70 mph	Defeated Stan Mizell (Rd. 1); Defeated Don Campanello (Rd. 2); Lost to Bruce Allen (Rd. 3)
NHRA Fall Nationals	No. 5; 7.699 at 178.92 mph	Defeated Harry Scribner (Rd. 1); Lost to Bob Glidden (Rd. 2)
NHRA World Finals	No. 6; 7.640 at 178.92 mph	Defeated Roy Hill (Rd. 1); Lost to Bruce Allen (Rd. 2)

*Top speed of the meet

My Merry Oldsmobile

Butch said, "By midseason [1985], John Callies wasn't real happy that we were still running the Chevy cylinder head, which he considered old-school technology. However, he wasn't quite ready to unleash his new Pontiac Pro Stock cylinder head either, so he sent us a couple of sets of the Warren Johnson DRCE Oldsmobile cylinder heads along with a couple of intake manifolds for me to be able to put together a couple of 500-ci 'Oldsmobile' engines.

"We primarily ran those engines while competing in NHRA's chain of national events known as the Western Swing. It [the Oldsmobile] ran alright. It made quite a bit of torque but wasn't real big on engine speed.

"When I went to the Mile High Nationals in Denver, I ran four runs in a row against Warren Johnson and beat him in qualifying with his own engine combination. That was great stuff. Then, I think I faced Warren in the third round of Pro Stock Eliminator on Sunday and beat him all over again. I ran that engine combination until the end of 1985 when the new Pro Stock Pontiac cylinder heads were ready."

1986: Put a Pontiac in Your Pro Stock Pontiac

John Callies and Pontiac engineers Al Feliska, John Erickson, and Tim Peterson had begun working on a Pro Stock Pontiac cylinder head as far back as early 1985.

"Cylinder head–wise, we had done the Pontiac I-4 cylinder head, the Pontiac V-6 cylinder head, the small-block NASCAR Pontiac V-8 cylinder head, and now the big-block Pontiac Pro Stock cylinder head (engineering number 10093378)," Callies said. "Man, were we ever busy!

In 1987, Butch, Pontiac's John Callies and the Rod Shop's Gil Kirk unleashed their new Pro Stock Pontiac cylinder head. NHRA Pro Stock racing was never the same.

"Our budget at Pontiac was small. The thing was, I made the program [continue to] work because I had been building and fabricating stuff since I was a kid and knew how to get the most out of the least. Developing those heads was a lot of fun. What I did was get hold of JV Brotherton at Brodix, Inc. and said, 'Here's a cylinder head I want to build. Build me five prototype sets, and that's going to pay for the production tooling. Then we'll buy product at the piece-part price.' That's how I

Butch, who was the No. 6 NHRA Summernationals qualifier at 7.623, defeats arch nemesis Warren Johnson in the second round. In the final, Butch lost to Bruce Allen. (Photo Courtesy Richard Shute, Auto Imagery)

got everybody interested because I made sure that they [Brodix] owned the tooling and I would back and support them in selling that product."

Brodix

Brodix cofounder J.V. Brotherton said, "We're a modest-size aftermarket cylinder head manufacturing company headquartered in the hills of Mena, Arkansas. In the mid-1980s John Callies contacted me, and we started our relationship with Pontiac [Motorsports] on the NASCAR Winston Cup small-block Pontiac cylinder head program. That project worked out pretty well in spite of the fact that we didn't have a large engineering department. John was able to streamline the process dealing with such a huge conglomerate by cutting through much of the red tape that is associated with projects like this.

"Once he got the NASCAR cylinder head program cleared through GM, I think it took us about six weeks to build him the first set of small-block Pontiac cylinder heads complete with a part number, and they were quite successful in NASCAR.

"When it came to the big-block Pontiac Pro Stock cylinder head program, racers had up until that point been highly modifying standard big-block Chevrolet aluminum cylinder heads by rolling them, welding up the ports, and modifying the heck out of them, which took a lot of time, work, and money. John set into motion a program to cast a Pro Stock big-block Pontiac cylinder head that you didn't have to do all that to. You just took them out of the box, sent them to your local cylinder head porters, fitted them with a Jesel valvetrain, and you were ready to go.

"Well, that was the intended goal. I flew up to see Dale Eicke in Ohio, and we started out with not even a complete cylinder head design. He gave us the basics of it [head], and we reverse engineered [and foundered] the first set of cylinder heads in a matter of six months without even a [formal] blueprint.

"I'm really proud of what we [Brodix and PMD] achieved and the [on-track] results that Pontiac Motorsports (and specifically the Rod Shop's Butch Leal) achieved. It was well worth all the time and effort."

Cylinder Head Specifications

Today, Brodix offers a highly refined version of the same big-block Pontiac Pro Stock cylinder head (engineering number 10045427) that Butch Leal and other big-name Pro Stock racers made famous. It is extremely popular with large-cubic-inch NHRA/IHRA Sportsman and bracket racers. The specifications listed below are as close to, but may not be exactly the same as, the original set of cylinder head prototypes delivered to Butch Leal and the Rod Shop, but they are considered ideally suited for their intended use.

Thanks to J.V. Brotherton and the staff at Brodix, Inc. for their technical assistance regarding the Brodix/Rod Shop Pontiac Pro Stock cylinder head.

- This head features raised intake and exhaust ports. The intake valve is set at 4- and 18-degree compound angles. The exhaust valve is set at 4- and 9-degree compound valve angles. This represents an 8-degree roll in comparison to the stock big-block Chevrolet cylinder head.
- 435-cc intake port volume
- 81-cc combustion chamber volume
- Valve seats are installed
- Accepts 2.400- and 1.940-inch-diameter intake and exhaust valves
- Requires special-length valves
- Accepts 14-mm-reach spark plugs
- A Jesel shaft roller rocker arm system is required
- Welded sheet-metal aluminum valve covers were first used by Leal and company, but today, Brodix offers special "Pontiac" signature valve covers for this application

John Callies later designed a spread-port big-block Pontiac cylinder head, engineering number 10093386.

Pontiac versus Chevrolet

"I wanted to beat Chevrolet any anyway I could," Callies said. "They [the Chevrolet Engineering Group] were a cast of thousands, while the Pontiac Engineering Group was very, very small. There were about 10 Chevrolet engineers to 1 Pontiac engineer, so it was always a big battle between the two divisions.

"When we developed the Pontiac Pro Stock [cylinder] head, it was very tight-lipped. We were out at the 1987 SEMA Show, and we [Pontiac] put up a huge display showing the Pro Stock Pontiac head and the NASCAR Pontiac head that we had done, and Chevrolet came over. I knew all those guys, and they said, 'What's this?'

"I said, 'It's our new Pro Stock cylinder head.'

"They said, 'You can't do that!'

"I said, 'Well, it's already done. Sorry, guys!'

"They responded, 'You're never going to sell it to GMPD.'

"I said, 'We already did, and everything's successful.'

"All you've got to do is tell me no, you can't do this,

so we did. When we brought out the [Pontiac] NASCAR head, it took the place of the Chevrolet head because the Chevrolet head wouldn't last 500 miles.

"So, when I said, 'I want to do a new Pro Stock Pontiac cylinder head,' GM typically would want you to use its purchase-ordering system so it would own the tooling, and that just wouldn't fly."

Building a Better Tin Indian

Much like the design and development work on the Brodix/Rod Shop Pro Stock Pontiac cylinder head itself, the very first Butch Leal–built 500-ci Rod Shop Pontiac engine was assembled in total secrecy behind closed doors. That is one of the reasons why technical photos of both cylinder head and engine are so rare.

"The foundation for the new Pontiac engine was a GM Performance Parts 427 Bowtie Race Block, which had thicker cylinder walls so that you could run the bigger [500-ci] bore," said Butch. "It was just a standard thing. Once again, we selected a Sonny Bryant stroker crank and a set of Bill Miller Enterprises [BME] billet aluminum connecting rods pressed on-to a set of 15.7:1-compression Venolia pistons. We also used a Cam Dynamics cam and, again, a Jesel belt drive. Lubrication was handled by a Weaver dry sump, circulating Castrol 10-30 racing oil housed in an Ed Hamburger oil pan.

"We had a slight problem with the first set of Pro Stock Pontiac [engineering number 10093378] cylinder heads. Danny Jesel got us set up with the latest in needle bearing roller rocker arm systems technology. Everything bolted up correctly. By that time, Mike Kennedy had the heads all ported and polished and ready for testing. Once we got the 2x4 sheet-metal intake manifold done, we bolted the engine onto the dyno, warmed it up, and ran it up to about 7,500 rpm. It [the engine] then decided it was going to pitch off some of the rocker arms—not all of 'em but at least four or five on each cylinder head.

"We pulled off the heads and figured out that the bolts that extended down into the head and held the rocker arm assembly [rocker arm pads or stands, rocker arms, and rocker arm shafts] in place weren't long enough. They were coming loose and pulling what threads there were out of the thread bosses at higher RPM. So, we heli-coiled those bosses and installed longer rocker arm bolts and it held it just perfectly.

"We also Heli-Coiled the bosses at each end of the rocker arm shafts and again installed longer bolts. Then everything was good. When we [Bob Riffle, Gil and the entire Rod Shop crew, and Butch] installed the engine back on the dyno, we proceeded to make some serious [more than 1,150] horsepower."

In this photo taken in the summer of 2021, engineering wizard John Callies reflects while holding the actual engineering book used in bringing that engineering program to fruition.

Box Score: 1986
Statistics compiled by Bob Frey

Overall record: 25-12
Points: 4th place

Event	Qualifier	Result
NHRA Winternationals	No. 3; 7.582 at 182.55 mph	Defeated Stan Mizzel (Rd. 1); Defeated Ken Dondero (Rd. 2); Lost to Frank Iaconio (Rd. 3)
NHRA Gatornationals	No. 3; 7.535 at 184.95 mph	Defeated David Hutchens (Rd. 1); Defeated Dempsey Hardy (Rd. 2); Defeated Bruce Allen (Rd. 3); Fouled to Don Campanello (final)
NHRA Southern Nationals	No. 4; 7.566 at 183.89 mph	Defeated Reid Whisnant (Rd. 1); Defeated Jerry Eckman (Rd. 2); Lost to Bob Glidden (Rd. 3)
NHRA Cajun Nationals	No. 4; 7.590 at 185.91 mph	Defeated Dempsey Hardy (Rd. 1); Defeated Don Coonce (Rd. 2); Defeated Reid Whisnant (Rd. 3); Fouled to Warren Johnson (final)
NHRA Springnationals	No. 2; 7.585 at 183.03 mph	Defeated Don Coonce (Rd. 1); Defeated Frank Iaconio (Rd. 2); Defeated Jerry Eckman (Rd. 3); Defeated Warren Johnson (final); set top speed of the meet (186.25)
NHRA Grandnationals	No. 5; 7.596 at 183.29 mph	Defeated Stan Mizell (Rd. 1); Defeated Gordie Rivera (Rd. 2); Defeated Joe Lepone (Rd. 3); Defeated David Hutchens (final)
NHRA Summernationals	No. 4; 7.518 at 183.59 mph	Defeated Ken Dean (Rd. 1); Defeated Ken Dondero (Rd. 2); Lost to Warren Johnson (Rd. 3)
NHRA Mile High Nationals	No. 3; 7.959 at 173.24 mph	Defeated Joe Sway (Rd. 1); Lost to Stan Mizell (Rd. 2)
NHRA Northstar Nationals	No. 10; 7.704 at 185.56 mph	Lost to Bruce Allen (Rd. 1)
NHRA U.S. Nationals	No. 5; 7.509 at 184.08 mph	Defeated Joe Clark (Rd. 1); Lost to Bob Glidden (Rd. 2)
NHRA Keystone Nationals	No. 8; 7.548 at 184.53 mph	Defeated Joe Sway (Rd. 1); Lost to Don Beverly (Rd. 2)
NHRA Chief Nationals	No. 9; 7.599 at 183.00 mph	Lost to Bob Glidden (Rd. 1)
NHRA Fall Nationals	No. 5; 7.596 at 182.00 mph	Defeated Joe Lepone (Rd. 1); Lost to Bob Glidden (Rd. 2)
NHRA World Finals	No. 5; 7.556 at 184.04 mph	Defeated Joe Lepone (Rd. 1); Lost to Bob Glidden (Rd. 2)

Shouting the News

Pontiac Motorsports published a quarterly newsletter (established in 1985) blanketing the world of Pontiac Motorsports known as the *Pontiac Winners Circle*. Edited by former *Hot Rod* magazine Tech Editor John Baechtel, *Winners Circle* contained race results (including coverage from Butch Leal's big wins at the 1986 NHRA Springnationals and 1986 NHRA Grandnationals), engine tech (including write-ups on Pontiac's I-4 engine and the NASCAR and NHRA Pro Stock Pontiac cylinder heads), tuning tips, new products, and anything having to do with high-performance news from the Tin Indian Tribe.

Today, pristine copies of these newsletters are highly prized by Pontiac memorabilia collectors.

A proud Butch Leal hoists the trophy for winning Pro Stock Eliminator at the 1986 NHRA Springnationals. He qualified No. 2 with an ET of 7.585 and defeated Don Coonce in the first round, Frank Iaconio in the second round, Jerry Eckman in the semifinal round, and Warren Johnson in the final. Butch also set the top speed of the meet for Pro Stocks at 186.25 mph. (Photo Courtesy Richard Shute, Auto Imagery)

This winner's circle photo underscores the joy and jubilation generated from Butch's Springnationals win over Warren Johnson. (Photo Courtesy Richard Shute, Auto Imagery)

APRIL 1987 — VOL 3. NO. 4

In 1985, Pontiac Motorsports debuted its quarterly publication Pontiac Winners Circle. It was edited by former Hot Rod magazine Technical Editor John Baechtal. It covered the world of Pontiac from A to Z, including Butch and the Rod Shop.

PONTIAC'S DOMINATE NHRA GATORNATIONALS

For the second race in a row, Pontiac's leading Pro Stock racer has come up victorious over the typically powerful Ford Thunderbird of Pro Stock champion Bob Glidden. Butch qualified second with a 7.44 second, 187mph blast; only a blink away from Glidden's 7.41, 186mph time. Perhaps Glidden was recalling their last meeting at Pomona when Leal caught him napping at the starting line in the second round. Whatever it was, he obviously wasn't confident about having only a few hundredths advantage when Leal is widely recognized as one of the most formidable starting line aces in drag racing. Shaving the tree a mite too close in the final round, Glidden left early and fouled out trying to prevent Butch from gaining the starting line advantage. Leal calmly took the green and streaked to a 7.47 at 186mph for the Gatornationals championship and a substantial lead in the 1987 NHRA Pro Stock championship points chase.

Leal's Nationwise/Valvoline sponsored entry has been the primary development car for Pontiac's aluminum big block cylinder heads and its performance thus far indicates the strength of the program and the effort that went into making the best big block cylinder head available. The team has also worked very hard to keep the Willie Rells chassis in top competitive form. Aerodynamic testing helped them create the required downforce on the rear wheels without incurring a substantial drag penalty and subtle chassis refinements have made the Trans Am one of the hardest leaving and smoothest cars in the class. Tire shake has virtually been eliminated leaving Butch free to concentrate on driving the car straight and fast; just like he did at the Gators.

In 1985 and 1986, the Flash finished fourth in both years in NHRA Winston Pro Stock points and put sponsors the Rod Shop, Pontiac, Nationwise, and Castrol solidly in the hunt to add an NHRA Winston Pro Stock World Championship. (Photo Courtesy Richard Shute, Auto Imagery)

1987: Pontiac on Track

Callies said, "Once we got the first set of heads race worthy, Butch assembled the 500-ci engine in time to compete in Pro Stock at the Winternationals in Pomona, California. Just hours before the event, I received a call from Chief NHRA Technical Inspector Bill 'Farmer' Dismuke informing me that he would not approve our new heads.

"I said, 'Well, you already did.'

"He said, 'No, Pontiac Motor Division never built a big-block V-8 in a G-Body Pontiac!'

"Of course, I had already spent all our money on the tooling, and Butch was already on his way from Ohio to California to attend the race, so I contacted GM's archivist for Pontiac and found out that we [Pontiac] had built 240 big-block 1962 Pontiac Gran Prixs. I got together the list and rushed it over to Farmer, and he approved the heads. Butch was the No. 3 qualifier at that race and made it all the way to the third round of competition. It was quite an auspicious debut."

PONTIAC TEAMS LOOKING VERY STRONG AT MID SEASON

Well into the 1987 racing season, Pontiac teams are looking stronger than ever with solid points leads in NHRA Pro Stock drag racing, IMSA GTP-L competition and the Charlotte/Daytona Dash Series. Three Pontiac teams are currently running in the top ten in NASCAR's Winston Cup series with two of them in the top five positions. Huffaker Racing's Terry Visger just picked up a win with his Fiero in the IMSA GTU category at Mid-Ohio where Don Bell and Jeff Klein were victorious again in GTP-L. Based on their consistent performances, Pontiac now holds a commanding lead in the manufacturers championship for GTP-L, and three Fiero drivers are in the top five positions for the drivers championship. In Europe, Gordon Spice and Fermin Velez continue to extend their Fiero's lead in the C-2 division of the Sports Prototype World Championship having just captured a stunning victory at the 24 hours of Le Mans. (See coverage next month).

Pontiacs are currently holding down second and fifth place in the Bendix Trans Am series thanks to Ken Murray and Bill Doyle, and Chris Kneifel drove the Bruce Jenner Racing team's Firebird to second place at Sears Point to put even more Pontiac points on the board. Bill Bayley and Andy Pilgrim are leading the Firestone Firehawk Endurance Championship with their Pontiac Trans Am while a pack of other Pontiacs are hot on their trail. Drag boat racers are putting Pontiac's aluminum big block cylinder heads to good use setting new records in jet boat racing, and land speed record holding Gale Banks Engineering will be back to the Bonneville salt flats in late August to try for 300 mph in their record setting big block Pontiac powered Trans Am. Pontiac excitement is everywhere this year as racers take advantage of solid performance hardware developed over the past two seasons. Diehard Pontiac enthusiasts can definitely look forward to multiple championships in what is fast becoming Pontiac's strongest season yet.

Pro Stock points leader Butch Leal has put the Nationwise/Valvoline Trans Am in the final round at all five events this year. With two wins and two runner up finishes, he leads the Pro Stock points race.

The AT&T/Collins & Aikman GTP-L /Fiero of Don Bell and Jeff Klein is the most formidable car ever to run in IMSA GTP-L category with five wins and seven pole positions including their latest win at Mid-Ohio.

Terry Visger put the Mr. Goodwrench Huffaker Racing GTU Fiero on the pole at Mid-Ohio and drove it to a solid victory over a screaming pack of Mazda powered competitors.

More Cylinder Head Drama

Butch said, "When I was at Pomona with the new Pontiac motor, the president of a well-known aftermarket cylinder head manufacturer (who shall remain nameless) walked up to me in the staging lanes and said, 'If you run those cylinder heads, I'm going to sue you!'

"It seemed that the NHRA didn't let him run the Pro Stock cylinder head that his company had designed without an NHRA-approved part number assigned to it and, apparently, those heads didn't have one.

"I said, 'Go get your attorney and get to suing. But first, stand there and watch me make this run, and you'll see just how quick this thing is.'

"Anyhow, nothing ever came of it after that."

Into the Wind

"The Don Ness car [1987] was Gil's doing and not mine," said Butch. "Everybody [the top-running GM cars in NHRA Pro Stock Eliminator] was running Don Ness cars. When Don built our car, he decided to change the chassis and try something a little different from what he had done before, and the car's driving characteristics were a bit spooky.

"I was making a decent run at the NHRA Winternationals, and this thing went down through there. I rolled it into high gear, and everything felt good. Then all of a sudden, the back end started coming around, and I was spinning the tires. I went through the lights, and I was the No. 5 qualifier with an ET of 7.514 at 184.48 mph.

Box Score: 1987 *Statistics compiled by Bob Frey*

Overall record: 37-16-39
Points: 2nd place

Event	Qualifier	Result
NHRA Winternationals	No. 5; 7.514 at 184.48 mph	Defeated Reid Whisnant (Rd. 1); Defeated Bob Glidden (Rd. 2); Defeated Don Coonce (Rd. 3); Lost to Warren Johnson (final)
NHRA Gatornationals	No. 2; 7.447 at 187.30 mph	Defeated Joe Sway (Rd. 1); Defeated Lee Dean (Rd. 2); Defeated Bruce Allen (Rd. 3); Defeated Bob Glidden (final)
NHRA Southern Nationals	No. 4; 7.498 at 185.29 mph	Defeated Nick Nikolis (Rd. 1); Defeated Lee Dean (Rd. 2); Defeated Tony Christian (Rd. 3); Fouled against Bob Glidden (final)
NHRA Cajun Nationals	No. 3; 7.520 at 185.41 mph	Defeated Steve Schmidt (Rd. 1); Defeated Larry Morgan (Rd. 2); Defeated Bob Glidden (Rd. 3); Defeated Bruce Allen (final)
NHRA Springnationals	No. 2; 7.528 at 183.71 mph	Defeated Jeff Velde (Rd. 1); Defeated Lee Dean (Rd. 2); Defeated Jerry Eckman (Rd. 3); Lost to Bob Glidden (final)
NHRA Grandnationals	No. 6; 7.606 at 184.65 mph	Defeated Ken Koretsky (Rd. 1); Defeated Warren Johnson (Rd. 2); Defeated Jeff Velde (Rd. 3); Defeated Bruce Allen (final)
NHRA Summernationals	No. 9; 7.553 at 184.57 mph	Lost to Bob Glidden (Rd. 1)
NHRA Mile High Nationals	No. 3; 7.963 at 173.67 mph	Defeated Don Campanello (Rd. 1); Defeated Dempsey Hardy (Rd. 2); Fouled to Bob Glidden (Rd. 3)
NHRA Northstar Nationals	No. 9; 7.622 at 181.96 mph	Lost to Bob Glidden (Rd. 1)
NHRA U.S. Nationals	No. 15; 7.553 at 184.61 mph	Defeated Joe Lepone (Rd. 1); Defeated Jerry Eckman (Rd. 2); Lost to Bob Glidden (Rd. 3)
NHRA Keystone Nationals	No. 10; 7.550 at 134.12 mph	Lost to Bruce Allen (Rd. 1)
NHRA Chief Nationals	No. 6; 7.418 at 186.48 mph	Defeated Don Coonce (Rd. 1); Defeated Warren Johnson (Rd. 2); Defeated Jerry Eckman (Rd. 3); Lost to Bob Glidden (final)
NHRA Fall Nationals	No. 2; 7.538 at 184.69 mph	Defeated Reid Whisnant (Rd. 1); Defeated Larry Morgan (Rd. 2); Defeated Warren Johnson (Rd. 3); Lost to Bob Glidden (final)
NHRA World Finals	No. 9; 7.472 at 186.24 mph	Lost to Bob Glidden (Rd. 1)

Box Score: 1988 *Statistics compiled by Bob Frey*

Overall record: 21-12

Points: 5th place

Event	Qualifier	Result
NHRA Winternationals	No. 8; 7.454 at 186.14 mph	Defeated Frank Sanchez (Rd. 1); Defeated Reid Whisnant (Rd. 2); Defeated Tony Christian (Rd. 3); Defeated Mark Pawuk (final)
NHRA Gatornationals	No. 13; 7.409 at 188.12 mph	Defeated Dempsey Hardy (Rd. 1); Defeated Warren Johnson (Rd. 2); Defeated Kenny Delco (Rd. 3); Lost to Bruce Allen (final)
NHRA Southern Nationals	No. 12; 7.552 at 184.04 mph	Lost to Bruce Allen (Rd. 1)
NHRA Mid South Nationals	No. 12; 7.491 at 186.06 mph	Defeated Larry Morgan (Rd. 1); Defeated Jerry Eckman (Rd. 2); Lost to Kenny Delco (Rd. 3)
NHRA Cajun Nationals	DNQ	
NHRA Springnationals	No. 14; 7.509 at 185.33 mph	Defeated Frank Iaconio (Rd. 1); Defeated Tony Christian (Rd. 2); Lost to Bruce Allen (Rd. 3)
NHRA Grandnationals	No. 12; 7,444 at 186.02 mph	Defeated Harry Scribner (Rd. 1); Defeated Frank Iaconio (Rd. 2); Defeated Tony Christian (Rd. 3); Lost to Morris Johnson Jr. (final)
NHRA Summernationals	DNQ	
NHRA California Nationals	No. 9; 7.444 at 187.46 mph	Defeated Bob Glidden (Rd. 1); Lost to Mark Pawuk (Rd. 2)
NHRA Seafair Nationals	No. 7; 7.406 at 187.14 mph	Defeated Harry Scribner (Rd. 1); Beat Morris Johnson Jr. (Rd. 2); Lost to Bob Glidden (Rd. 3)
NHRA Northstar Nationals	No. 11; 7.543 at 183.73 mph	Lost to Jerry Eckman (Rd. 1)
NHRA U.S. Nationals	No. 16; 7.488 at 185.49 mph	Defeated Bruce Allen (Rd. 1); Lost to Morris Johnson Jr. (Rd. 2)
NHRA Keystone Nationals	DNQ	
NHRA Supernationals	No. 8; 7.326 at 189.11 mph	Defeated Frank Iaconio (Rd. 1); Lost to Tony Christian (Rd. 2)
NHRA Fall Nationals	No. 5; 7.503 at 185.68 mph	Defeated Frank Iaconio (Rd. 1); Lost to Bob Glidden (Rd. 2)
NHRA World Finals	No. 6; 7.423 at 187.78 mph	Defeated Kenny Delco (Rd. 1); Fouled to Bob Glidden (Rd. 2)

Once Butch worked out all the bugs, the Rod Shop's 500-ci big-block Poncho produced 1,150 hp on the dyno. (Photo Courtesy Mark "Willie Boy" Wilson)

Butch wins another one! He accepts the winner's check from 1987 NHRA Gatornationals associate sponsor Ford Motorcraft, which posted an $8,000 check to the winner. (Photo Courtesy Richard Shute, Auto Imagery)

Butch celebrates his 1987 Cajun Nationals win over Bruce Allen. Also shown is Bob Riffle, the Rod Shop's chief engine builder and a championship driver in his own right, and Team Manager Phil Polotti (right). (Photo Courtesy Richard Shute, Auto Imagery)

"I went back Sunday and the same thing happened. I was driving the thing sideways through the lights because I was winning. I mean, the car was really quick up to the 1,000-foot mark, and then it started spinning the tires and I lost to Warren Johnson in the final. Bob Riffle and I adjusted the rear spoiler way up (about as far as you could go), and I was still getting sideways at 185 mph, just smoking the heck out of the tires! After that, I called Willie Rells and told him to build me another car.

"In the meantime, John Callies called the shop and said, 'Bring it to the [Milford, Michigan] wind tunnel [the largest wind tunnel in the world]. Well, I had never been in a wind tunnel before. It was like something out of *Star Wars*. The only thing I knew was that with Mickey's [Thompson] cars, he ran a full belly pan underneath. I belly panned the [one-piece lift off] front end on the car all the way up to the oil pan. Then, after the engine and transmission, the weight bars were flat up against the bottom of the car, so everything was tucked in and really beautifully. It was aerodynamically efficient, right?"

Well, not quite.

Callies said, "Butch and those other fellows never had the opportunity to go to the wind tunnel before, so it was more fun than work for them. At the time, it was costing me [PMD] $15,000 an hour to go into the wind tunnel, so when I would bring a race car there for testing, you had to be prepared with all the parts you wanted to try. It was like you were making a pit stop at the Indy 500. When the wind thrust from its massive 4,500-hp variable-speed motor slowed down and the buzzer blew, you ran inside like you were at a NASCAR race changing tires. Once you got the next part installed, you would haul tail outside and get the wind speed up again."

Butch said, "We got the car tied down in the wind tunnel and everything was cool. We went back inside, and they started the wind turbine. It took a while to get that thing going. It got about halfway up to speed and the 'whiz kids' [wind tunnel operators] flipped the switch and turned the thing off. They turned around and looked at me and said, 'Butch, you've got the car in the tunnel backward.' It was crazy. It was lifting the back end, and it damned near blew out the door of the wind tunnel!"

"Now, those folks at the General Motors wind tunnel have got just about anything and everything you needed to test a car, but they didn't have a part to compensate for stupid."

Testing revealed that Butch's prized front belly pan was causing the Trans Am to lift in the lights.

"We pulled the nose off the car, got a blanket, and turned it upside down," Butch said. " John Callies said, 'Cut that panel out!'

"I said, 'I'm not cutting that panel out.'

"Callies said, 'Butch, trust me, cut the panel out.

"We sawed the panel out, installed the front end back on, and the car never moved. It turned out there was 1,200 pounds of down force on the nose, and it was lifting up the back end of the car. By doing that, it took it [the car] to neutral and applied equal downforce on the back."

"When we took the car to the wind tunnel, we not only got the car pointed in the right direction but wind-tunnel testing helped get the pitch movement right," said Callies. "Second, we developed the Pro Stock hood scoop, which extended all the way back to the windshield and greatly improved the car's aerodynamics. We also developed a rear spoiler, which, for a time, was exclusive to Butch's car only."

1988: It Was Fun While It Lasted

By 1988, Nationwise began splintering off in different sponsorship directions.

"We held on for as long as we could," said Gil Kirk. "By the time our contract had expired,

In 1987, Butch's Pontiac won all the marbles at the NHRA Grandnationals where Butch qualified No. 6 at 7.606 and defeated Kenny Koretsky in the first round, Warren Johnson in the second round, Jeff Velde in the semifinals, and Bruce Allen in the final. In the end, Butch finished No. 2 in Pro Stock World Championship points to winner Bob Glidden. (Photo Courtesy Richard Shute, Auto Imagery)

At the 1988 NHRA Winternationals, Butch and the Rod Shop debuted Valvoline as one of their major sponsors and qualified No. 8 in the eliminator with an ET of 7.454. This photo was taken on a qualifying run.

On Sunday, Butch defeated Frank Sanchez in round one, Reid Whisnant in round two, Tony Christian in round three, and Mark Pawuk in the final.

Nationwise had gone into NASCAR with the sponsorship of driver Lake Speed, so I knew what we were up against. We raced for Nationwise and Castrol [and then for Valvoline] up to the end of the 1988 NHRA Pro Stock Eliminator season. Overall, I would say, it was a good run."

1989: ACDelco Goes Pro Stock Racing

When John S. Zwerner left Pontiac Motor Division in 1989 and moved on to GM's ACDelco Parts Division, one of his goals was to jazz up the image of the 79-year-old OEM replacement and accessory parts manufacturer.

Zwerner decided to try something new, namely, drag racing! After all, Ford's Motorcraft Parts Division (formerly known as Ford-Autolite) had been a major player in the quarter-mile arena for two decades and currently sponsored multi–NHRA Pro Stock World Champ Bob Glidden, so why not an ACDelco–sponsored Pro Stock entry? Not surprisingly, John Zwerner turned to John Callies and Callies turned to the Rod Shop's Gil Kirk for the answer.

Callies said, "The Rod Shop's Gil Kirk was a most amazing guy when it came to putting sponsorship deals together. After experiencing huge success with the team concept, Gil wanted to solely concentrate on NHRA Pro

It's party time at Pomona! Butch and company celebrate in the winner's circle after winning Pro Stock Eliminator against Mark Pawuk. (Photo Courtesy Richard Shute, Auto Imagery)

Stock racing, and the ACDelco sponsorship just made good sense from both a racing standpoint and a marketing standpoint."

Of course, Butch Leal continued to drive. However, gone was the familiar Refrigerator White paint scheme with flowing red flag motif. In its place was a Larry Shinoda–designed red [the primary color] with white [the secondary color] paint scheme accented by touches of blue with the huge letters "ACDelco" emblazoned across the Trans Am's hood and side flanks.

Also new to the program was Kendall GT1 Racing Oil (returning as one of Butch's earliest sponsors), which would be replacing departing one-year-sponsor Valvoline, and more data testing.

"I wanted to have recording data on the car, but Butch hated the idea," said Callies. "For some reason, he felt that I was looking at what he was doing and thought that I was going to criticize his driving style when all I wanted to do was see what the car was doing and make it perform better. We went head-to-head on that subject more than a few times. Corporate sponsor ACDelco was also quite keen on the idea and scheduled dyno time at its expansive high-tech engineering facility in Lansing, Michigan."

Unfortunately, ACDelco's computer software was more geared to OEM street driving and not the extreme rigors of high performance, such as drag racing. After sev-

eral test sessions, Butch suggested using one of pioneer Funny Car driver-turned-computer guru Ray Alley's Race Pac data-recording programs instead, which was more ideally suited to achieve the desired test data.

Callies said, "I installed the data recorder in the car for the very first time at the NHRA Winternationals at Pomona, California. Butch went out, made a qualifying run, came back, and we printed out the data sheet. I said, 'Alright Butch, what RPM did you leave at?'

"He said, 'Well, I left at 8,800.'

"I asked, 'What did you shift from first to second at.'

"'About 9,200.'

"How about second to third?

"'It was about 9,200.'

"And what about third to fourth?

"'About 9,250.'

"And we just kept going through the list. I looked at the data, and he didn't miss any of those shift points by 2 rpm. That's how good of a driver Butch Leal was.

"In finite analysis, the computer testing program made for a more driveable car. In testing at the track, we used a truck with remote sensors, and everything on the chassis was wired. We learned that the rear axle housing was flexing, and we came up with a pair of sleeves that we welded inside the housing, which effectively eliminated that problem.

"We also installed an angular brace in back of Butch, which changed the frequency of where the tire shake would occur and relocated that frequency to a more advantageous location where it would reduce tire shake. But that could only have been done in finite analysis by modeling the entire chassis."

Today, any Pro Stock driver worth his salt wouldn't be caught dead without one of these onboard diagnostic systems, and you can thank Butch Leal, Gil Kirk, John Callies, the technicians at ACDelco, and Ray Alley for that one.

Tracking Down Lost Horsepower Through Finite Analysis

"Another thing we found out through finite analysis was that once Butch would leave the starting line, he would lose 50 hp by the time he got to the other end," Callies said. "What I found out was the water [cooling] was not getting across the combustion chamber and back out of the head, and we were getting a hot spot and detonation.

"I came up with a series of cooling tubes that ran above the combustion chamber to relieve this and then went back into the radiator, which instantly fixed the horsepower loss. After discovering that, Butch told me that he felt out of all the engineering people he had worked with, I was one of the best in helping to make the car go faster. To me, that meant a lot."

1990: Subdued but Still Serious

Butch lights up the tires at Indy during U.S. Nationals Pro Stock qualifying. Ultimately, he qualified in the No. 16 spot with an ET of 7.488, besting Bruce Allen in the first round and losing to Morris Johnson in the second round.

Wheels-up and getting after it, Butch squares off against Steve Schmidt during 1988 NHRA U.S. Nationals qualifying. The competition in Pro Stock qualifying was tough that year.

In 1990, Callies resigned from his position at Pontiac Motorsports and started his own custom crankshaft business known as Callies Crankshaft Company. From there, he went into the cam core business and after that, his current gig, private-label manufacturing roller lifters and other assorted high-performance valvetrain hardware known as Morel Lifters. All three endeavors have been highly successful. In Callies' absence, John Erickson was appointed to the directorship of Pontiac Motorsports.

"John Erickson was a good guy and knew his business," Callies said. "Ultimately, John moved on to work with the NHRA and then on to Penske Motorsports to run its NASCAR program. Unfortunately, due to extenuating circumstances, the programs that Pontiac Motorsports

Box Score: 1989
Statistics compiled by Bob Frey

Overall record: 41-11
Points: 8th place

Event	Qualifier	Result
NHRA Winternationals	No. 9; 7.387 at 187.81 mph	Lost to Don Beverly (Rd. 1)
NHRA Supernationals	No. 6; 7.345 at 187.42 mph	Defeated Chuck Echmalian, Lost to Bob Glidden (Rd. 1)
NHRA Gatornationals	No. 8; 7.374 at 187.85 mph	Defeated Carlos Gonzales (Rd. 1); Lost to Frank Iaconio (Rd. 2)
NHRA Southern Nationals	No. 13; 7.425 at 186.10 mph	Lost to Reid Whisnant (Rd. 1)
NHRA Mid South Nationals	No. 6; 7.364 at 187.22 mph	Defeated Joe Folgore (Rd. 1); Fouled to Warren Johnson (Rd. 2)
NHRA Cajun Nationals	No. 4; 7.440 at 184.80 mph	Defeated Don Beverly (Rd. 1); Defeated Kenny Delco (Rd. 2); Defeated Larry Morgan (Rd. 3); Lost to Bruce Allen (final)
NHRA Springnationals	No. 16; 7.440 at 184.53 mph	Lost to Don Coonce (Rd. 1)
NHRA Grandnationals	No. 4; 7.395 at 186.02 mph	Defeated Joe Lepone (Rd. 1); Lost to Ken Koretsky (Rd. 2)
NHRA Summernationals	No. 9; 7.413 at 187.11 mph	Defeated Bob Glidden (Rd. 1); Fouled to Joe Lepone (Rd. 2)
NHRA Mile High Nationals	No. 6; 7.867 at 174.45 mph	Lost to Rickie Smith (Rd. 1)
NHRA California Nationals	No. 5; 7.363 at 188.24 mph	Defeated Frank Iaconio (Rd. 1); Lost to Rickie Smith (Rd. 2)
NHRA Seafair Nationals	No. 8; 7.384 at 186.56 mph	Defeated Jerry Eckman (Rd. 1); Defeated Larry Morgan (Rd. 2); Fouled to Warren Johnson (Rd. 3)
NHRA Northstar Nationals	No. 11; 7.487 at 183.89 mph	Defeated Reid Whisnant (Rd. 1); Lost to Frank Iaconio (Rd. 2)
NHRA U.S. Nationals	No. 12; 7.413 at 186.06 mph	Defeated Kenny Delco (Rd. 1); Lost to Don Beverly (Rd. 2)
NHRA Keystone Nationals	DNQ	
NHRA Heartland Nationals	No. 12; 7.427 at 185.87 mph	Lost to Bruce Allen (Rd. 1)
NHRA Chief Nationals	No. 10; 7.337 at 187.26 mph	Fouled to Larry Morgan (Rd. 1)
NHRA Fall Nationals	No. 9; 7.474 at 184.95 mph	Lost to Darrell Alderman (Rd. 1)
NHRA Word Finals	DNQ (alternate)	Lost to Mark Pawuk (Rd. 1)

was running began to change and/or be canceled. Unfortunately, the Rod Shop sponsorship was one of them. What a shame—those were some fast and furious times. When you look back at it, guys like Butch Leal, Warren Johnson, Bob Glidden, and Lee Shepherd were the [stock-body] heroes of the day."

Flying Solo

It's been frequently said that "it's not over until it's over." If there ever was such a thing as a hardcore "race-a-phobe," then both Butch Leal and Gil Kirk were it. Nationwise was gone, Castrol and Valvoline were gone, and now ACDelco was gone. Still, Leal and Kirk pressed on furiously.

Although ACDelco had departed, the two decided to retain the rather expensive

Butch races Joe Lepone Jr.'s Chevy Beretta during qualifying. Butch ran an ET of 7.498 and won the race.

Butch and the 'Bird dump the laundry in the lights at the 1988 U.S. Nationals. After an aggravating week of qualifying blasts in an attempt to better his spot, Butch lost to Morris Johnson, Jr. in the second round. Butch ultimately qualified 16th at 7.488. (Photo Courtesy Les Welch)

Larry Shinoda–designed red, white, and blue paint scheme that they ran the previous season. This time, it carried the "California Flash" and "Rod Shop" lettering on the Firebird's side flanks. It was the last of a long line of Rod Shop Pontiac Trans Am Firebirds.

The Ideal Boss

"Butch was my hero when I was growing up, and it was just by chance that I met him when I was working at Groveport Golf Course outside of Columbus," Mark "Willie Boy" Wilson said. "Butch was a really great guy and always treated me like an equal, maybe even like a king. After years of being his golfing buddy, I went to work for him in 1990. Mike Stryker was Butch's crew chief, and I basically did whatever Mike and Butch wanted done. We went from race to race, and I never had more fun than when I was racing with the California Flash.

"However, I think that first year on the road was the worst year for weather that I ever saw. First, when we got to Houston, it was snowing. Then, we went to Phoenix, it was 40 degrees and windy. It wasn't any better in Pomona, either. There's nothing worse than lying on the ice-cold ground working on an extremely hot race car. However, there were plenty of good times too.

"Every time something really cool would be happening, Butch would make sure that I was included. One time, I remember we were at Sonoma Raceway. Butch came running up to me in the pits and said, 'Willis, Willis, come here, come here!'

"I replied, 'What? I'm in the middle of doing something, Butch.'

"He said, 'Hurry, hurry, come with me!'

"We ran across the pits and came up to an elderly gentleman standing there. Butch said, 'I want you to meet Ed Iskenderian.'

"I was like, 'Oh, my God.' I mean, it was so cool, and Butch would always do that. He would go out of his way to introduce people to me who were big-time hitters in drag racing, and I always thought it was cool!"

The Last Car

"With our Pontiac deal gone, we decided to order a Chevrolet Beretta from Willie Rells," Gil Kirk said. "It was our last car. I got the car in the middle of 1990, and

Box Score: 1990
Statistics compiled by Bob Frey

Overall record: 3-8
Points: 17th place

Event	Qualifier	Result
NHRA Winternationals	No. 13; 7.388 at 187.73 mph	Lost to Darrell Alderman (Rd. 1)
NHRA Motor Craft Nationals	No. 16; 7.404 at 186.18 mph	Lost to Bob Glidden (Rd. 1)
NHRA Supernationals	DNQ	
NHRA Gatornationals	DNQ	
NHRA Southern Nationals	DNQ	
NHRA Mid South Nationals	DNQ	
NHRA Springnationals	DNQ	
NHRA Mile High Nationals	No. 6; 7.793 at 176.64 mph	Lost to Buddy Ingersoll (Rd. 1)
NHRA Motorcraft Ford Nationals	No. 10; 7.339 at 188.83 mph	Lost to Rickie Smith (Rd. 1)
NHRA Seafair Nationals	No. 12; 7.395 at 187.72 mph	Lost to Mark Pawuk (Rd. 1)
NHRA U.S. Nationals	No. 12; 7.417 at 186.45 mph	Defeated Bruce Allen (Rd. 1); Fouled to Jerry Eckman (Rd. 2)
NHRA Heartland Nationals	No. 15; 7.371 at 187.03 mph	Lost to Darrell Alderman (Rd. 1)
NHRA Chief Auto Parts Nationals	DNQ	
NHRA World Finals	No. 13; 7.365 at 188.24 mph	Lost to Larry Morgan (Rd. 1)

we tested it at Houston Raceway on the way home. I had installed my old faithful Chevrolet big-block that was darned near worn out, and the car ran 7.30 at 190 mph on the first lap down through there, so I was feeling pretty good about making the change. Since the Pontiac deal was over (even though we were still running the 500-ci Pontiac cylinder head engine combination), we got a little help from Chevrolet, and we put their name on the door. I started out my racing career with Chevrolet, so I was going to end it with Chevrolet."

Butch said, "When 1991 came along, we ran the full NHRA national event schedule but didn't have much luck in spite of the fact that we ran consistently in the low-7s at 190 mph, which were national-event winning times. Gil sold everything at the end of the season and briefly toyed

In 1989, Nationwise, Castrol, and Valvoline were gone. ACDelco stepped up to the plate and signed on. Shown is the original Larry Shinoda-designed conceptual drawing.

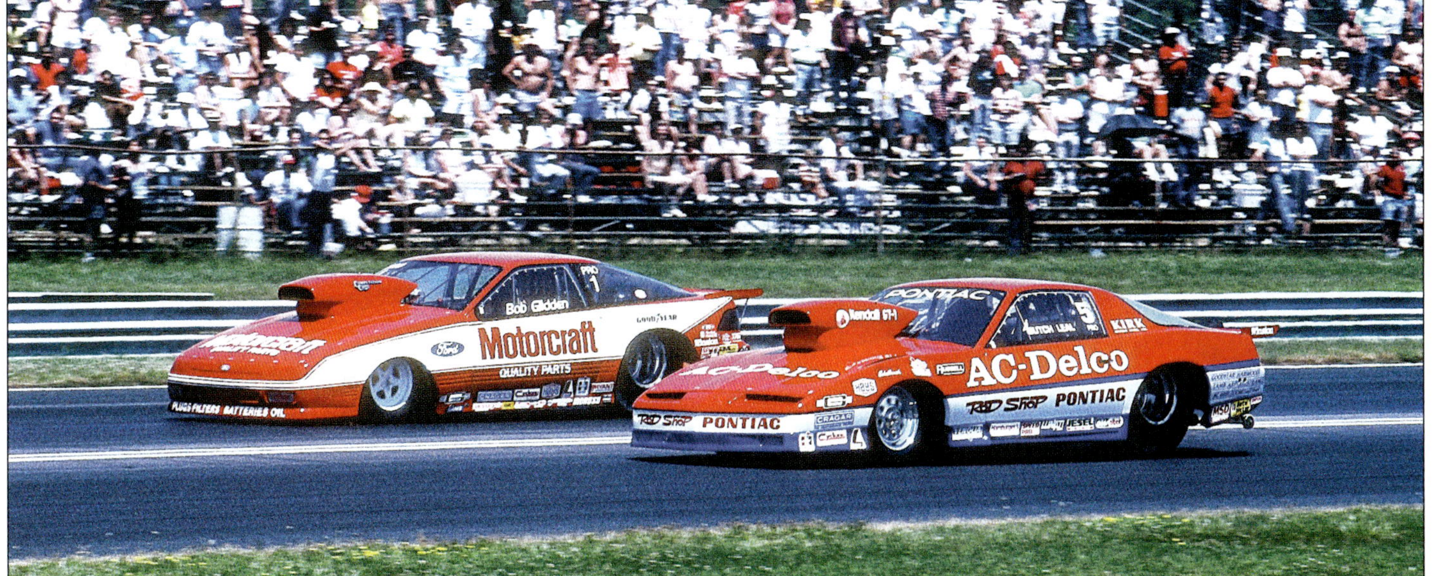

It's the classic battle of the century: Ford versus General Motors and ACDelco versus Ford Motorcraft. It all unfolded at the 1989 NHRA Summernationals where Butch defeated arch nemesis Bob Glidden in the first round. (Photo Courtesy Norman Blake)

with the idea of going NASCAR racing but thought better of it and decided to spend more time with his family and concentrate on his growing real estate business instead.

"I hung up my helmet and driving gloves and hit the links in an effort to improve my golf game. Needless to say, racing with Gil Kirk and the Rod Shop was a great partnership, and it was fun while it lasted."

Box Score: 1991
Statistics compiled by Bob Frey

Overall record: 4-13
Points: 15th place

Event	Qualifier	Result
NHRA Winternationals	DNQ	
NHRA Motorcraft Nationals	No. 12; 7.383 at 186.52 mph	Defeated Joe Lepone (Rd. 1); Lost to Jerry Eckman (Rd. 2)
NHRA FRAM Supernationals	DNQ	
NHRA Gatornationals	No. 13; 7.283 at 189.27 mph	Defeated Scott Geoffrion (Rd. 1); Lost to Bob Glidden (Rd. 2)
NHRA Southern Nationals	No. 10; 7.341 at 186.79 mph	Lost to Jerry Eckman (Rd. 1)
NHRA Mid South Nationals	No. 16; 7.419 at 186.27 mph	Lost to Darrell Alderman (Rd. 1)
NHRA Springnationals	No. 9; 7.376 at 189.91 mph	Fouled to Jerry Eckman (Rd. 1)
NHRA Grandnationals	No. 14; 7.298 at 188.52 mph	Lost to Warren Johnson (Rd. 1)
NHRA Summernationals	DNQ	
NHRA Mile High National	No. 10; 7.774 at 176.74 mph	Lost to Jim Yates (Rd. 1)
NHRA California Nationals	No. 12; 7.299 at 191.00 mph	Lost to Bruce Allen (Rd. 1)
NHRA Northwest Nationals	No. 14; 7.341 at 188.00 mph	Lost to Larry Morgan (Rd. 1)
NHRA Northstar Nationals	No. 13; 7.449 at 185.22 mph	Lost to Bruce Allen (Rd. 1)
NHRA U.S. Nationals	No. 6; 7.350 at 187.77 mph	Lost to Scott Geoffrion (Rd. 1)
NHRA Keystone Nationals	DNQ	
NHRA Heartland Nationals	DNQ	
NHRA Chief Auto Parts Nationals	No. 11; 7.301 at 190.11 mph	Lost to Jerry Eckman (Rd. 1)
NHRA World Finals	No. 8; 7.289 at 190.11 mph	Defeated Bob Glidden (Rd. 1); Defeated Frank Iaconio (Rd. 2); Lost to Jerry Eckman (Rd. 3)

Butch's 1,174-hp 500-inch Pontiac is shown. (Photo Courtesy Mark "Willie Boy" Wilson)

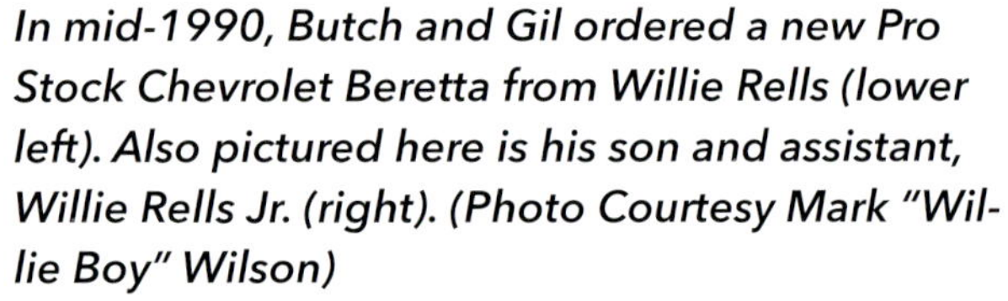

It was the same paint job with different lettering. With ACDelco's departure, Butch brought back the "California Flash" name. (Photo Courtesy Mark "Willie Boy" Wilson)

In mid-1990, Butch and Gil ordered a new Pro Stock Chevrolet Beretta from Willie Rells (lower left). Also pictured here is his son and assistant, Willie Rells Jr. (right). (Photo Courtesy Mark "Willie Boy" Wilson)

When the Beretta was debuted, it set the Pro Stock world on its ear with its low, swoopy center of gravity and clutchless 5-speed transmission. Yes, the Flash was back to manually banging gears again. "I had installed my faithful big-block Chevy [also known as Red] for testing, and we stopped at Houston Dragway on our way back to Ohio," Butch said. "I was amazed when the car ran 7.30 at 190 mph right out of the box."

Painted in the familiar Rod Shop flag motif, Butch slogged on throughout the end of the 1990 NHRA season and the entire 1991 season, but the writing was on the wall. As team owner Gil Kirk philosophically said, "I started with a Chevrolet (as did Butch), so I'm going to end it with a Chevrolet."

The year 1990 was tough for the Rod Shop team. All told, the team had six DNQs that season, making it look as though Butch had lost his magic touch.

Fortunately, things looked up in 1991, as the team qualified for 14 out of 18 events, albeit in the middle of the eliminator, making them cannon fodder for all the fast cars. The best qualifying effort for the year was at the U.S. Nationals, holding on to the No. 6 position at 7.350, which unfortunately wasn't strong enough when facing first-round opponent Scott Geoffrion.

CHAPTER 17

LEAL FAMILY SCRAPBOOK

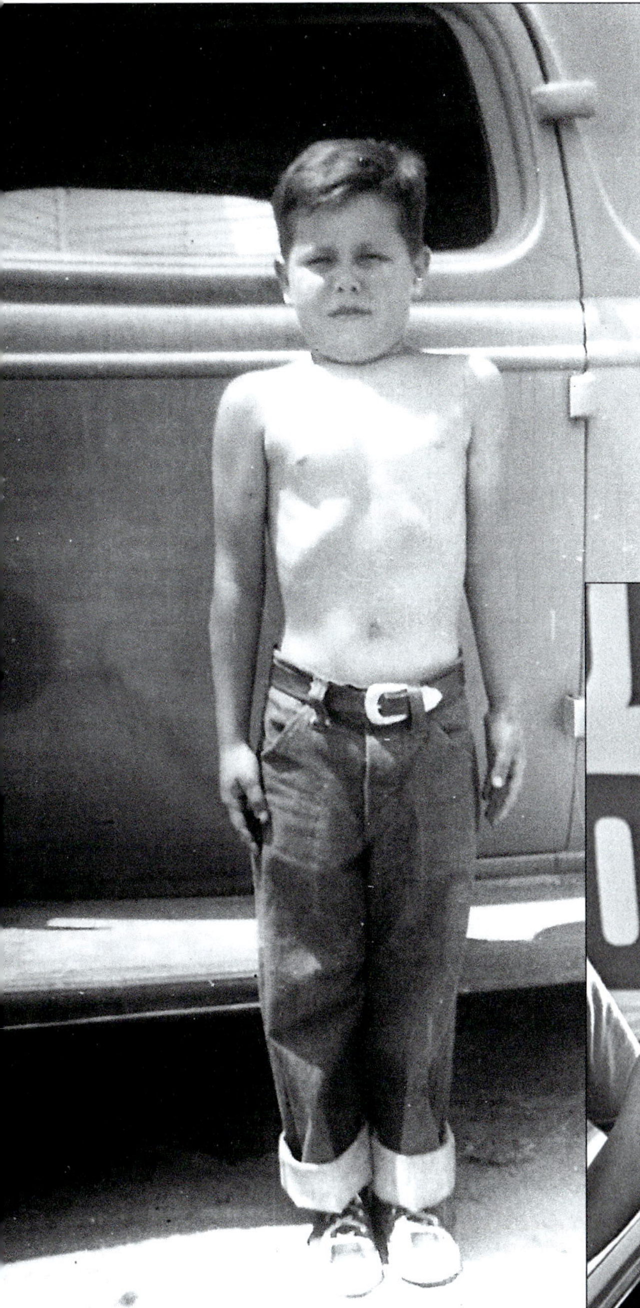

Circa 1953, a young Larry "Butch" Leal strikes a pose in front of his uncle's 1935 Ford coupe at his grandfather's dairy farm known as the Frank Leal Dairy in Hanford, California.

After selling his 1973 Plymouth Duster Pro Stocker to Roy Hill, Butch freelanced for the remainder of the season. One of his assignments included driving the Tomlinson & Toplentz GT1 Dodge Dart, which captured the eliminator at the IHRA Longhorn Nationals at Dallas International Motor Speedway. (Photo Courtesy Steve Reyes)

From the get-go, Larry "Butch" Butch was a natural-born athlete, as these certificates of achievement from Pixley Grammar School attest. Between 1957 and 1958, Butch was a dominant figure in baseball, basketball, and track. "When it came to throwing the ball, catching it, and running the bases, I was one of the best," Butch said. "I also had a pretty good throwing arm (I really liked throwing the shot [put]), and as a junior, I played quarterback with and against the seniors."

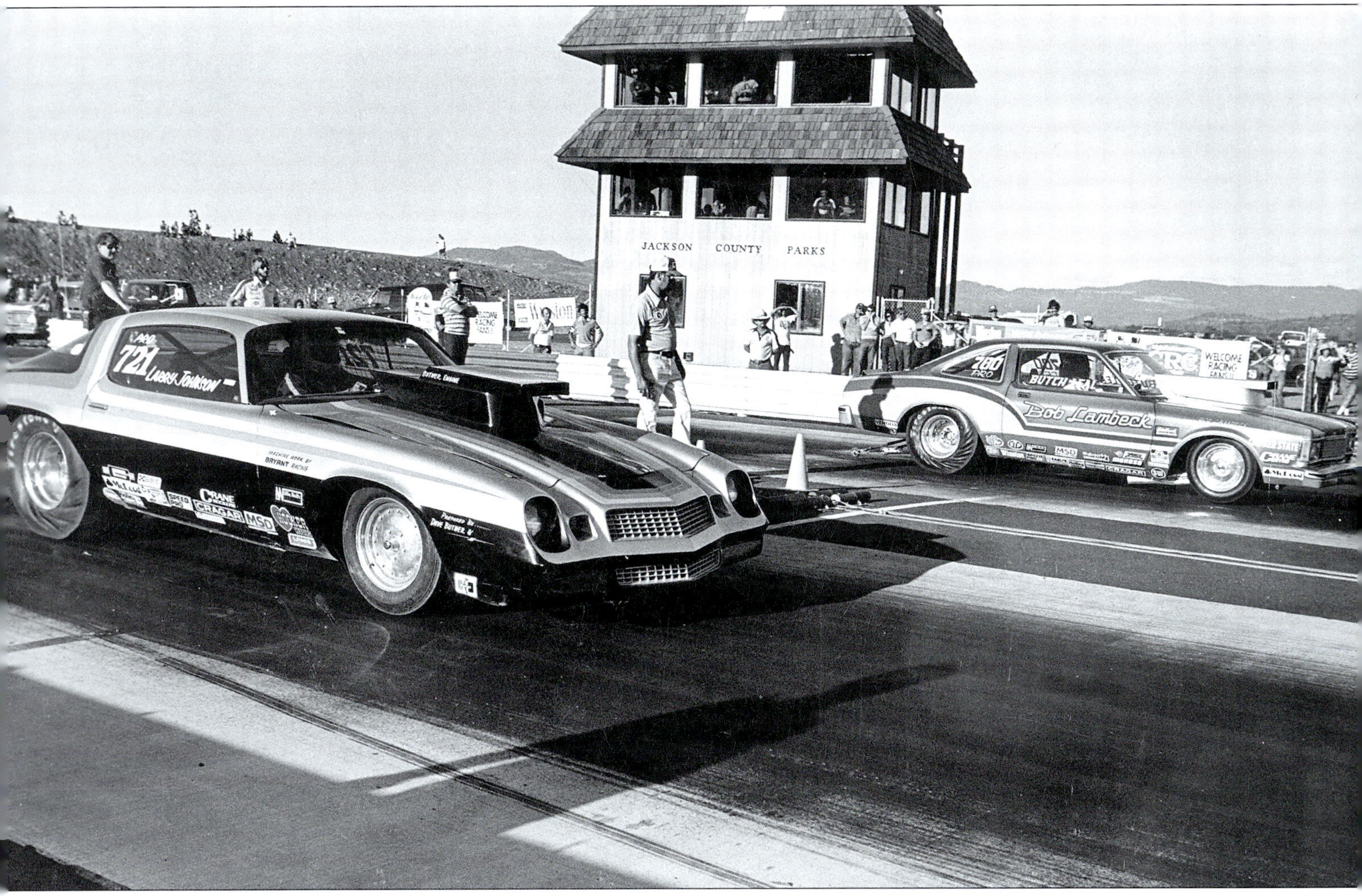

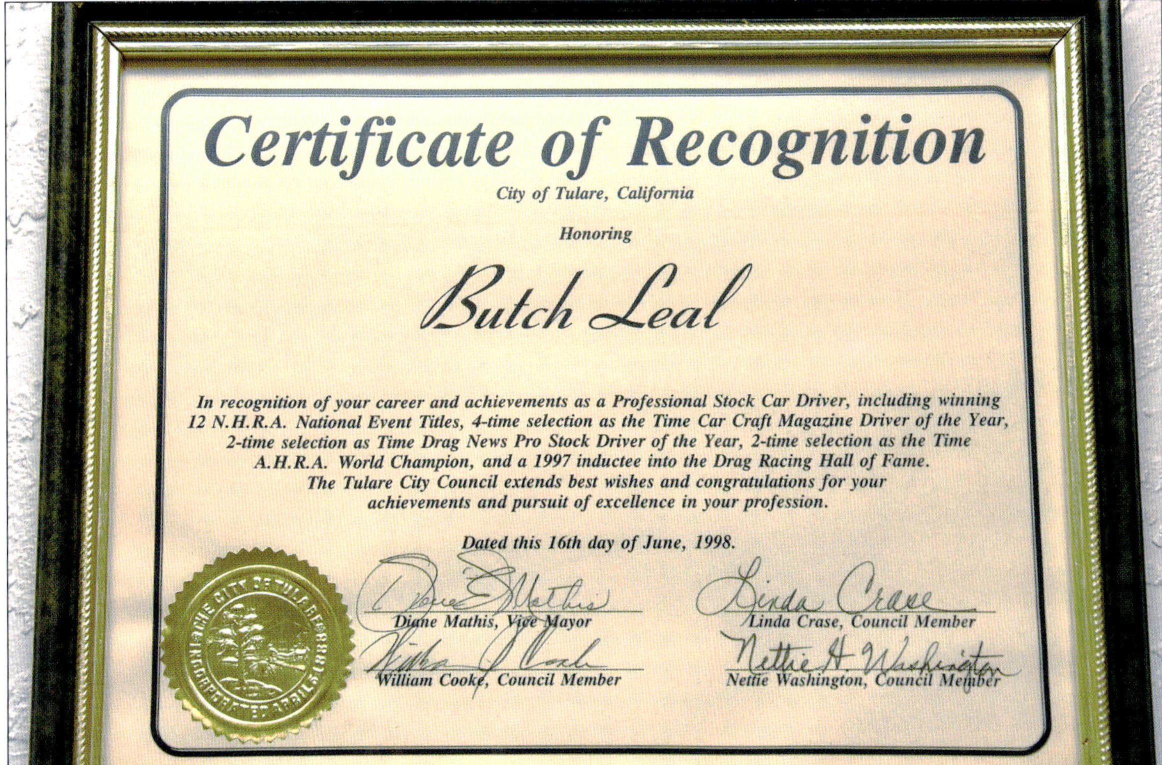

Another driving gig for Butch included driving Bob Lambeck's 1980 Plymouth Pro Stock Volare (shown here racing Larry Johnson at Medford Dragway in Medford, Oregon), which captured the 1980 NHRA Division 7 Winston World Championship Series (WWCS) title.

Certificate of Recognition

City of Tulare, California

Honoring

Butch Leal

In recognition of your career and achievements as a Professional Stock Car Driver, including winning 12 N.H.R.A. National Event Titles, 4-time selection as the Time Car Craft Magazine Driver of the Year, 2-time selection as Time Drag News Pro Stock Driver of the Year, 2-time selection as the Time A.H.R.A. World Champion, and a 1997 inductee into the Drag Racing Hall of Fame. The Tulare City Council extends best wishes and congratulations for your achievements and pursuit of excellence in your profession.

Dated this 16th day of June, 1998.

Diane Mathis, Vice Mayor

Linda Crase, Council Member

William Cooke, Council Member

Nettie Washington, Council Member

Honorariums come from all kinds of interesting places. For example, this June 1998 certificate of recognition was bestowed on Butch by the City of Tulare, California.

Ford stars the late Hubert Platt (far left), Gas Ronda (second to the right), and Tommy Grove (far right) pose with Linda "Miss Hurst Golden Shifter" Vaughn (third from right) during the 2006 Southwest All Ford Classic event at Cardinal Stadium, Phoenix, Arizona.

Butch poses with the Rod Shop Pro Stock Pontiac Trans Am at Indy for this Castrol Oil Company advertisement.

Butch and "Dandy" Dick Landy flash their best Ipana smiles while attending Fred Engle-hart's muscle car show in 2007.

Butch (left) and "TV" Tommy Ivo chat at the 2013 California Hot Rod Reunion. "When I was 13 or 14 years old, there was an ad in Hot Rod magazine advertising "TV" Tommy Ivo's '23 T-Bucket for sale for $2,500," Butch said. "I wanted that thing so badly, but my dad just laughed and said, 'You'll kill yourself driving that crazy thing.'"

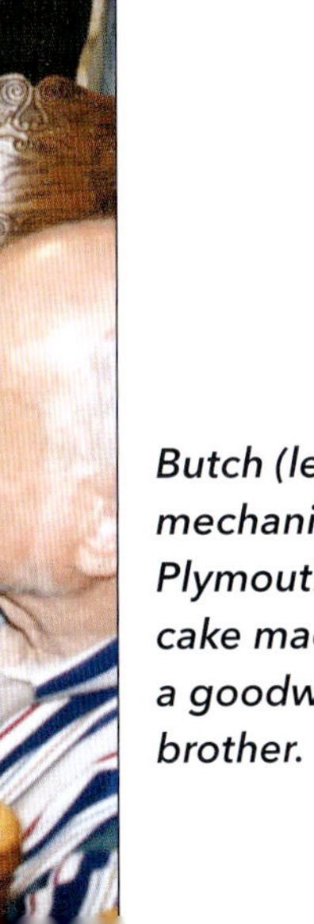

Butch (left) and famed race car mechanic Joe Smith (Fenner-Tubbs Plymouth) prepare to slice into a cake made by Butch's sister Pam as a goodwill gesture to her visiting brother.

Butch is interviewed by California Hot Rod Reunion Master of Ceremonies Dave McClelland during the 2013 event where Butch was being inducted as grand marshal. (Photo Courtesy Mark Gewertz)

Part of the California Hot Rod Reunion (CHRR) grand marshal selection process was inscribing Butch's name along with other 2013 CHRR inductees on a bench permanently erected in Famoso Raceway's famed "grove." Butch and Donna's grandchildren Maddison and Harrison Leal check out the finished product.

Butch was inducted into the 2014 Mopar Hall of Fame in Carlisle, Pennsylvania. From left to right, are Herb McCandless, Ramo Stott, Butch, Shirley Shahan-Bridges, Norm Krause, Joe Smith, Don Grotheer, and Kenny Black.

Shirley "the Dragon Lady" Shahan and Butch are lifelong friends. In fact, they live across the street from each other in Tulare, California. In this autographed photo, Shirley and Butch pose with the Drag-On Lady Dodge Dart in the pits at Bakersfield.

Butch (left) and famed NASCAR star David Pearson pose alongside Pearson's No. 21 Mercury Grand National stock car on display during Dick Brannan's All Ford Show at Atlanta Motor Speedway in Atlanta, Georgia.

When Roy Hill Drag Racing School head master and vintage Pro Stock superstar Roy Hill celebrated his 50th anniversary in drag racing, he sent out this letter of thanks.

Butch,

   To my brother, Butch Leal, to the knowledge and times we have shared together!

This is a small token of what your friendship means to me!

Thanks,

Roy Hill

Roy Hill

Roy Hill Drag Racing School

This beautiful ring was sent to Butch and a number of other lucky participants.

To the victor go the spoils (along with a nice, fat check), and to the crew goes a champagne bubble bath. Butch lives it up after winning another major event with the Rod Shop Pontiac.

Judging from the disgusted look on Butch's face he must be saying, "Rain, rain, go away."

Part of Butch's trophy collection is this rare Sounds of Drag Racing record album that features Butch's Rod Shop Pontiac Trans Am Pro Stocker on the face of the pressing.

In 2020, the NHRA celebrated 50 years of Pro Stock Eliminator during the NHRA Winternationals, and Butch was one of the celebrated drivers interviewed by Fox Sports. (Photo Courtesy Andy Willsheer)

This is the afterlife of a genuine drag racing icon. Butch and his restored 1965 SS/B Plymouth make an appearance at the 2021 Muscle Car and Corvette Nationals in Chicago, Illinois. In retirement, Butch travels the country to vintage racing and muscle car events, signing model kits, glossy photos, and books.

Butch proudly poses next to the 1965 Plymouth at the 2021 Muscle Car and Corvette Nationals. (Photo Courtesy Chuck Hanson)

Often making appearances with Butch at events are his restored race cars. In addition to the 1965 Plymouth at the Muscle Car and Corvette Nationals show, the 1975 Pro Stock Duster joined the party. Follow Butch's appearance schedule by joining his Facebook group: Butch Leal "The California Flash."

APPENDIX
BUTCH LEAL'S RACING ACCOMPLISHMENTS

- **• 12-time NHRA National Champion**

1964
- NHRA Winternationals Super Stock (S/S) Runner Up
- NHRA U.S. Nationals S/S Champion/NHRA National Record Holder
- Won 21 races (11 weeks in a row) at Lions Drag Strip

1965
- NHRA U.S. Nationals S/S Champion
- Quickest and Fastest Funny Car on gas (9.69 at 144.92 mph)
- Green Valley, Texas, S/S Champion

1966
- Hot Rod Magazine S/S Eliminator Champion

1967
- Quickest and Fastest Injected Funny Car (7.82 at 182.41 mph)

1968
- Dodge Dart Price & Leal raced three times (2 wins and 1 runner-up finish)

1969
- First Boss 429 Ford Hemi

1970
- Carlsbad, California, World Championship Series Champion
- Bakersfield, California, World Championship Series Champion
- Phoenix, Arizona, AHRA GT-1 Champion
- AHRA Grand American Series Champion

1971
- NHRA Western Conference Champion
- NHRA Pro Stock National Record Holder (9.57 at 144.92 mph)
- NHRA Division 7 Champion
- Fremont, California, World Championship Series Champion
- Amarillo, Texas, World Championship Series Champion
- Orange County International Raceway (OCIR) Points Champion

1972
- NHRA Pro Stock Division 7 Champion
- *Drag News* Pro Stock Driver of the Year
- Popular Hot Rod Meet Champion
- Bakersfield, California, March Meet Champion
- NHRA National Pro Stock Top Speed Record (145.86 mph)
- Orange County/OCIR All-Pro Championship Series
- Fremont, California, AHRA World Champion
- Phoenix, California, NHRA Winternationals Pro Stock Champion
- Detroit, Michigan, UHRA Pro Stock Champion (9.29 at 148.20 mph)
- Bonneville, Utah, World Championship Series Pro Stock Champion
- Sacramento, California, World Championship Series Pro Stock Champion
- OCIR Pro Stock Match Race Showdown winner
- First Pro Stock car to run 9.11 at 150.50 mph
- Las Vegas, Nevada, World Championship Series Pro Stock Champion

1973
- Montreal, Canada, NHRA Grand Nationals Pro Stock Champion
- Popular Hot Rod Meet Champion
- Bakersfield, California, March Meet Champion
- AHRA National Pro Stock Record Holder (8.88 at 154.10 mph)
- *Drag News* Pro Stock Driver of the Year
- NHRA National Pro Stock Top Speed Record Holder (151.77 mph)
- Englishtown, New Jersey, First Pro Stock car to go in the 8s (8.98 at 151.0 mph)
- Fremont, California, Grand American Final Pro Stock Champion (8.91 at 153.75 mph)
- Irwindale, California, Grand Prix Pro Stock Champion
- NHRA Summernationals Pro Stock Runner Up
- NHRA Springnationals Pro Stock Runner Up

1974
- NHRA Summer Nationals S/S Eliminator Champion
- AHRA S/S Winter Nationals Eliminator Champion
- *Car Craft* magazine's All Star Drag Racing Team Super Stock Driver of the Year
- NHRA Springnationals Super Stock Runner Up

1975
- NHRA Gatornationals Modified Eliminator Champion
- *Car Craft* magazine's All Star Drag Racing Team Super Stock Driver of the Year

1976
- NHRA Phoenix Winter Classic Modified Eliminator Champion
- NHRA Winternationals Modified Eliminator Champion
- *Car Craft* magazine All Star Drag Racing Team Modified Driver of the Year
- Popular Hot Rodding Modified Eliminator Champion

1977
- NHRA National Record Holder B/G (8.387 at 156.25 mph)
- *Car Craft* magazine All Star Drag Racing Team Modified Driver of the Year
- First match race Pro Stock car to run in the 7s (7.96 at 172.91 mph)

1984
- NHRA Winston Finals Pro Stock Runner Up
- NHRA Cajun Nationals Pro Stock Runner Up

1985
- NHRA Mile High Nationals Pro Stock Runner Up
- NHRA Summernationals Pro Stock Runner Up
- NHRA Grandnationals Pro Stock Runner Up
- NHRA Southern Nationals Pro Stock Champion

1986
- NHRA Grandnationals Pro Stock Champion
- NHRA Springnationals Pro Stock Champion
- NHRA Cajun Nationals Pro Stock Runner Up
- NHRA Gatornationals Pro Stock Runner Up

1987
- NHRA Fallnationals Pro Stock Runner Up
- NHRA Chief Nationals Pro Stock Runner Up
- NHRA Grandnationals Pro Stock Champion
- NHRA Springnationals Pro Stock Champion
- NHRA Cajun Nationals Pro Stock Champion
- NHRA Southern Nationals Pro Stock Runner Up
- NHRA Gatornationals Pro Stock Champion
- NHRA Winternationals Pro Stock Runner Up

1988
- NHRA Grandnationals Pro Stock Runner Up
- NHRA Gatornationals Pro Stock Runner Up
- NHRA Winternationals Pro Stock Champion

1989
- NHRA Cajun Nationals Pro Stock Runner Up

2014
- Inducted into the Mopar Hall of Fame

2015
- Inducted into the International Drag Racing Hall of Fame

Butch Leal by the Numbers

- Butch's 1967 Barracuda Funny Car was one of the first in the seven- and eight-second zone.
- In the 1970s, he was the first driver to win in three NHRA National categories (Super Stock, Modified, and Pro Stock).
- In 1972, he won 16 match race eliminator shows.
- In 1973, he won the NHRA Pro Stock title at the "Molson," driving a 1973 Duster with Hemi power, but that was the last time a Mopar with a Hemi engine won.
- Frank Iaconio and Butch Leal debuted Funny Car–style roll cages in their Pro Stockers, which are now a permanent fixture in the category's chassis design.
- On April 21, 1985, Butch Leal became the first racer other than Bob Glidden, Warren Johnson, Lee Shepherd, or Frank Iaconio to win an NHRA Pro Stock national event since 1979. Leal's Castrol GTX/Nationwise Pontiac Trans Am defeated Glidden's 7-11/Chief Auto Parts Ford Thunderbird in the final round of the NHRA Southern Nationals at Atlanta, Georgia, with a 7.73 at 179.71 mph to a 7.80 at 167.72 mph.

Additional books that may interest you...

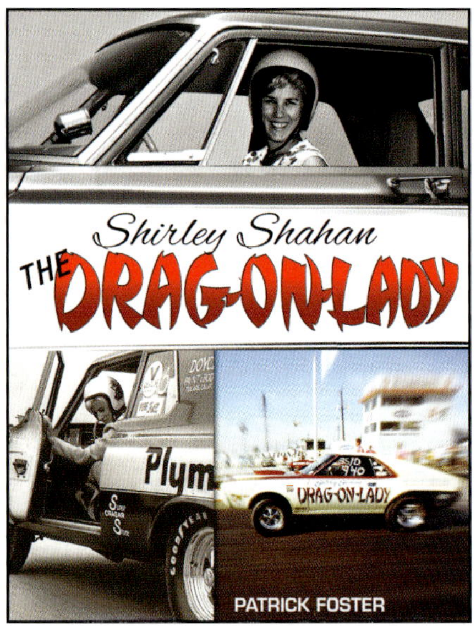

SHIRLEY SHAHAN: The Drag-On Lady
by Patrick Foster
Meet drag racing legend and pioneer Shirley Shahan, the Drag-On Lady! As the first woman to win an NHRA national event when she was named Top Stock Eliminator at the 1966 Winternationals, Shirley Shahan blazed a trail for women in drag racing. 8.5 x 11", 176 pgs, 300 photos, Sftbd. ISBN 9781613255810 Part # CT675S

HEMI UNDER GLASS: Bob Riggle and His Wheel-Standing Mopars
by Rich Truesdell & Mark Fletcher
Bob Riggle campaigned wheel-standing Mopars for more than 60 straight years. This is a new must-have history book on *Hemi Under Glass.* 8.5 x 11", 176 pgs, 350 photos, Sftbd. ISBN 9781613255612 Part # CT670

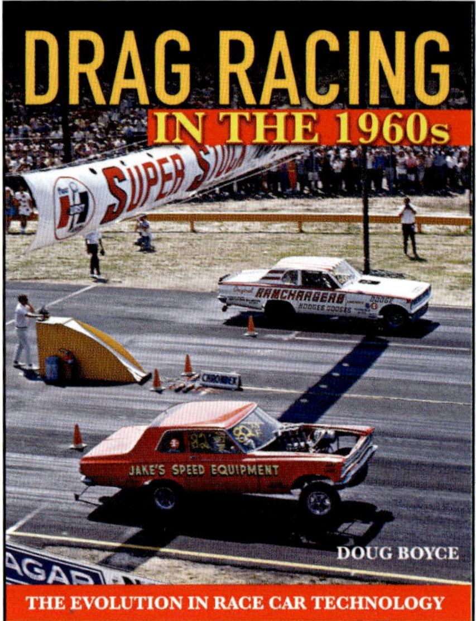

DRAG RACING IN THE 1960s: The Evolution in Race Car Technology
by Doug Boyce
In this book veteran author Doug Boyce takes you on a ride through the entire decade from a technological point of view rather than a results-based one. 8.5 x 11", 176 pgs, 350 photos, Sftbd. ISBN 9781613255827 Part # CT674

Check out our website:

CarTechBooks.com

✓ **Find our newest books before anyone else**

✓ **Get weekly tech tips from our experts**

✓ **Featuring a new deal each week!**

Exclusive Promotions and Giveaways at www.CarTechBooks.com!

www.cartechbooks.com or 1-800-551-4754

DRAG RACING'S WARREN "THE PROFESSOR" JOHNSON: The Cars, People, & Wins Behind His Pro Stock Success
by Kelly Wade
Go behind the scenes for a look at Warren Johnson's path to becoming *The Professor of Pro Stock.* This new book illuminates the life and career of one of the most prolific engine builders and racers ever to compete in the ultra-competitive Pro Stock category, drag racing's most technologically advanced class. 8.5 x 11", 176 pgs, 350 photos, Sftbd. ISBN 9781613255704 Part # CT672